Routledge Revivals

A Handbook for History Teachers

First Published in 1929, *A Handbook for History Teachers* is an attempt on the part of a number of teachers (many of them members of the S. E. London branch of the Historical Association) to offer some practical help in the choice of historical material for children. It discusses themes like schemes of work in elementary junior and senior schools, textbooks for pupils under fifteen, class library books for pupils under fifteen, book lists for teachers, and sources for the preparation of history stories by the teacher. This is an essential read for history teachers.

A Handbook for History Teachers

Edited by Dorothy Dymond

Routledge
Taylor & Francis Group
ROUTLEDGE REVIVALS

First published in 1929
by Methuen and Co Ltd.

This edition first published in 2023 by Routledge
4 Park Square, Milton Park, Abingdon, Oxon, OX14 4RN

and by Routledge
605 Third Avenue, New York, NY 10017

Routledge is an imprint of the Taylor & Francis Group, an informa business

Publisher's Note
The publisher has gone to great lengths to ensure the quality of this reprint but points out that some imperfections in the original copies may be apparent.

Disclaimer
The publisher has made every effort to trace copyright holders and welcomes correspondence from those they have been unable to contact.

A Library of Congress record exists under LCCN:

ISBN: 978-1-032-61611-7 (hbk)
ISBN: 978-1-032-61613-1 (ebk)
ISBN: 978-1-032-61612-4 (pbk)

Book DOI 10.4324/9781032616131

A HANDBOOK FOR HISTORY TEACHERS

EDITED BY

D. DYMOND, M.A.

LECTURER AT GOLDSMITHS' COLLEGE, UNIVERSITY OF LONDON

SECOND EDITION, REVISED

METHUEN & CO. LTD.
36 ESSEX STREET W.C.
LONDON

First Published . . . . May 1929
Second Edition, Revised . 1929

PRINTED IN GREAT BRITAIN

EDITOR'S PREFACE

THIS book is an attempt on the part of a number of teachers (many of them members of the S.E. London branch of the Historical Association) to offer some practical help in the choice of historical material for children. There was never an age more rich in historical knowledge and publications than our own. But this very richness is an embarrassment to the non-specialist, who does not know how to find his way among the wealth of material offered to him. While the authors hope that the handbook may prove useful to all teachers of children under fifteen, it is more particularly dedicated to those non-specialist general teachers for whom the standard bibliographies are too technical, and who yet hold the responsibility of teaching history to the vast majority of English children. Such teachers are asked not to be alarmed at the number of books recommended. The aim is not that a teacher should use them all, but that he should find among them exactly the book that he needs. The expert, on the other hand, who may chance to pick up the handbook, is asked to remember that it is not meant for him, and, while he smiles, to make the smile a kind one.

Children's books (all of which have been examined by experienced elementary school teachers to judge of their suitability as well as by history specialists to judge of their soundness) are generally grouped as useful for Juniors (age 7 + to 11 +) or Seniors (age 11 + to 15). For the convenience of readers the prices of children's books, cheaper books for teachers and source books are generally added : but while pains have been taken to ensure accuracy, prices undergo such variation that it cannot be guaranteed.

In conclusion, the warmest thanks are offered to Dr. Rachel Reid, Dr. Delisle Burns, Professor Hearnshaw, Mr. R. H. Tawney, Mr. A. S. Turberville, Mr. A. Farquharson and Mr. C. H. Williams for help and advice generously bestowed on various sections of the Handbook, and to Miss Graveson, Vice-Principal, and Mr. A. E. Dean, Warden of Goldsmiths' College, and the headquarters of the Historical Association for continued help and encouragement throughout.

D. DYMOND

GOLDSMITHS' COLLEGE
April, 1929

LIST OF COLLABORATORS

N.B.—The names of those who acted as Secretaries of Committees or who undertook some special piece of work are distinguished by an asterisk.

Miss ADAM, B.A. (Oliver Goldsmith School).
J. ARMITAGE, Esq., M.A. (Balgowan Central School).
H. W. ARMSTRONG, Esq. (Joseph Barrett School).
A. J. ARNOLD, Esq. (Childeric Road School).
Miss BARTON, B.A.* (formerly of Blackheath High School).
Miss BENTLEY (Rutland Street School).
Miss BOSLEY (Durham Hill Senior School).
Miss BRUNTON (Brixton Central School).
Miss N. CARTER, M.A.* (Goldsmiths' College).
Miss CATTY, M.A. (formerly of Goldsmiths' College).
Miss CHAPMAN, B.A.* (Dulwich High School).
Dr. CURZON * (Goldsmiths' College).
Mrs. DANE (Forest Hill Central School).
Miss DYER, F.R.Hist.S.
G. EADES,* Esq. M.A. (Faunce Street School).
Miss ELLABY, B.A. (formerly of Avery Hill Training College).
Miss K. M. GARDINER, M.A.* (Whitelands Training College).
A. P. W. GAYFORD, Esq., B.A. (Dulwich College).
C. GERRED, Esq., (The Medburn Senior School).
Miss GIBSON * (S. James' School).
Mrs. GOODRICH * (Mitcham Lane School).
Miss GRICE, M.A. (Beckenham Secondary School).
T. S. GUNTON, Esq., B.Sc. (Franciscan Road School).
Miss HAIGH * (Mantle Road School).
Miss E. HARRISON * (Heath Clark Central School).
Miss E. M. HARRISON.
Miss M. L. HARRISON (Glengall Road School).
Miss HAWKES (Scawfell Road School).
Miss F. HIGHFIELD * (Childeric Road School).
Miss HOUGH, B.A. (Roan Girls' School).
G. E. HUTCHINGS, Esq., F.G.S.* (Junior Technical School, Rochester).
C. E. IRVING, Esq. (Invicta Road School).
E. H. JENKINS, Esq., M.A. (Hackney Downs (formerly the Grocers' Company) School).

D. Jones, Esq., B.A.* (Addey and Stanhope School).
Miss M. E. Monckton Jones, M.A., F.R.Hist.S. (Hockerill College).
Dr. R. Jones * (Bermondsey Central School).
Miss Kennedy, B.A. (Mary Datchelor School).
W. Lee, Esq., B.A.* (formerly of Bermondsey Central School).
Miss Lofvengren, B.A.* (Morning Lane School).
Miss Lovett (Leo Street School).
Miss Lumb, M.A.* (Beckenham Secondary School).
Mrs. Macfarlane.
Miss Mackay, M.A. (Sydenham High School).
Dr. D. Marshall.
Miss Newton, B.A. (Aske's Hatcham Girls' School).
Miss Nicholas (John Evelyn School).
E. G. Peal, Esq. (Rathfern Road School).
Miss Pike * (Childeric Road School).
Dr. Rees * (Goldsmiths' College).
Miss Revell (Fair Street School).
S. Ridout, Esq., M.A.* (Goldsmiths' College).
Miss Rowland, B.A. (Lewisham Prendergast School).
Miss A. Russell, M.A.*
Mrs. Sidley, M.A. (Streatham County Secondary School).
Mrs. M. E. Smith * (Mantle Road School).
Miss Taylor, B.A.* (Aske's Hatcham Girls' School).
Miss E. White, B.Sc.* (Childeric Road School).
Miss Wiggins (Waller Road School).
W. T. Williams, Esq., M.A. (Beckenham Secondary School)
Miss Wyon, M.A. (formerly of Roan Girls' School).

LIST OF ABBREVIATIONS

C.U.P., Cambridge University Press.
O.U.P., Oxford University Press.

CONTENTS

A HANDBOOK FOR HISTORY TEACHERS

I

SYLLABUSES AND SCHEMES OF WORK IN ELEMENTARY JUNIOR AND SENIOR SCHOOLS

1. Introduction: The Present Situation in England and France

'They order', said I, 'this matter better in France.'
'You have been in France?' said my gentleman, turning quick upon me.

IF the English teacher of history should decide to take up the challenge given to Sterne and study the official suggestions for history teaching across the Channel,[1] there is no doubt that he would be struck with a certain envy. He would find there, besides general suggestions on method and subject-matter, an authorized scheme of study which would take his worst problems out of his hands and solve them by methods at once bold, logical and scholarly. He would find at his disposal 'interpretations' of these schemes by expert teachers, working out the general course into detailed monthly and weekly assignments; and the more history he knew, the more admiration he would feel for the powers of selection and the thorough methods which these assignments display. There are some mistakes which the French general teacher cannot make; the specialist protects

[1] The official courses and interpretations have been translated into English under the following title: *French Elementary Schools: Official Courses of Study*, edited by P. H. Gay and O. Mortreux. Translated by I. L. Kandel. Published by Columbia University, 1926.

him against them. He can accept the outline of his syllabus with a simple faith, undisturbed by the fear that he may be missing the main point of his period, and concentrate his mind entirely on the subject-matter of the lessons set down for him to teach.

The French authorities organize their schools after the infant stage into three courses of two years each. The *elementary* course deals with the 'principal facts and principal dates of French history up to 1610'. The *middle* course carries on this study to our own times. The *upper* children are to be given 'a very simple notion of ancient history', which is considered indispensable to their obtaining 'a modest but genuine culture', and a revision of the outstanding events of national history in their relation to the history of the world. During this period, too, a good part of the time given to moral instruction is devoted to learning about the machinery of present-day government: a proceeding which would not strike a Frenchman as in the least funny. The official suggestions emphasize strongly the importance of teaching 'general' or international history and of giving the greatest time and care to a study of the most recent age. The aim of the scheme as a whole is that the pupils shall develop into well-informed, civilized people and good citizens of France.

The 'interpretations' of the syllabus work out into detail these general ideas. They are very full, contain frequent allotments of time and schemes for revision, and evidently aim at great thoroughness. A specimen month's work at the lowest and highest stage is appended:—

ELEMENTARY COURSE. *First Year* (i.e. children of 7).
First month (*October*).

1. Gaul. Boundaries, aspects, frontiers.
2. The Gauls. Organization, customs, beliefs. Their spirit of adventure.
3. The Roman Conquest. Caesar and Vercingetorix (58–50 B.C.). Fall of Alesia.
4. Roman Gaul. Cities, monuments. The language.

UPPER COURSE. *Second Year. April.*

N.B.—It must be remembered that this is in part a revision course.

1. The two revolutions in England (1648 and 1688). Magna

Carta (1215). Parliament. Charles I. Cromwell. Restoration. Flight of James II.

2. The wars of Louis XIV. Treaties. Aix la Chapelle (1668) ; Nimègue (1678) ; Ryswick (1697) ; Utrecht (1713). Territorial expansion : Flanders, Franche-Comté, Strasbourg.

3. Age of Louis XIV. Literature, art and science. The court.

4. Colonial rivalry between France and England in the eighteenth century. Canada, the Indies. The Treaty of Paris (1763). The bad government of Louis XV.

It is impossible to withhold admiration for these comprehensive, logical arrangements of fact. It is impossible not to praise the lucid treatment which succeeds in including the general history of civilization and of other lands without confusion and without unduly distorting chronological sequence. Nor can we doubt that from the practical point of view the ready-made outline syllabus and the optional detailed interpretations must save the general teacher in a primary school from many a blunder and many a headache.

Yet our praise is not insincere because it stops short of imitation. This is a good way, but it is not our way ; we prefer something else, even at the cost of blunders and headaches. France admires clarity and reason : we admire individuality and action. We know that our syllabuses often err through confusion and want of specialized knowledge : does not her syllabus perhaps err a little through over-specialization ? Was the spirit of childhood present at its making ? Was it not planned from the beginning from an adult point of view ? Will it not tend, in spite of official warnings to the contrary, towards constant oral exposition from the teacher and receptive learning by the child ? Each nation worships its own national gods in its approach to history. We remember the difference between the swift changes of the Revolution, when every young man fresh from college had a constitution in his pocket, and the slow development of English democracy, created by events and never written down at all by anybody. There is a real difference of national temperament between the unwritten constitution and history syllabuses of England and the well-defined constitutions and history syllabus of France.

Our system has the enormous advantage that a history syllabus can be related to the district and conditions in which it is being used. The needs of the children, the particular character of their environment, the special interests of the teacher, can all be considered. Above all, the experienced teacher knows what is possible in his school and if the syllabus is entrusted to his making he can produce something that is genuine and practicable. But this system has the corresponding danger of 'blunders and headaches'. There is no doubt that it imposes a very heavy burden on the head mistress or head master who is an expert teacher and organizer but can hardly be expected to be a history specialist as well. The making of a history syllabus depends on the power to select and arrange parts of the vast contents of history, as well as on a competent knowledge of the subject and an understanding of the child mind. There is no recognized elementary material with which the learning of history *must* begin, and which will lead naturally to more advanced studies. Without considerable knowledge of the general programme of events and of the alternatives and possibilities to be weighed in making a selection, the task of syllabus making is extremely difficult.

History is comparatively a new-comer to our curriculum. It made its appearance in English elementary education in 1871, as one of a number of specific subjects for which an additional grant might be earned, and it held this optional position until it was made part of the regular course of instruction in 1900. The subject was not a popular one. Professor Withers calculated that 'in the year ending at Lady Day 1899 about four London children out of every hundred took History as a class subject'. The syllabus was meagre: Standard VI, the highest standard in those days, had only to master the details of 'three or four events of importance in the history of England since the conquest, and the general sequence of the landmarks of history'. English history teaching began as a thing of shreds and patches, in the highest possible contrast with the ambitious syllabus of the French. We aimed at what was immediately practicable; they at what was to be desired. Their danger might be that their syllabus on paper did not always correspond with the facts of real life; ours, that we might not be quick enough to pass on from our early simple standards as soon as higher ones were possible. In 1875 a more definite syllabus began to be formed, but it still had obvious limitations: English history only was to be studied, and even of that nothing after 1820. Standard IV studied the outlines of English history as far as 1066, Standard V from

1066 to 1485, Standard VI from 1485 to the death of George III. It is clear that the idea of bringing the child to some understanding of his present environment by means of history can hardly have existed, for modern history was both crowded and incomplete. In 1881, when Standard VII was added, history was made one of a number of class subjects from which each school must choose two; and soon afterwards a specified syllabus was issued, whose memory still governs the content of history teaching in many schools. It was confined to English history and for Standard II consisted of simple stories of no definite period. Standard III got twelve stories from Early English history to 1066; IV had twenty studies and biographies from 1066–1485; V the Tudor period; VI the Stuart period, with special reference to the Civil War and the constitution and functions of Parliament, and with biographies of six leading statesmen; Standard VII studied the Hanoverian period, with special reference to the acquisition and growth of the Colonies and foreign possessions, and six more biographies. The scheme of work had by this time succeeded in reaching 'the present day', and in the general instructions emphasis had begun to be placed on a sympathetic and vivid treatment. But it was still purely national and there was little attempt, even with the older children, to represent History as a continuous growth instead of a series of incidents.

In 1900, when history was made a regular class subject, it was laid down that teachers might deviate from this scheme to suit local convenience, or might produce schemes of their own 'similar to it as to length and clear arrangement'. In 1901 the whole schedule was cancelled and complete freedom of syllabus making was allowed. A few specimen schemes of instruction were appended to serve as guides; but as they generally consisted of the words 'Oral exposition of Historical Reading Book', they were far from helpful. Finally in 1902 the new freedom was definitely inaugurated. 'All that has been said . . . is given as advice and not as imperative. The course of instruction to be followed in all schools was once prescribed in minute detail and practically little variety, even of method, was attempted by any teacher. Teachers have now to consider for themselves what shall be the scope of their instruction. . . . They may, if they choose, deviate little from the routine which has become a second nature, or they may introduce innovations both numerous and various. But whether they adopt either of these extreme courses or a judicious modification of both of them, they must remember that the responsibility is theirs.'

These rather sinister closing words indicate the price teachers had and still have to pay for freedom. They have no regular opportunity of consulting specialists while making their plans and yet they are constantly having to meet specialist criticism of the finished scheme. They know well what is possible in their schools, but how can they know the full possibilities of every subject ? Many of the dark places may be illuminated by study of the Board's Suggestions ; but from the very nature of the system teachers will not find their individual problem solved there.

The Suggestions of 1927 are an able, imaginative piece of work which it would be an impertinence to praise. But they leave the greatest practical difficulty untouched. They rightly object to the '*overloading of the syllabus*' as causing the gravest faults in history teaching, and they insist that the right principle of selection is not '*How much can I put in ?*' but '*What can I leave out ?*' But they go on to make a list of '*what should be known by the end of the course*' which would overload any syllabus. By the time the pupil leaves the elementary school he is to have gained 'a connected and definite knowledge of the story of Britain and of the British commonwealth of nations' with an understanding of social and industrial as well as political aspects and 'some knowledge of the growth of free institutions at home and overseas' ; he is 'not to neglect overseas history' ; he is 'not to ignore ancient history' ; and his course is to include wherever possible 'such explanation of the outstanding movements of general history as is necessary for the understanding of our own story at home and overseas'. There is not a word here with which one disagrees. But it must be admitted that to aim at such results in a course lasting from 11 + to 14 without overloading the syllabus would require both the very nicest and best-informed powers of selection.

2. The Aim of the Handbook

In view of all this, the members of the Syllabus Committee felt that the most pressing need of the teachers was for constructive help. They realized that it is easier, and safer, to criticize : but they were convinced that large numbers of keen non-specialist teachers are perfectly aware of their difficulties, and require not so much a re-statement of the problem as some practical help in its solution. They therefore decided to ask schools to lend their syllabuses anonymously as a basis for discussion, in the hope of discovering, among the multitude of counsellors, some wise suggestions for the help of others. About sixty syllabuses from various types of schools were submitted, and were handed round among members of the committee for analysis and comment. A report form was drawn up which required each reader to review the syllabus as regards its general plan and choice of subject-matter (especially on the teaching of social and international history); as to the degree in which historical unity and continuity were preserved throughout the course; as to whether the syllabus were overcrowded on the whole course or in any part; whether it were well graded; what opportunities were given for individual work and reading; and finally what general conclusion could be reached as to its excellence, and what special features it contained that might be of interest to other teachers. These reports were discussed in frequent committee meetings, extending over the course of two years: the members of the committee were teachers of all types, some history specialists in elementary or more advanced education and others teachers of general subjects. The Committee had the advantage of meeting in discussion experts of various kinds. It is needless to say that no syllabus emerged unscathed by any criticism, and the committee members do not propose to announce the discovery of an ideal syllabus in real life. What they do propose is to consider the difficulties confronting a teacher who has to frame a history syllabus, and to show in what various ways these are met in some of the best syllabuses submitted. One of their main aims has been to consider how the history scheme will be affected by reorganization; but in quoting from syllabuses they have retained the nomenclature of the seven "standards", since this nomenclature is most familiar to teachers.

3. General Plan of Syllabus

Having determined his aim, the first problem the teacher has to solve is the arrangement of his general scheme. Only two syllabuses out of the sixty had adopted the plan known as the *concentric*, which, in its extreme form, was unanimously condemned by the committee. This plan, which dooms its victims to survey the whole course of history each year from a different point of view, is satisfactory neither on the practical nor the academic side. The attempt to scramble through the whole of history in forty weeks' work means that an event can never be studied with leisure in its proper context and in the atmosphere of its period, and such enormous gaps have to be left that the syllabus often gives the impression of a haphazard assortment of incidents. The children's minds are at once staled by frequent repetition of a few stories and utterly confused as to the general sequence and relationship of outstanding events. Richard's crusade, for instance, makes an annual appearance in one syllabus, but it is never connected with any other crusade, or with the religious life of the age, or with the development of foreign trade and exploration: it is sandwiched in one standard between Henry II's Irish policy and Magna Carta, and in another between Henry's French dominions and Simon de Montfort. One of the few dogmatic conclusions reached by the committee was that the extreme concentric arrangement should not be recommended.

Our teacher has therefore to frame some kind of periodic arrangement and he will first have to consider whether it is wise to cover the ground once or twice during the course of a child's career. Each plan presents some difficulties. It was evidently felt by many teachers that a thorough treatment of modern history, and especially of the nineteenth century, in the senior stage was essential to a child's understanding of the present time, and therefore they must content themselves with a story treatment of ancient and medieval history in the junior forms, covering the whole ground once only during the child's school life. The plan of syllabuses based on this principle follows on page 9. The dates are of course intended only as a rough indication of the ends of periods.

The great value of such a plan is that it avoids overcrowding the syllabus. The advantages of having time to work thoroughly in the upper classes and above all of giving the last year of school life to a study of nineteenth-century and present-day history are obvious: but obvious too are the disadvantages of studying no early history after the junior stage. Either formal history must be begun at far too early a date or the children's knowledge of the earlier

	Standard II. (8 years+)	III. (9 years+)	IV. (10 years+)
First Example .	Stories of Ancient Times	55 B.C.–A.D. 1066	1066–1485
Second Example	Primitive Man–A.D. 1066	1066–1485	1485–1603
Third Example	Primitive Man–decline of Greece	Rome–1066	1066–1485

	Standard V. (11 years+)	VI. (12 years+)	VII. (13 years+)
First Example .	1485–1603	1603–1714	1714–present day
Second Example	1603–1715	1715–1815	1815–present day
Third Example	1485–1688	1688–1815	1815–present day

periods must be fragmentary, childish and practically forgotten by the time they reach the senior classes. Even the careful annual revision prescribed in several syllabuses of this type would not meet the case, for children are apt to despise and lose intimacy with work taken 'when we were little'.

The alternative to one continuous periodic scheme is to divide the syllabus at 11 +, taking an introductory survey of history through stories for the junior and a more connected treatment for the senior stage, a plan which accords with the general reorganization into Junior and Senior Schools, and permits some connected treatment of earlier history. This plan is in use in several schools, and an analysis of some of their schemes follows on page 10.

Some such division into junior and senior stages is assumed by the Board of Education's Suggestions, and the establishment of separate Junior and Senior schools will tend to make it the universal plan. The importance of making a fresh start in the new Senior Schools is more true of history than of almost any subject. We have now the opportunity for a definite break between a 'story' history built up on episodes and a 'connected' history which gives a sense of development and continuity between present and past. It seems naturally appropriate that this change in method

First Example	Standard II. Stories of world history from Primitive Man to about A.D. 1327	III. Stories from about 1327–the present day	IV. More connected history of ancient and medieval times up to about 1272
Second Example	Biographies taken from world history	Biographies continued	*c.* 55 B.C.–1485
Third Example	English stories from early times to A.D. 1154	Stories from 1154–1603	IIIA. Stories from 1603 to the Industrial Revolution
Fourth Example	Stories covering all range of history	Stories of medieval social history	IV. Stories of modern social history

First Example	Standard V. 1272–1553	VI. 1553–1783	VII. 1783 to the present day		
Second Example	*c.* 1485–1715	*c.* 1715–1832	1832 to the present day.		
Third Example	IV. Stories from the Industrial Revolution to to-day	V. Connected history from early times to A.D. 1154	VI. 1154–1603	VII. 1603–1815	Ex-VII. 1815–to-day
Fourth Example	V. 1066–1485	VI. 1485–1750	VII. 1750–the present day		

should be accompanied by a fresh start in syllabus, and that Senior teachers should try to survey all the ground from a fresh standpoint instead of relegating the important early periods to be studied in the Junior schools only. This plan, however, has the great disadvantage of encouraging an overcrowding of the syllabus. If the whole course of history is covered, on however definite a principle of selection, in the three years of a Senior School course or the three top standards of an 8–14-year-old School, there is very little elbow room: and in fact it might almost be said that until the leaving age is raised a satisfactory syllabus of this type is impossible. A four-year Senior course is more manageable, and might run:—

First Year.	Second Year.	Third Year.	Fourth Year.
Ancient times to the fall of Rome	The Middle Ages	c. 1485–1715	1715 to the present day
or Ancient and early medieval times to 1066	c. 1066–1603	1603–1815	1815 to the present day

4. Some Practical Difficulties

The greatest of all the practical difficulties awaiting our author is indeed the difficulty of *avoiding overcrowding*. His salvation will be to find some principle of selection dictated by his own ideals and experience. One syllabus aimed at 'selection on the principle of what affects our own environment'. This is the point of view taken by the French authorities who exclude from their elementary syllabus details of the French religious civil war, which they consider to have little bearing upon modern conditions, but include a study of the English constitutional struggles of the seventeenth century as containing ideas essential to the understanding of modern democracy. Another teacher opposes the idea that the history syllabus should attempt to cover the whole field. 'The mistake we teachers have made has been in aiming at completion. We have visualized a finished education at twelve, at fourteen, at seventeen, at twenty-one, and so have failed, for we have tried to crowd in too much. Especially true is this of history. Looking at the vast amount to be done, at the demands made by this or that specialist, we have almost thrown up our hands in despair, declaring it could never be done in the limited time at our disposal. But neither could it be completed in the longest lifetime; so why try to crowd it into the years before leaving the Elementary School at fourteen, or even the University ten years later? Why, in fact, try to complete it at all—why not aim chiefly at giving a zest for historical studies and let Nature and Opportunity do the rest?'

This does not mean that the committee would advise the omission of whole periods of history from the curriculum. It is true that a case might be made out for doing so, for we should not choose to teach eighteenth and nineteenth century history to children of thirteen and fourteen if there were any reasonable chance of their studying it at a later time; children leave the elementary school at an age when the more expensively educated child has hardly begun the study of serious history, and they are always in danger of being treated as more mature than they really are. But the solution of this difficulty lies in the raising of the leaving age rather than in the omission of the difficult modern periods from the syllabus: the children have a right to learn the connected outline of the story of their own past. What the teacher can do, is to abandon the attempt to teach all parts of history in equal detail, and to concentrate on those movements and events that are of outstanding interest, showing their sequence by time charts and diagrams rather than by plodding through intermediary events of secondary importance, and explaining a movement not by telling as many facts as possible in connexion with it, but by choosing the most vivid incident to stand as symbol for the rest. The relief given to the syllabus by the use of this '*symbol lesson*' can hardly be exaggerated: so much is gained and so little lost. The whole issue between Crown and Parliament in the reign of James I can be conveyed by a well-prepared treatment of the Parliament of 1621; the very spirit of Roman civilization and government is implicit in the story of Agricola in Britain. One interesting syllabus was drawn up entirely on the basis of the 'symbol' lesson. It was divided into two columns, headed 'From the grown-up point of view' and 'From the child's point of view'. The first column contained a chronological analysis of the great movements of history; the second column showed the title of a 'symbol' story or piece of work by which the movement could be made intelligible to the child's mind, so slow to classify, and so quick to apprehend.

The next practical difficulty that faces our author is the question of the *six-months' promotion system* which is in force in some localities and notably in London. It is obviously unsuitable to arrange a syllabus which allots a period of history for a year's work in each standard if large numbers of the children are to be moved up when the work is half done. Nor was the committee successful in finding any simple solution of this difficulty. Some schools aim at covering the period twice in each standard so that the brighter children study it once and pass on, while the slower ones repeat the work. But this obviously doubles the difficulty of the overcrowded syllabus: the periods are generally fully long enough for a year's study and could not be covered satisfactorily in six months. One school had made an ingenious adaptation of the concentric plan; the year's work was studied from the social point of view in the first six months and from the political point of view in the second. This plan did at least ensure that there should be no gaps of centuries in the individual child's curriculum. Other schools expected the brighter children to fill in the gaps for themselves by individual reading from a simple book. None of these solutions is really satisfactory, and it was the general conclusion of the committee that the six-months' promotion system is definitely harmful to the continuity of history teaching. It is hoped, however, that the evils of the system will disappear during reorganization. In one of the new Senior Schools known to the committee the children were grouped (with the exception of two special classes for retarded children) in six consecutive and separate classes, each pursuing its work without interruption from a newly promoted group. Schools organized in this way might adopt the following scheme:—

First Year.	First half. Ancient and Early Times to A.D. 1066.
	Second half. 1066–1485.
Second Year.	First half. 1485–1603.
	Second half. 1603–1714.
Third Year.	First half. 1714–1830.
	Second half. 1830–the present day.

Or, to much more advantage, if a fourth year is possible:—

First Year.	First half. Ancient Times to the birth of Christ.
	Second half. From the birth of Christ to A.D. 1066.
Second Year.	First half. 1066–1399.
	Second half. 1399–1603

Third Year. First half. 1603–1688.
Second half. 1688–1783.

Fourth Year. First half / Second half — 1783 to the present day, divided on the basis of topics rather than periods.

A further practical difficulty is often found in the presence of *Standard Ex-VII* children who cannot form a separate class and who are in danger of marking time. In every school that mentioned the point, this difficulty was solved by individual work. One school allowed boys working individually or in pairs to use a reference library and to draw up an illustrated note-book on such topics as :—The History of Westminster : The Industrial Revolution : the Growth of the Empire. Another school set boys to work on individual revision from the point of view of a new text-book. This difficulty too will disappear with reorganization.

If our author is framing a *country-school syllabus* the arrangement of the general plan is still further complicated by the grouping together of two or more standards. If, for instance, Standards V, VI, and VII are to work together and are to study modern history in three periods, only one group in three will study them in their proper order, and the difficulty of giving a sense of continuity (a difficulty great enough in any case with children under fifteen) will be insuperable. Country schools are meeting this problem in various ways. Many use time charts to make clear to the children the whereabouts of the period they are studying and to show the unfortunates who begin in the middle exactly what gap they have left and when it is to be filled in. One school prefaces each year's work with a short summary of the whole course in broadest outline, taken by the old pupils as revision and by the new-comers as introductory. This plan seemed to the committee much to be commended. Another school combined the periodic with the concentric plan :—

Standards I and II.	Standards III and IV.	Standards V, VI and VII.
A two-year course; stories of world history.	A two-year course on medieval history: first year, social; second year, political.	A three-year course on modern history: first year, social; second year, political; third year, imperial.

Others advise that pupils should work individually as much as possible, so that several schemes of work should go on in the same room at the same time. This plan is excellent in good hands and if there is an adequate class library: it requires a high standard of knowledge and organizing power on the part of the teacher, and imposes a heavy burden of correction. It is the solution of the enthusiast.

5. Choice of Subject-Matter

It is generally agreed that at the *Junior Stage* history should be told or read in story form. At this stage the child delights in action, both in himself and in others; he can picture incidents but not sequences. He can project himself into other scenes so thoroughly as to lose his own personality, but he has little sense of time, cause or effect. The natural aim of the teacher is to use this imaginative power to awaken a zest for the learning of history and to create bright picturesque centres of interest round which the general plan of history can later be revealed. But he must also have in mind the development of a sense of time and proportion, and this second aim will be important in determining his choice and grouping of stories. The best syllabuses showed clearly the attempt to find *stories that were not merely anecdotal in character, but significant of some great outstanding character and event.* One syllabus is arranged on biographical lines, each character chosen to introduce some historical movement: S. Augustine stands as spokesman for the conversion of the barbarians, Richard I for the crusades, and Raleigh for the age of Elizabeth. Another aims at 'giving an early acquaintance with the great names and characteristics of the history of all nations', and arranges the stories in geographical groups which preserve a rough time order: one or two typical groups from different parts of the syllabus follow:—

Egypt: The Nile; the Pharaohs; the Pyramids; the story of the Israelites.
Greece: The Siege of Troy; Sparta and Athens; Marathon; Salamis; Alexander the Great.
Norway: Eric the Red; Greenland; America.
Spain: the Moors in Europe; Christopher Columbus; the Spanish Armada.

In the majority of cases the stories were drawn from a wide range, both in time and space. A considerable number opened with stories of the ancient world and made the connexion with early British history through the figure of Julius Caesar, as is illustrated below :—

Standard II. Stories of Heroes from Ancient and English History.

Greece. The Story of Troy
The Story of Marathon
The Story of Thermopylae
The Story of Alexander
Rome. The Story of Romulus and Remus
The Story of Horatius
The Story of Regulus and the Carthaginians
The Story of Julius Caesar
Britain. The Ancient Britons and how they lived
The coming of Julius Caesar to Britain
The Story of Caractacus, etc.

This *width of range* seemed to the committee much to be commended: at a time when the children have not arrived at national consciousness but enter readily into dramatic stories of every age and sphere it seems natural and sensible that they should be given access to the many mansions of history.

Children at the junior stage enjoy *the connexion of history with handwork,* and this was recognized in several of the syllabuses submitted. In one school the whole course was planned as a history of everyday things: the development of ships, land transport, crafts, agriculture and houses was traced from their primitive beginnings by a series of stories told in the history lesson and a series of models made in handwork time. The stories were not too general in their character, but illustrated development from actual historical events: as is shown, for instance, by two stories from the section on transport—'How the first crusade marched across Europe' and 'How the third crusade went by sea'. The advantage of historical handwork is that it gives the children a sense of the concrete reality of life long ago. The danger is that it may proceed so slowly as seriously to hamper the pace of the course.

The difficulty of developing the *time sense* at the junior stage is very great. Some schools begin to use time charts as early as Standard III: this would require careful teaching. In one case children are taught to make time charts, as they are taught to make maps, by beginning with small familiar units: they plan out, first a school morning into hours, then their own lives into years, and finally the life lines of their grandfathers, fathers and themselves using the decade and century units. This school has produced some very successful charts and diagrams among the older children. Another school has an arrangement of world history stories for Standard II so grouped that in the course of a year the children learn a few broad divisions of historical time:—

Standard II: (i) Stories of long ago, before the birth of Christ. (The children are to learn to divide 'long ago' into B.C. and A.D. and understand the meaning of the abbreviation.) The detailed list of stories follows.

(ii) Stories of long ago after the birth of Christ and before the Norman Conquest. (The children learn to make a division of time A.D. at the Conquest, nearly eleven centuries after the birth of Christ.)

(iii) Stories after the birth of Christ, after the Conquest and before the reign of Queen Victoria. (The children learn to make another division at Queen Victoria's accession, roughly eight centuries after the Conquest.)

(iv) Stories of recent times. (Nearly a century: the children grasp the century unit as consisting roughly of three generations.)

A number of schools showed very careful *correlation between the junior and senior stages* of their scheme. This seemed to the committee an important point, and one which should not be forgotten during the reorganization. In one case a separate junior school was already shaping its scheme to accord with the scheme of the senior department, and it is to be hoped that this co-operation will be universal.

At the *Senior Stage* the choice of subject-matter becomes increasingly difficult. The committee does not propose to consider the general lines on which each individual period should be treated, because this work has been admirably sketched out on pages 127–34 of the Board's Handbook of Suggestions: and the teacher would be wise to have these pages open before him as he frames his syllabus. But it was felt that many teachers are in doubt as to how the various aspects of history—the social, local, imperial and international—should be envisaged in the syllabus, and that an account of the treatment of this problem by certain picked schools might help to lessen their difficulties.

There were some teachers who solved the problem in each case by a special course. One school finished its survey of English history by the end of Standard VI, so that Standard VII could take a simple course in modern European and

Imperial history. Others covered the field of history on the social side in Standards IV and V and again on the political side in Standards VI and VII. Others introduced short separate courses on local or imperial history. It was felt by the committee that none of these was really satisfactory, partly because the introduction of separate courses tends to overcrowd the rest of the scheme, but chiefly because they deny the essential unity of history to a child's view and obscure the widespread influences of the very theme they wish to emphasize.

To teach history truthfully it is necessary to teach it as a whole. We do not hold simply that English history *should* not be isolated from the history of the outside world, but that it *cannot* be so isolated without destroying its very roots. Almost all the great movements of earlier times—the ideas of Rome, Christianity, monasticism, to some extent feudalism, crusading and commercial enterprise, the Renaissance, the Reformation—passed from Europe to England, and without the story of their origins in Rome or France, Florence or Germany, the English version loses half its meaning. And in the great movements of later history—the development of a European system, the growth of trade and industry and above all the Europeanization of huge areas of the sister continents—England has been more than a recipient : she has been a primary actor, and how can we describe her part without describing the play as a whole ? Historical truth in the past and common sense in the present age make the same demand upon us, that we should teach the history of co-operation and international relationship, of an instinct towards peaceful intercourse more strong and persistent even than our instinct towards war.

The teacher's aim then should not be to give separate courses in 'European' and 'English', 'political' and 'social', 'local' and 'national' history, but to frame one course which shall introduce the great facts of civilization in their true universal bearing, with stories from English history chosen to illustrate them more fully, and stories from local history to make the picture intimate and concrete. Such a course as found in one of the syllabuses submitted runs :—

Standards II and III. Stories from earliest prehistoric times to the Norman Conquest. Stories arranged in chronological order and dealing chiefly with persons.

Standards IV and V (Two-Year Course). *Study of Medieval Times* from the Conquest to the close of the Tudor period. Still largely biographical, but gradually changing in treatment and introducing more formal history and reading.

Standard VI. The Stuart and Bourbon periods. Social and political changes in Britain from 1603 to 1750; and in Europe in the days of Richelieu and Louis XIV. Interest is centred in England on the constitutional struggle, the growth of the first British Empire, and trade progress; in Europe on the struggle of France for domination and on the French leadership in science and art.

Standard VII and ex-VII. [Most boys spend the greater part of two years on this course.] *The Modern World, the Age of Revolutions.* The French Revolution and the rise of democracy. The Industrial and Commercial Revolutions and consequent social changes. The spread of European civilization, modern overseas Empires and world changes in consequence.

To show the balance kept between general, national and local history, an analysis of the syllabus in one standard is subjoined:—

STANDARD IV.

General	*British*	*Local*
A. FEUDALISM. Lord and Vassal. Manors, Crown and Barons. Chivalry.	A. The Normans. Domesday Book. Magna Carta. Simon de Montfort. Edward and Hundred Years' War. Peasants' Revolt.	A. Norman London. Tower. London and the Charter.
B. THE CHURCH. Popes and Kings. Monks. Friars. The Crusades.	B. The Church in England. Anselm. Becket. Monks and Friars. Schools.	B. London Monasteries. S. Bartholomew's. Westminster. Lambeth Palace. Parish Churches.
C. TOWNS AND TRADE. The Hanse, Italian and Belgian Towns. Great traders.	C. English Commerce. Wool and Wine. English towns.	C. London Trades and Gilds. Civic government. Social life. Great Londoners.

This syllabus is worked in a boys' school in a fairly good district, where one hour a week is allotted to history in the lower classes, one hour and a half in the middle and two hours in the upper. The treatment is by oral stories in the lower school, by oral lessons with reading in the middle school, and by reading supplemented by oral lessons in the top classes. The lessons are illustrated throughout by reference to the history of London, by visits to museums and places of interest, by pictures, models and sketches, by references to contemporary literature and for the older boys by a school journey to a place chosen for its historical associations. Important anniversaries are mentioned by the History Master at Assembly. The main purpose of the course is 'to arouse interest in historical studies generally and in particular in the part played by the British people in the growth of modern civilization, so that whilst the chief emphasis is laid on British History this is considered in relation to the whole history of civilization, particularly in Western Europe, and is illustrated by constant reference to the history of London'.

It is fully recognized that this combination of national and international history is not easy for the non-specialist to plan, and that many teachers may be holding to a conventional English outline merely because they feel at home there and dread losing themselves in the mazes of universal history. Such teachers would find practical help in studying Marten & Carter's 'Elementary Histories' where the main movements of general history are very cleverly connected with the national story, and Delisle Burns' 'International Intercourse' which gives valuable suggestive material for the teacher. They might also find helpful the following extracts from syllabuses, showing how particular topics are dealt with from the world history point of view.

1. A boys' school in a poor district begins the senior course of history by a 'brief outline of Ancient History to show how and when England stepped on the stage of history'.

A. Ancient History :—

I. *Egypt : Assyria : Babylon : Persia.*

II. *Greece* (1) Crete the forerunner of Greece—the early Greek world.
(2) Greece saves Europe from Persia.
(3) Fall of Greek City States.
(4) Alexander the Great: spread of Greek influence and learning.

III. *Rome* (1) Rise to power. Patricians and Plebeians. Rise of republic.

(2) Conflict with Carthage.
(3) Julius Caesar and conquest of Gaul.

B. ENGLAND BEFORE 1066 (with some reference to Europe) :—

I. *Britons* at time of Roman invasion.
II. *Romans in Britain*—
(1) Great characters and events.
(2) The work of the Romans in Britain.
(3) Why the Romans left Britain, etc.

2. Another school prefaces the Tudor period in English history with a description of the continental movements without which the careers of Henry VIII or Cranmer, Drake or Raleigh, must be unintelligible to the beginner :—

THE BEGINNINGS OF MODERN HISTORY

(i) Discovery. The new map. Portuguese exploration to the East : Spaniards to the West : England to the North-west.
The great names : Prince Henry the Navigator; Columbus ; Diaz ; Da Gama ; Cabot.
(ii) Learning. Painting, Sculpture, and Art : Angelo and Titian. Literature : More and Erasmus. Science : Bacon and Copernicus.
(iii) Religion. The Reformation : substitution of national churches for a world Church. The state of the Church and the Lutheran revolt.

3. A girls' school in a fairly good district gives the Standard VII year to a study of nineteenth-century history taken in two parts. The first part, which is entitled '*The Worker and the State*', is concerned with home history considered mainly from the social point of view. The second part, '*Nations and Empires*', deals with outstanding events of imperial and European history and concludes with a picture of the modern world which is quoted here :—

THE GREAT WAR AND AFTER

Before the War. The Armament Race. The Triple Alliance.
The War. Murder of the Austrian archduke and outbreak of war.
The Colonies and the Mother Country.
The Eastern and Western fronts. The Russian Revolution. The entry of America. The Armistice. The German Revolution.

After the War. Treaty of Versailles. President Wilson and the fourteen points.

The formation of the League of Nations.

The British Empire to-day; the self-governing Colonies; the Irish Free State; the problem of India and Egypt; the Imperial Conference.

In the same way that European history cannot be separated from English, social history cannot be separated from political in the elementary syllabus. Children are not ready for these artificial divisions which enable the adult to specialize his interests. But the balance between social and political in a combined course is not always easy to keep. Where social history is supreme, the work is in danger of becoming vague, lacking in clear outline and chronology; but it is equally futile to go to the other extreme, treat social history as a poor relation, and put it off with an occasional trivial lesson on manners and customs. The study of social history should give not only a vivid picture of the conditions of the period but a sense of those great public grievances, desires or beliefs which have inspired political events. It is not necessary, for instance, to spare one group of lessons for the description of town and country life in early Stuart times and another for discussing the causes of the Civil War: the life of the countryside can be treated in the course of a story showing what happened when Hampden's estate in Stoke Mandeville was assessed at 20 shillings ship money, or what a village felt like when Laud's metropolitan commissioners visited it: and the life of the town can be described when the Five Members enter the City after their retreat from Westminster, and find enthusiastic welcome there. The aim should not be to add social history to political as another burden on the already heavily burdened syllabus, but to socialize the whole treatment of political events so that the great facts of history are seen not only through the minds of statesmen but as they affect the lives of humble people.

This combination of social and political history was attempted in a large number of syllabuses. In one school each block of political history was revised from the point of view of its social effects. Another school gave an extra fortnightly period to history, which was devoted to considering the social aspect of the political events under review: an instance follows:—

Political Aspect	*Social Aspect*
The Reformation on the Continent: Luther, Calvin, Knox.	
The English Reformation: political aspect; religious aspect.	Effect of the dissolution of the monasteries.

Another syllabus was arranged in parallel columns showing the analysis of a single course into its political and social elements :—

Political Aspect	*Social Aspect*
1. William of Normandy conquers England.	Norman architecture—the Abbey and Tower. Feudalism. Domesday Book. Norman amusements. Tournament and Hunt. The New Forest. Norman village and castle.

The same principle was found in regard to local history: Roman Britain is illustrated from the history of Greenwich and Charlton, Norman England from the Tower of London, the Stuart period from Greenwich Hospital, the eighteenth century from Lincoln's Inn Fields, and nineteenth-century changes from the development of the suburbs. The idea of the combined syllabus was well expressed by the notes written by one head master at the head of his syllabus :—

(*a*) Special stress laid on social and industrial development.
(*b*) European viewpoint taken where possible.
(*c*) History of locality taken in conjunction with national events.

A brief analysis follows of the events which might be considered essential to include in the senior school work: this analysis is not in any sense of the word a syllabus, nor are the topics always arranged in a suitable order for teaching: it is simply a list from which teachers may test the comprehensiveness of their own scheme.

The First Year might contain a series of lessons, based largely upon the work already done in story form at the junior stage, beginning with Early Man and coming down to the Norman Conquest.

1. The Stone and Bronze Ages
2. Egypt, Babylon and the Jews
3. The Greeks
4. The Roman Republic
5. Early Britain
6. The Roman Empire and Roman Britain
7. The Barbarian Invasions and Settlements; the Saxon village
8. Religions of East and West. (*a*) The Conversion of the Barbarians to Christianity: early Monasticism. (*b*) Mahomet and Islam
9. The Barbarian Empire: Charles the Great
10. The Danish Invasions and the Age of Alfred and his house
11. The coming of Feudalism
12. The Norman Conquest

The Second Year would deal with the Middle Ages to the time of the great discoveries.

The late eleventh and twelfth centuries (Romanesque architecture: Norman)

1. Norman and early Angevin government
2. Feudalism: castle and manor
3. The Church: wars of Church and State in Europe and England: monasticism: architecture
4. The First Three Crusades
5. Intercourse between England and Europe: (*a*) peaceful, (*b*) warlike: the empire of Henry II

The thirteenth century (Gothic architecture: Early English style)

1. The rise of the French monarchy under Philip II and S. Louis
2. The greatness of the Papacy under Innocent III
3. The development of the constitution in the times of John, Henry III and Edward I
4. The Friars
5. First attempts at the union of the British Isles

The fourteenth century (Gothic architecture: decorated style)

1. Trade and town life in Italy, Germany and England
2. The first part of the Hundred Years' War
3. Decline of the influence of the Church: the Pope at Avignon; Wyclif
4. Social changes in the manor; the Peasants' Revolt

The fifteenth century (Gothic architecture: perpendicular style)

1. Social changes: the 'overmighty subject'; the decay of villeinage
2. Second part of the Hundred Years' War: revival of France
3. The Wars of the Roses

4. Islam victorious in Constantinople and defeated in Spain
5. The Italian Renaissance

Third Year

The sixteenth century (Transition from Gothic to Renaissance architecture)

1. The Renaissance in Italy, France and England
2. The Great Discoveries
3. The New Monarchy in Spain and England
4. The Reformation in Germany, France and England
5. Social and economic changes in town and country
6. The Age of Elizabeth
7. The Revolt of the Netherlands

The seventeenth and eighteenth centuries to 1783.

1. The Age of Richelieu and the Rise of France
2. The political and religious causes of the English Civil Wars
3. The Civil War and Commonwealth
4. Expansion of Commerce and Colonization
5. The Restoration and Revolution
6. The Age of Louis XIV in Europe
7. The Foundations of Russia and Prussia
8. The Wesleyan Revival
9. Developments of Agriculture and Science
10. The First British Empire and Anglo-French wars
11. The Loss of America

Fourth Year. The Age of Revolution and Change from 1783 to the present day.

A. The Political Revolutions :—
   1. The French Revolution
   2. The English Constitutional Revolution from 1832

B. The Mechanical Revolution :—
   1. Textiles
   2. Machinery and Engineering
   3. Transport and Communications

C. The Social Revolution :—
   1. Social conditions in the early nineteenth century
   2. The State and remedial legislation
   3. Trade Unionism

D. The International Revolution, which is barely begun :—
   1. Napoleon and Europe
   2. The settlement of 1815 and its immediate effects
   3. Europe in 1848–70
   4. The causes of the great war, 1870–1914
   5. The War: the treaties
   6. The New Europe and the League of Nations

E. Europe and the World :—
1. The world bound together by trade and transport
2. The United States: the civil war and the negro question; the immigration problem
3. The British Commonwealth :—
(a) The colonies and self-government
(b) The dependencies and their problems
(c) Mandated territories under the League of Nations
(d) The Imperial Conference

6. Detailed Arrangement

Having got out his general plan and considered his subject-matter, our author will now have to consider the detailed arrangement. This will vary, and full scope must be left to individual teachers: but at the same time there should be some common principle of arrangement. The old-fashioned division into the reigns of kings had the merit of simplicity and regular chronological sequence. But it involved much overlapping and tended to fill the lesson with miscellaneous material instead of presenting the one clear, well-illustrated point that the child's imagination can grasp. This arrangement by reigns is most satisfactory in those periods, such as the Tudor age, when the king's power was so great that a change of monarch did really affect the course of events: it is definitely unsatisfactory in early times or in the eighteenth and nineteenth centuries. Very few of the syllabuses submitted had adopted such an arrangement. The majority had grouped their facts in topics, arranged in a time order. The aim of this grouping is to avoid scrappiness and to allow time for an intelligent understanding of each subject. But there is danger that if the topics are made too full, the time order may be lost and the child's mind confused. To take the whole of the Hundred Years' War in one dose, and the whole of the religious unrest of the same period in another, for instance, must leave the child with a strong tendency to feel that Wyclif lived after Joan of Arc. Chronological sequence is the first consideration in the normal syllabus, and the 'topic' treatment of facts can only be used with safety so long as it fits into a chronological framework. This point is strongly emphasized by the French authorities, and we should do well to imitate them. Care should also be taken that the topics are of equal value, not a medley of great movements and small episodes: the historical balance is destroyed if, for instance, the Reformation is set down as one single topic and the Pilgrimage of Grace as another.

7. The Children's Attitude Towards the Syllabus

And now, having drafted his syllabus, our author must at once end and begin his work by introducing it to the children. For there is no reason why the school plan of work should be treated as a state secret, known only to the teaching caste. The children gain both in interest and in general grasp of the work if they understand their programme : and alternatively it is extraordinary what ignorance of the main historical sequence may be shown by a well-informed child who has never realized his syllabus as a whole.

In one school an introductory lesson was given yearly to the children on the outline programme of work throughout their course, while a fuller terminal programme was pinned up for inspection. In another school a large class-room chart is begun in Standard III and carried up the school until the course is completely shown in Standard VII. In yet another a time chart is made in each standard showing the whole range of historical time, so that the class can definitely 'place' the period it is studying. The child's knowledge of the syllabus is closely connected with that essential factor in the learning of history, knowledge of time order and continuity of events. A large number of schools advocate the use of *time charts* and a short *list of important dates* to be memorized each term. This shows a welcome reaction from the vague history of recent fashions. Certain dates are milestones in the course of history, and without them the young student easily loses his way. Other schools stress the importance of *revision*: one school begins each year with a general revision. Many teachers have pointed out the importance of a well-kept *note-book* : without this, indeed, it is difficult to see how revision could be carried out or how the elementary school child who possesses no text-book can gain any idea of the march of events. One head master writes, 'No history lesson should be considered complete until the boys have some definite record of it in their own note-books. These notes need not necessarily be in literary form. The subject of each lesson will suggest to the teacher and boys its particular form.' In another school each boy has a time chart note-book which goes up the school with him. Several other schools note that their younger children keep history picture books and the older children note-books, using class libraries, public libraries and books of reference as their work develops.

In every case, the aim of the course must be to give the children a living interest in the past, present and future state of the world : to give them, as one head mistress writes, 'enough knowledge, pride, interest and perhaps dissatisfaction in regard to the past to make them good citizens in the future'. To this end it is essential both that they work with interest and that they work hard. Interest and hard work should not be regarded as two alternative and mutually exclusive principles dividing teachers into hostile camps : no one can work really hard unless he is interested, and no one can come to possess a lasting interest without hard work. The aim of an attractive syllabus, like the aim of modern methods in the class-room, is to bring into education (to use the words of our colleagues in France) 'plus d'air, plus d'aisance, plus de liberté, plus de joie *et partant plus de travail*'.

II

TEXT-BOOKS FOR PUPILS UNDER FIFTEEN

Arranged in alphabetical order under publishers' names

Bell. State and Commons. Vol. I, by Allsopp, H., 180 pp., 2*s.* 3*d.* Vol. II, by Mowat, R., 131 pp., 2*s.* 8*d.* Vol. III, by Cameron, S. S., 161 pp., 2*s.* 3*d.* 1926.

A periodic series, which gives a sound narrative of English history, combining economic and political aspects : too hard for individual reading by the average Senior School child, but useful for reference.

Black. Finnemore, J. Social Life in England. 2 vols., about 260 pp. each. 2*s.* 6*d.* each.

Rather an old, but still useful series ; vividly and simply told, and containing some interesting extracts from sources. Illustrations of varying value ; those from contemporary sources good. For the upper classes of Junior and for Senior Schools.

Blackie. Britain and her Neighbours. I. Tales from Far and Near. 1*s.* 9*d.* II. Tales of Long Ago. 1*s.* 10*d.* Simple romantic stories covering the whole field of history. III. The Beginnings. 55 B.C.–1066. 2*s.* 2*d.* IV. Lord and Vassal. 1066–1485. 2*s.* 4*d.* V. The New Liberty. 1485–1688. 2*s.* 8*d.* VI. The Modern World. 2*s.* 10*d.* VII. The Twentieth Century. 3*s.* 6*d.*

The first two volumes are useful for reading by very young children, though the stories are not always of great historical importance. Books III, IV and V are quite well suited to use in an elementary school ; they are simple and interesting, and their most valuable feature, as the name of the series suggests, is the correlation of National and European History. The main episodes, however, are sometimes disproportionately treated, and the series is most valuable used in conjunction with some other. The last two volumes are considerably harder. The series is undated, but is not new.

Blackie. Lands and their Stories. A series combining History and Geography. Could not be used as the only text-book, but valuable for supplementary reading. The most useful volumes are :—Vol. IV. Scotland and Ireland and Britain Overseas. By Berry, A. J. 240 pp. 1923 (current issue). 2*s.* 7*d.* Vol. V. Europe and its Peoples. By Palmer, H. W. 288 pp. 1925 (latest issue). 2*s.* 10*d.* Vol. VI. Our Empire Overseas. By Palmer, H. W. 1924 (latest issue). 3*s.*

Blackwell. Elementary Histories. By Marten, C. H. K. and Carter, E. H. Can be obtained in one, two, three or four volumes. The four vol. arrangement runs :—I. Our Heritage. 2*s.* II. The Middle Ages. 2*s.* 6*d.* III. New Worlds. 2*s.* 9*d.* IV. The Latest Age. 3*s.* 1927–8. Or, I. To 1485. 2*s.* 9*d.* II. 1485–1688. 2*s.* 9*d.* III. 1688–1927. 3*s.*

This is a new series of outstanding merit, both as regards the character of its contents and the beauty of its illustrations. It covers the whole ground of history from ancient times to to-day, ' setting the British story in the story of mankind ' and not neglecting the social background. The subject-matter is very skilfully chosen and arranged, and the numerous excellent contemporary pictures go far to solve the whole problem of illustrations for the teacher. The grading is rather steep. Book I is delightfully simple and vivid reading, suited for Junior School children, while Book IV requires the intelligent co-operation of the teacher, and probably the average Senior School would not study the whole of it. Highly recommended as text-books.

C.U.P. The Story of the People of Britain. Book I. 55 B.C.–1485. By Sarson, M. 182 pp. Book II. 1485–1688. By Sarson, M. 197 pp. Book III. 1689–1815. By Hanson, L. 250 pp. Book IV. By Hanson, L. 240 pp. Books I and II, 2*s.* 6*d.* each. Books III and IV, 3*s.* each. Original date, 1916–18. Current issues, 1924–8.

A good and simply written series, specially emphasizing social history. Excellent pictures and charts. Specially useful for supplementary reading.

Collins. The New World History Series. Ed. Manning, B. L. Book I. To 1485. By Power, E. 227 pp., 2*s.* Book II. 1485–1688. By Jones, M. G. 280 pp., 2*s.* 3*d.* Book III. 1688–1815. By Gardner, A. 260 pp., 2*s.* 6*d.* Book IV. By Hanson, L. 296 pp., 2*s.* 6*d.* Original date 1920. Date of current issue, 1925.

A series covering the ground of political and social English History. The first three vols. contain appendices of illustrative extracts, very useful for individual work. The first volume is outstandingly the best—simple, vivid and original in treatment. It is also the best illustrated.

Collins. The Path to History. By Niemeyer, N. Book I. The Dawn of History to Imperial Rome. 96 pp., 1*s.* 6*d.*

Book II. Stories from Early and Medieval History. 112 pp., 1s. 8d. Book III. Stories from Modern History. 160 pp. 2s. 1928–9.

A series of very charming stories for private reading in Junior Schools.

Collins. The Way of History. Ed. Bell, K. N. Book I. To 1485. By Gorham, M. A. C. 210 pp. 1s. 9d. Book II. By Blake, W. J. 1485–1660. 256 pp. 2s. Book III. 1680–1815. By Otley, A. M. 256 pp. 2s. 3d. Book IV. To the present day. By Bell, K. N. 324 pp. 2s. 6d. 1924–6.

A good clear outline of English and Imperial history, containing maps, date lists, and some very useful extracts from sources. The illustrations not particularly good. Not always interesting to read, but distinguished for their unbiased treatment of controversial eras. A useful text-book.

Ginn. England and the Empire. Book I. To 1485. By Stevinson, E. 160 pp. 1s. 9d. Book II. 1485–1660. By Field, E. M. 192 pp. 2s. Book III. By Field, E. M. 256 pp. 2s. 6d. Book IV. 1815–1925. 320 pp. 2s. 9d. 1920–5.

A good series, simple, clear, and containing suggestions for further individual work and reading. Illustrations fairly good. Useful for children's reading, especially in conjunction with another book, as not all essential topics are dealt with.

Harrap. Stone Age Readers. I. The Cave Boy of the Age of Stone. By McIntyre, M. A. 160 pp. 1927. 1s. 6d. II. Days Before History. By Hall, H. R. New enlarged ed. 1927. 1s. 6d. III. The Threshold of History. By Hall, H. R. 160 pp. 1s. 6d. IV. Man Before History. By Boyle, M. 128 pp. 1924. 2s.

Far the best series of elementary text-books on prehistory, especially the last three. Good illustrations.

Heinemann. The People of England ; a Social History for Schools. By Leathes, S. 3 vols. I. The People in the Making. 289 pp. 1921. 3s. 6d. II. The People in Adventure (to the French Revolution). 302 pp. 1924. 3s. 6d. III. The People on its Trial. 470 pp. 1923. 6s.

This admirable series is too difficult to be used regularly as a text-book by elementary school children. But it should be in the school library for reference ; the first two volumes could be read in part by the older children, and all by the teacher. A story of the development of English civilization and society. Good illustrations, especially in the first two volumes.

Longmans. The Grip-Fast History Books. I. The Beginnings of Christian Britain. By Forbes, F. A. 104 pp.

1924. 1*s.* 6*d.* II. Medieval Britain. By Kerr, C. 149 pp. 1924. 2*s.* III. The Building of the British Empire. By Kerr, C. 141 pp. 1927. 2*s.* IV. The Middle Ages and the Renaissance. By Forbes, F. A. 195 pp. 2*s.* 6*d.* 1928. V. United Britain. By Cunnington, S. 219 pp. 1928. 2*s.* 9*d.*

An attractive series for the use of Roman Catholic Schools. The history of the Church is taken as a guiding thread, particularly in the earlier volumes. Illustrations of uneven value; some merely fanciful. The dates given are of the last impressions; the original dates are not stated.

McDougall's Educational Co. The March of History. I. Little Folks of To-day and Long Ago. By Bryson, E. L. 144 pp. 1928. 2*s.* II. Little Folks through the Ages. By Bryson, E. L. 160 pp. 1928. 2*s.* 2*d.* III. From the Beginnings to the End of the Middle Ages. By Dance, E. H. 240 pp. 1928. 2*s.* 4*d.* IV. From the Middle Ages to the End of the Seventeenth Century. By Futers, F. T. and Martin, C. M. 240 pp. 1928. 2*s.* 6*d.* V. From the end of the Seventeenth Century to the Early Nineteenth. By McHaffie, W. H. 256 pp. 1929.

A new and attractive series which is well suited to the ages for which it is written. The two earliest volumes are very slight, pretty stories suited for the youngest children. There is a considerable gap before Book III, which begins the course of continuous history, and which is suited for children of ten or eleven. The books contain a good deal of social history, constant easy quotations from sources, and useful charts, exercises, and references to historical novels. Illustrations useful when taken from contemporary sources.

Macmillan. The Progress to History. 6 vols. This series is on the concentric plan, and therefore would not agree with the syllabus of most schools. But certain volumes are excellent for class reading. I. Pictures of Long, Long Ago. 128 pp. 1916. Latest impression, 1927. 1*s.* 9*d.*, and II. Peeps into Old Books. 176 pp. 1916 (1925). 2*s.*, are two most charming and useful books for small children. They are beautifully illustrated, and the child is taught to use the pictures as evidence for knowledge of social life. The episodes in Book I are chosen from the period from Joseph to Becket, and form a good background to early world history stories; the episodes in Book II are taken from medieval and Tudor history. Book V. Children of the Seven Seas. 288 pp. 1916 (1923). 2*s.* 6*d.*, is also very useful for supplementary reading on the Empire at a later date. The whole series is edited by R. Wilson.

Nelson. History Practice. I. Then and Now. 96 pp. 1*s.* 3*d.* Semi-fictitious stories which aim above all at giving young children a sense of time. Pass from present to further and further distant past. II. Milestones of History. 95 pp. 1*s.* 3*d.* Simple episodes of British History. Very fanciful illustrations. III. From Ancient Britain to British Empire. 127 pp. 1*s.* 6*d.* IV. The Building of the United Kingdom. 127 pp. 1*s.* 6*d.* V. The Building of Modern Britain. 128 pp. 1*s.* 8*d.* VI. From Napoleon to Yesterday. 128 pp. 1*s.* 8*d.* Compiled by R. Wilson. 1923. Quite useful for supplementary reading.

Nisbet. Self Help Series. By Synge, M. B., Ewing, J., Gaskoin, C., and others. Old Britain and Early England. 208 pp. 2*s.* 6*d.* Normans and Plantagenet. 240 pp. 2*s.* 8*d.* The Tudors. 260 pp. 2*s.* 10*d.* The Stuarts. 300 pp. 3*s.* The Hanoverians. 320 pp. 3*s.* 3*d.* Britain in the Modern World. By Gaskoin, C. J. B. 328 pp. 3*s.* 6*d.* 1911. For children of eleven and upwards. The language of the later volumes is difficult. Sound, and useful for reference. Many illustrations ; the contemporary ones good. Coloured time charts. The Tudors and Stuarts can also be obtained in one abridged vol., 304 pp. 3*s.* There is also a shorter and simpler series in 5 vols., 132 pp. each, 11*d.* or 1*s.* 2*d.* each.

Nisbet. Through the Ages Series. Europe through the Ages. 132 pp. The British Empire through the Ages. By Hill, Wentworth. 132 pp. English Writers through the Ages. By Burton, H. M. 132 pp. The English Citizen through the Ages. By Hill, Wentworth. 132 pp. British Women through the Ages. By Edwards, E. A. 132 pp. 1*s.* or 1*s.* 3*d.* Quite useful for supplementary reading on their subjects, but much compressed.

O.U.P. Mowat, R. B. Graphic History of Great Britain. Part I. To 1603. 160 pp. 1*s.* 6*d.* Part II. 1603–1815. 204 pp. 1*s.* 9*d.* Part III. 1815–1914. 216 pp. 2*s.* 1927.

An abridgement of his larger work, specially intended for Elementary Schools. A clear, straightforward, up-to-date text-book for Senior Schools. Language not easy. Can be obtained in one volume, 4*s.* 6*d.*

O.U.P. Oxford History Readers. 11 parts. 1*s.* 4*d.*, 1*s.* 6*d.*, 1*s.* 8*d.*, 2*s.* and all the rest 2*s.* 4*d.*, except part 10, 1*s.*

The first four parts consist of stories for junior school children on concentric lines : the last five deal with modern English History in periods, with special books on the Empire. For supplementary reading.

Philip. Piers Plowman Histories. General Editor, Spalding, E. H. Junior Book I. 1*s.* 6*d.* Coloured pictures with brief well-written comments for very young children. Junior

Book II. By Sarson, M. and Paine, M. Simple stories from ancient and early medieval history. 1*s.* 6*d.* Junior Book III. Stories chosen from English History from 1066 to the nineteenth century. By Keary, M. and Wragge, P. 1*s.* 9*d.* Junior Book IV. The Social History of England from the Earliest Times to 1485. By Bell, J. J. 2*s.* Junior Book V. The Social History of England from 1485 to the present day. By Spalding, E. H. 2*s.* 6*d.* Junior Book VI. The Nation and its Government from the Time of the Romans to 1485. By Bell, J. J. 2*s.* 9*d.* Junior Book VII. The Nation and its Government from 1485 to the present day. By Spalding, E. H. and Wragge, P. 2*s.* 9*d.* The Teacher's Story Book. By Ramsay, M. and Keary, M. R. 536 pp. 8*s.* 6*d.*, corresponds with Junior Books I, II and III, and the Social and Economic Histories which are detailed in the teachers' section correspond with Junior Books IV and V.

This well-known series is unequalled for the beauty of its illustrations and the simplicity and skill with which it is told ; it is one of the few series that children can really read alone with ease. As it has a definite bias throughout towards social national history, and aims at making certain episodes real rather than including the essential facts of continuous history, it is best used in conjunction with some other series. Books IV and V are especially useful.

Philip. Individual Work Assignments. The 'Individual' History. By Marriott, E. S. A four-year course ; contracts one and two, 7*d.* each ; contracts three and four, 8*d.* each. The working out of a Dalton plan in an elementary school. Interesting ; but such plans are necessarily individual.

Philip. Living History. By Bell, J. J. In progress. Jimmie's Story Book. 120 pp. 1*s.* 6*d.* A History of Homely Things. 154 pp. 1*s.* 9*d.* 1928. Simply told introductory volumes which interest children in the past of everyday things. For very young children.

Pitman. Britain and the World. I. Children of Other Days. By Engvall, E. 40 pp. 1*s.* 6*d.* Simple sketches of boys through the ages, each sketch connected with a picture. For very little children. II. Makers of Britain. By King, E. M. 177 pp. 2*s.* A group of delightfully told stories from English History. III. Twenty Centuries of Travel. By Power, E. and R. 194 pp. 2*s.* 3*d.* Another more advanced series of stories from English and European History. Excellently chosen and told ; suitable for private reading by juniors, yet would give a valuable background for later work. IV. The Growth of a Nation. By Curtis, S. J. 224 pp. 2*s.* 6*d.* V. The Changing Order. By Bowman, F. L. 227 pp. 2*s.* 9*d.* VI. Britain in the nineteenth century and after. By Morris, G. W. 288 pp.

3*s*. These volumes cover the ground of British History in an interesting survey enlivened with delightful illustrations from contemporary sources. Contain useful charts and references for further reading. A very good and attractive new series. Highly recommended.

University of London Press. The Headway Histories. Ed. by Tickner, F. W. Book I. People of Long Ago. By Polkinghorne, R. K. and M. I. R. 100 pp. 1*s*. 8*d*. and 1*s*. 6*d*. Book II. Famous Men and Famous Deeds. By Polkinghorne, R. K. and M. I. R. 128 pp. 1*s*. 10*d*. and 1*s*. 8*d*. Book III. Making the English Homeland. By Tickner, F. W. 128 pp. 1*s*. 10*d*. and 1*s*. 8*d*. Book IV. Building the British Empire. By Tickner, F. W. In preparation. 1928–9.

A very attractive new series for juniors. The history is simply told in story form, yet the subject-matter is not merely anecdotal but of real historical significance. Well graded, and contains exercises. Book I gives simple stories of ancient and Book II a little more substantial stories of modern world history; Book III is an elementary history of England to the end of the Tudor period. Attractive but not contemporary illustrations.

2. SHORTER TEXT-BOOKS OF ENGLISH HISTORY

(*a*) Mainly Political

Davis, M. O. The Story of England. 336 pp. O.U.P. 1924. 3*s*. 6*d*.

Excellent and attractive. A straightforward political history text-book arranged under kings' reigns. The characters, although briefly introduced, are made to live by a few deft phrases. Very good maps, charts and pictures. For Seniors.

Gayford, A. W. P. A Junior History of England. 232 pp. Methuen. 1926. 3*s*. 6*d*.

A well-written book, condensed, but bringing out the essentials. Intended for Secondary School work. Could be used as a reference book in the top class of a Senior School.

Guest, G. Outlines of British History. 248 pp. O.U.P. 1922. 2*s*. 6*d*.

Good matter, but not always easy reading.

Keatinge, M. W. A First History of England. 189 pp. Black. 1926 (3rd ed.). 2*s*. 6*d*.

A good, clear elementary sketch. Its special feature is that it combines political and social history by tracing the fortunes of the imaginary village of Oakwood through the ages. Simply and clearly written for children of about eleven. Contains maps and numerous illustrations of varying value.

Jones, Dr. R. The English People : A Junior History. 220 pp. Dent. 1928. 2*s*. 6*d*.

A lively, direct little sketch.

Miller, E. W. A Beginner's History of England. 280 pp. Harrap. 1921. 2*s*. 6*d*.

A good, straightforward little text-book for Seniors. As well as the narrative of English History, social aspects are described and the leaders of European thought introduced. Events are brought down to the end of the Great War. Contains illustrations, maps, exercises and list of dates.

Thomson, C. L. The Child's Story of Great Britain. 173 pp. Marshall. 1910. 2*s*.

A charming elementary sketch for young children.

Thomson, C. L. A First History of England. In 7 parts. Marshall. The first 5 parts 2*s*. 6*d*., the last 2, 3*s*. 6*d*. each.

Rather old, but still holds its own by its attractive, pleasant style.

Tickner, F. W. Outlines of British History. 2 vols. Univ. of London Press. 1924. 3*s*. 6*d*. each.

An excellent, sound narrative of English social and political history ; this makes it the more annoying that the language is needlessly difficult. The book would be of value to teachers in planning a course, especially as the exercises at the end of each chapter suggest some interesting and stimulating individual work. Contains illustrations from contemporary sources.

Warner, G. Townsend. A Brief Survey of British History. 272 pages. Blackie. 1920 (latest impression ; original date, 1912). 2*s*. 9*d*.

This, although an old book, still deserves mention as a clear, succinct account of English History by a great teacher.

Wilmot-Buxton, E. M. A Junior History of Great Britain. 302 pp. Methuen. 1927 (9th ed. ; original date, 1910). 3*s*. 6*d*.

Quite a useful political narrative for Senior Schools ; subjects generally well chosen, and given as realistic and interesting treatment as is possible in the space. Useful summary at ends of chapters. 6 maps. No illustrations.

(*b*) Social and Economic

Allsopp, H. Introduction to English Industrial History. 172 pp. Bell. 1925. 2*s*.

A good interesting survey for the top classes of Senior Schools. Contains extracts from sources. No illustrations.

Burrows, H. L. The Story of English Industry and Trade. 208 pp. Black. 1914. 3*s*.

Concise, comprehensive and interesting ; deals with Medieval

Times, Tudor and Stuart Times, the Industrial Revolution and After. Good illustrations. For Senior Schools.

Court, H. and L. The Story of British Trade and Commerce. 150 pp. Sampson, Low, etc. 1927. 2*s.* 6*d.*

Very good and interesting. Covers new ground, especially as regards the nineteenth and twentieth centuries. Has the great advantage for children just going out into commercial life that it brings the story up to date—mentioning, for instance, the coal troubles of 1926 and the Finance Bill of 1925. Good illustrations. For top classes of Senior Schools.

Dance, E. H. Outlines of British Social History. 232 pp. Longmans. 1927. 3*s.*

A good sketch of social conditions from the Stone Age to the days of Trade Unions and Co-operative Societies. Some suggestive exercises and extracts from sources. Well illustrated. For Senior Schools.

Doorly, E. England in her Days of Peace. 254 pp. Philip. 1920. 2*s.* 6*d.*

Contains much interesting illustrative social material. A useful class library book for the top classes of Senior Schools and their teachers.

Finnemore, J. Social Life in England. 2 vols. Black. 1924. 3*s.* each.

An oldish, but still very interesting and comprehensive book, which holds its own among the new-comers for soundness and vividness. For top classes of Senior Schools.

Guest, G. A Social History of England. 230 pp. Bell. 2*s.* 6*d.*

A good and simple survey for Senior Schools. Well illustrated.

Hall, H. R. W. Social Life in England through the Centuries. 216 pp. Blackie. 1919. 2*s.* 9*d.*

A simple and interesting survey. Contains useful chapters on architecture. Good illustrations. For Senior Schools.

Hope, Ellis. A Short History of English Life and Labour. 240 pp. Nisbet. 1925. 3*s.*

A sound and very interesting book, containing generous extracts from sources. Of special value to children who are about to enter commerce or industry, since it explains how modern conditions arose. Very good illustrations. Too difficult as a whole for a text-book, but a most delightful class library book for teachers and the children of the top class.

Ramsay, A. A. W. Social and Industrial History of Britain. 322 pp. Chambers. 1926. 3*s.*

A good and reliable social history from Roman to modern times. Author makes use of original sources. Good illustrations and booklists. For top classes of Senior Schools.

Warner, G. Townsend. Tillage, Trade and Invention. 198 pp. Blackie. 1920 (latest ed.; original date, 1912). 3*s.*

A rather old but still valuable outline of Economic History.

3. TEXT-BOOKS ON WORLD HISTORY AND EUROPEAN HISTORY

Corke, H. Class Books of World History. O.U.P. Book I. The World's Family. 183 pp. 1927. 2*s.* 6*d.* Book II. The Home Builders. 244 pp. 1928.

An interesting series for the upper classes of Junior and the lower classes of Senior Schools. The great aim is to make the children feel the unity as well as the variety of world history. Book I introduces the reader to the great peoples and outstanding eras of world history, Book II to the development of homes. For individual supplementary reading: too general and too highly selective for text-books.

Cory, Harper. The Story of Civilization. 110 pp. Sampson Low. 1927. 2*s.* 6*d.*

An interesting book that should arouse thought. Written to show the general development of society; 'the hero of the book is man in general, not the king or bishop'. First part specially useful. Very good illustrations. For Seniors.

Davis, M. O. Outlines of European History. 149 pp. O.U.P. 1922. 3*s.* 6*d.*

Since this little book contains the outstanding facts of European history from ancient times to the Great War it is necessarily much compressed; but it is excellent of its kind and would be most useful for reference among Senior children and for clear, short accounts of such great movements as the unification of Germany and Italy. Excellent illustrations, maps and charts of contemporary rulers.

Gordon, D. K. A Junior History of Europe. 352 pp. Methuen. 1928. 5*s.* Part I, 2*s.* 6*d.* Part II, 3*s.*

A clear, well-written, interesting outline from the fall of Rome to the League of Nations. Intended for middle forms of Secondary Schools, but could be used for reference by older Senior School pupils. Contains maps and date lists.

Happold, F. C. The Adventure of Man: a Brief History of the World. 242 pp. Christophers. 1926. 3*s.*

A skilfully made text-book, which covers the ground from the earliest times to the League of Nations, and aims at showing children the unity and continuity of man's past. Contains illustrations and some interesting diagrammatic maps. For top classes of Senior Schools.

Ikin, R. G. A Pageant of History. 270 pp. Nelson. 1928. 2*s.* 9*d.*

A good concise survey, including the brief outline of social and intellectual progress; political history necessarily very much compressed. Contains charts and exercises and many excellent contemporary pictures as well as a few fancy ones. A useful book for the top class of Senior Schools, either as an outline text-book or to supplement a revision of English History.

Niver, H. H. Brief History of the World. 284 pp. 3*s*. 6*d*. Or in two parts: Ancient Peoples and their Heroes. Modern Nations and their Famous Men. Harrap. 1926. 2*s*. each.

A good introduction on biographical lines; necessarily very much compressed. Includes history of East as well as West. Illustrations, some merely fanciful. For top classes of Senior Schools.

Tickner, F. W. Stories of World History. 280 pp. London Univ. Press. 1925. 3*s*. and 3*s*. 6*d*.

Stories covering the early ages, the classical period, the Middle Ages, and the Modern World. Good illustrations. For top class of Senior Schools.

4. HISTORICAL ATLASES FOR CHILDREN

Marshall. A First School Atlas of English History: by Darbishire, B. D. 1*s*. 4*d*.

Philip. Junior Historical Atlas. The maps are coloured and most useful descriptive notes are given. Contains much information in a simple form. 2*s*. and 3*s*.

Philip. School Atlas of Modern History. By Muir, J. Ramsay. A good atlas, fuller than the Junior. 5*s*.

Wheaton. Atlas of British and World History. By Rennard, T. A. Clear, but uncoloured. 1*s*. 6*d*.

III

CLASS LIBRARY BOOKS FOR PUPILS UNDER FIFTEEN AND FOR TEACHERS

THIS section, which it is hoped will be among the most generally useful parts of the Handbook, is intended as a guide to supplementary reading. This is, of course, far the most valuable when undertaken by the children individually; but children's powers vary so greatly that it is impossible to draw a hard and fast line between books which can be studied by the children themselves and books whose material must be re-told by the teacher. Such a volume as Miss Stawell's *Story of the Iliad*, for instance, is valuable for teachers to tell or read to very young children and for older children to read by themselves. The ideal would be for every class-room to contain in a separate case or rest a number of the books recommended in this section for the period to be studied, and for some of these books to be read by the children in private study periods, while others are used by the teacher for story telling, or for illustrative material to give life and interest to lessons.

1. BOOKS COVERING A NUMBER OF PERIODS

A. WORLD HISTORY AND EUROPEAN HISTORY

Andrews J. Ten Boys who Lived on the Road from Long Ago till Now. 248 pp. Ginn. 1928 (latest edition). 2*s*. 9*d*.

Stories of eleven boys from ancient to modern times; details of life in Persia and Greece particularly good. For Seniors.

Canton, W. The Child's Book of Saints. Dent. Everyman's Library. 1898. 2*s*.

Charmingly and simply told.

Creighton, L. Heroes of European History. 196 pp. Longmans. 1922. 2*s*. 6*d*.

Short biographies, with a thread of history running through

them. From ancient times to the foundation of the German Empire. Interesting though compressed. Useful as giving the European background to an English syllabus (e.g., in the sixteenth century tells the stories of Isabella of Castile, Columbus, Luther, the Revolt of the Netherlands and Henry IV of France). For top classes of Senior Schools.

Dale, L. Stories from European History. 144 pp. Longmans. 1910. 2*s.* 6*d.*

A good series of simple biographies covering the ground from Marathon to Waterloo. Illustrations (some fanciful). For top classes of Junior and low classes of Senior Schools.

Dark, S. The Child's Book of France. 224 pp. Chapman and Hall. 1921. Out of print.

A simply and vividly told survey of French history from Roman times to to-day, suited for private reading by Seniors. Useful to read in connexion with the great crises of French History (e.g., the Revolution) even if there is not time to read all the book.

Guerber, H. A. The Book of the Epic. 640 pp. Harrap. 1916. 10*s.* 6*d.*

Very useful to teachers from its comprehensive character; gives clear, condensed versions of the great epics of all ages and all countries.

Moncrieff, A. R. Hope. Heroes of European History. 256 pp. Blackie. 2*s.* 9*d.*

Stories from ancient times to the present day. Subjects well chosen, but treatment sometimes lacking in interest. Illustrations. For top classes of Senior Schools.

Ponsonby, A. and **D. Rebels and Reformers.** 307 pp. Allen and Unwin. 1917. 2*s.* 6*d.*

Stimulating and graphic stories of some of the great leaders of European thought from Savonarola to Tolstoy. Very useful for teachers' preparation.

Power, E. and **R. Cities and their Stories.** 160 pp. Black. 1927. 3*s.* 6*d.*

The stories of twelve cities, delightfully and sympathetically told. Excellent in giving a background of European civilization. For top classes of Senior Schools and teachers.

Price, E. C. Stories from French History. 256 pp. Harrap. 1921. 7*s.* 6*d.*, 3*s.* 6*d.*, or 2*s.* 6*d.*

Spirited sketches illustrating French history from Vercingetorix to Napoleon. Although intended for young people they are not really juvenile in language; they would be most useful for the teacher's preparation on such subjects as Charles the Great, Richelieu, the Revolution.

Scales, L. Boys of the Ages. 216 pp. Ginn. 1922. 3*s.* 3*d.*

Interesting stories of nine boys from the age of Egypt to America. Good social background. For Seniors.

Stuart, D. M. The Boy Through the Ages. 288 pp. Harrap. 1927. *7s. 6d.* and *10s. 6d.*

Interesting though popular studies of child life from ancient Egypt to the nineteenth century. For top classes of Senior Schools and for the teacher to re-tell.

Wilmot-Buxton, E. M. Stories from Modern History. 122 pp. Methuen. 4th ed. *2s. 3d.*

Well-written and interesting biographies from Alaric to Napoleon; includes Charlemagne, S. Francis, Joan of Arc, Columbus, Savonarola, Luther, etc. For top classes of Senior Schools.

B. ENGLISH HISTORY

Bowman, F. L. Peeps at Children of Long Ago. 84 pp. Black. 1927. *2s. 6d.*

Very brief, pretty snapshots of a moment in the life of some child (real or fictitious) from cave times to to-day. Contain little history, but might be used as private reading by Standard III children leading up to the telling of a longer story.

Calvert, C. V., and **Henderson, B. L. K. Days of History.** 213 pp. Methuen. 1919. *2s. 6d.*

Thirty-nine scenes (from the Flint Knapper to the first Railway train) dealing imaginatively with the development of social and national life. Has a fictitious element, but is graphic and likely to arouse interest in history. For Seniors.

Dale, L. Illustrated Easy Stories from English History. 248 pp. Harrap. 1926 (latest issue). *2s. 6d.* Or in two parts, *1s. 6d.* each.

Good, well-chosen and simply told stories. For top classes of Junior and for Senior Schools.

Finnemore, J. Men of Renown. Or in two vols. under the title of **Famous Englishmen.** Black. *3s.*

Interesting and simply told biographies of heroes of warfare, politics and literature. Brought up to date by the life of Kitchener. Illustrations old-fashioned. For Seniors.

Hayens, H. Children of Other Times. 3 vols. Collins. *1s. 6d.*, *1s. 6d.*, *1s. 9d.*

Short stories of boyhood, generally of some famous historical personage. Do not contain much history, but would serve as an introduction to private reading for young children. Books I and II deal with English history and are for very young children. Book III, which is rather more advanced, contains stories of boys from world history from Greece to the nineteenth century, and includes some figures not found in the conventional scheme of history teaching—e.g., Giotto, Michael Angelo and Mozart.

Power, E. and **R. Boys and Girls of History.** 346 pp. C.U.P. 1926. 7*s*. 6*d*.

Most charming stories of child life by writers who combine knowledge of history with a gift of seeing the child's point of view. Contains a list of authorities which would be useful to the teacher. Illustrates social life from Roman Britain to to-day. For the top class of Junior Schools and for Seniors. Can be obtained in two vols. 2*s*. 6*d*. each. A further volume on the same lines has been published, entitled **More Boys and Girls of History.** (See p. 59.)

Price, E. C. Stories from English History. 256 pp. Harrap. 1924. 2*s*. 6*d*., 3*s*. 6*d*. and 7*s*. 6*d*.

Vividly and finely told stories of selected episodes from Cæsar to Waterloo. Diction at times hard for Seniors, but they would gain tremendously by making the effort. Excellent for the teacher to read aloud.

Quennell, M. and **C. H. B. A History of Everyday Things in England.** 2 vols. 201, 204 pp. Batsford. 1918 and 1919. 8*s*. 6*d*. each. Or in one vol., 16*s*. 6*d*. Or in six vols. 3*s*. each.

Picturesque volumes whose value to children lies in their illustrations.

Russell, A. History of the People of England from the Earliest Times to 1066. The Bede Histories. Series II. Sheldon Press. 1926. 2*s*. 6*d*.

A most interesting volume, full of vivid detail: specially emphasizes the lives of saints and scholars. For the teacher, and in parts for the children. Other volumes of the series are in preparation.

Tickner, F. W. Schools and Scholars in History. 128 pp. Nelson. 1*s*.

A very useful and illuminating little collection of selected passages describing school life from the Renaissance to the Nineteenth Century.

Wilmot-Buxton, E. M. Easy Stories from English History. 128 pp. Methuen. 12th ed. 2*s*. 3*d*.

Thirty-five well-told biographies covering the ground from Caradoc to Gordon. Story of Cromwell not free from anti-Puritan bias. For upper classes of Juniors and for Seniors. The stories are connected by a useful date list.

Wilson, R. Servants of the People. 224 pp. Dent. 1926 (latest issue). 2*s*.

A group of charmingly told biographies from Bede to Nurse Cavell, well varied in subject; illustrates heroes of exploration, war, social reform, and literature. For Seniors.

2. PREHISTORIC

Boyle, M. E. Man before History. 128 pp. Harrap. 1924. 2*s*. and 3*s*. 6*d*.

A charming and sound little book which could be read by children of eleven plus. Illustrated.

Fleming, R. M. See the volumes of folk tales recommended in the teacher's bibliography, p. 64.

Hall, H. R. Days before History. 159 pp. Harrap. 1927 (2nd ed.). 1*s*. 6*d*., 3*s*. 6*d*. **The Threshold of History.** 160 pp. Harrap. 1914. 1*s*. 6*d*.

Still the best books of their kind. Vividly and interestingly written, well founded, and distinguish between fact and fiction. For Juniors.

Hall, H. R. Unwritten History. Book I. The Age of Stone. 186 pp. Nelson. 1928. 2*s*. 6*d*.

A very good, interesting and up-to-date introduction to the subject. The pictures of past times are vivid without unduly drawing on the imagination. Most useful for Seniors, and also for teachers of younger children. The series is to be continued.

Quennell, M. and **C. H. B. Everyday Life in the Old Stone Age.** 128 pp. Batsford. 1921. 5*s*. **Everyday Life in the New Stone, Bronze and Early Iron Ages.** 109 pp. Batsford. 1922. 5*s*.

Picturesque volumes whose value to children lies in their illustrations.

3. ANCIENT TIMES

A. General

Bowyer, E. Stories from Ancient History. 134 pp. Methuen. 1910 (6th ed., 1926). 2*s*. 3*d*.

Stories of ancient civilization from 4000 B.C. to A.D. 337. Interestingly told in clear and simple diction. For Seniors.

Breasted, J. H. Abridged and edited by L. Hughes Jones. **A Brief History of Ancient Times.** 320 pp. Ginn. 1927. 3*s*.

Highly recommended for use by Seniors. It is a much-simplified form of the famous 'Ancient Times', and is therefore based on real scholarship; yet it is wonderfully simple and realistic in the telling. The valuable illustrations in themselves form a history of civilization.

Chandler, A. Magic Pictures of Long Ago. 160 pp. Harrap. 1921. 1*s*. 6*d*.

Introductory stories from the history of Egypt, Greece, Rome, France, Holland. Good contemporary illustrations. For Seniors.

Dale, A. M. A Junior Ancient History. 224 pp. Methuen. 1928. 3*s*. 6*d*.

A clear, interesting and fairly full narrative. Intended for middle forms of Secondary Schools. Useful as reference book for Senior Schools.

Farjeon, E. Mighty Men. Vol. I. From Achilles to Julius Caesar. 104 pp. Blackwell. 1924. 1*s*. 8*d*.

Charming stories with a literary flavour. Each one ends with a rhyme by the authoress in the marching rhythms loved by young children. For Juniors.

Gardner, A. Friends of the Olden Time. 180 pp. Arnold. 1903 (5th ed.). 2*s*. 6*d*.

One of the best children's books ever written—scholarly yet childlike, romantic and picturesque yet true to fact. Stories of the old Egyptians and of Greek and Roman heroes.

Hodgdon, J. R. The Enchanted Past. 230 pp. Ginn. 1922. 3*s*. 9*d*.

Very good. Gives an introduction to ancient literatures as well as history. Deals with Hindus, Egyptians, Chinese, peoples of the Fertile Crescent, Hebrews, Greeks and Romans. For Seniors.

Hutchinson, H. G. Old World Story. 208 pp. Murray. 1927. 2*s*. 6*d*.

A very interesting and simple account of civilization from the earliest times to the fall of Rome. Includes more detail than the time usually given to this period would allow, but most useful for supplementary reading; sets the Bible stories in their historical context. For Seniors.

Reed, G. H. Ancient World Stories. 95 pp. Black. 1927. 1*s*. and 1*s*. 3*d*.

A good, simple introduction for Juniors, consisting of short separate stories with a thread of continuous history running through them. Suggestions for children's work.

Vaughan, D. M. Outlines of Ancient History. 214 pp. Longmans. 1928. 2*s*. 6*d*.

A clear outline from the earliest times to the barbarian invasions. Intended as one year's course for children of twelve or thirteen. Material skilfully chosen so that in spite of great compression interest is not lost nor social background neglected. Good illustrations and maps.

B. THE EARLY EMPIRES

Baikie, J. Ancient Egypt. 88 pp. 1912. **Ancient Assyria.** 92 pp. 1916. **Ancient Palestine.** 92 pp. 1927. Black. 2*s*. 6*d*. each.

The first two volumes are suited for private reading by children of eleven plus. They consist mainly of vivid descriptions of social life in different classes, making the age and country live to the reader, and connecting with Bible history. The third volume, while equally good, is more difficult reading.

Baikie, J. Wonder Tales of the Ancient World. 248 pp. Black. 1924. 3*s*. 6*d*.

Delightfully and intimately told stories from Egyptian literature. They do not, of course, add to historical knowledge, but illustrate the character of the civilization. For teachers to tell to young children, or for children over ten to read to themselves.

Burke, E. The Shining East. 166 pp. 1915. Russell. 2*s*. 3*d*.

The best simple text-book on the period. Vividly written. Intended for children of eleven plus. Numerous excellent contemporary illustrations.

Burry, V. Old World Empires. 216 pp. Chambers. 1927. 2*s*.

Well and simply told stories of the ancient world for juniors. Illustrations poor.

Lamprey, L. Children of Ancient Egypt. 224 pp. Harrap. 1922. 2*s*. or 3*s*. 6*d*.

An interesting little book for juniors. Has a fictitious setting, but the background is quite good. Deals with period of eighteenth dynasty.

Mackenzie, D. A. The Story of Ancient Egypt. 80 pp. 1927. **The Story of Ancient Babylon and Assyria.** 80 pp. 1927. Blackie. 1*s*. 3*d*. each.

Clear, straightforward little narratives, introducing connexions with Hebrew history and now and then dealing interestingly with excavations (e.g., Mr. Carter and the tomb of Tutankh-amen). Contain too many names to act as reading books, but would be useful as class library books for the teacher and the children's reference. Contemporary illustrations.

Trotter, E. Life in Olden Times in Babylon and Assyria. 232 pp. Macdonald and Evans. 1913. 1*s*. 6*d*.

Based on sound knowledge and simply written; could be read by Senior School children. Forms an excellent background to Scripture lessons. Specially useful to children who are going to visit the British Museum, which contains many of the originals of the excellent illustrations.

Vaughan, D. M. Great Peoples of the Ancient World. 178 pp. Longmans. 1925. 3*s*. 6*d*.

A valuable and interesting little book containing simple accounts of the ancient peoples (in Babylon, Crete, Palestine, Egypt, etc.), which are at once graphically told and based on careful information. Excellent pictures.

C. GREECE

Baikie, J. Ancient Greece. 92 pp. Black. 1920. 2*s*. 6*d*.
A graphic description of the social life and spirit of Athens. Pictures of unequal value. For Seniors.

Ancient Crete. 92 pp. Black. 1924. 2*s*. 6*d*. See note above.

Burke, E. M. The Violet Crown and the Seven Hills. 183 pp. Russell. 1919. 2*s*. 8*d*.
Very good. Contains an outline of the essential facts of Greek and Roman History, yet wonderfully interesting and sympathetic. Numerous good contemporary pictures. For Seniors.

Burry, V. Gods and Heroes. 176 pp. Chambers. 1926–7. 1*s*. 9*d*.
Greek and Scandinavian legends well and simply told. Poor illustrations. For Juniors.

Church, A. J. Although many of the books of this author are getting old, the classical spirit is so well preserved in them that they are still valuable as sources for stories. Among them are :—**Helmet and Spear.** 380 pp. Seeley. 1900. Stories of the wars of the Greeks and Romans. 5*s*.

Stories of the Persian Wars from Herodotus. 292 pp. Seeley. 1882. 5*s*.

The Story of the Iliad. 160 pp. Seeley. 1892. 10*d*. or 1*s*. 8*d*.

The Story of the Odyssey. 160 pp. Seeley. 1892. 10*d*. or 1*s*. 8*d*.

The Children's Iliad. 304 pp. Seeley. 1907. 5*s*.

The Children's Odyssey. 308 pp. Seeley. 1907. 5*s*.

Havell, H. L. This author has produced a number of competent tales from Greek history. They are all published by Harrap, about 256 pp., from 1905–10 in date. They comprise :—
Stories from Greek History; retold from Herodotus. **Stories from the Iliad. Stories from the Odyssey. Stories from Thucydides. Stories from Xenophon. Stories from Greek Tragedy.** 2*s*. 6*d*. each.

Kingsley, C. The Heroes. Macmillan. 2*s*., 3*s*. 6*d*. and 6*s*.
The stories of Greek legendary heroes, Perseus, Jason and Theseus, gloriously told.

Lang, A. Tales of Troy and Greece. 287 pp. Longmans. 1907. 5*s*.
A splendid book; stories of the Homeric Age, told simply, yet instinct with poetry and romance. In two separate vols., 3*s*. each.

Moncrieff, A. R. Hope. Classic Myth and Legend. 440 pp. Gresham Publishing Co. 1912. 12*s*. 6*d*.
A useful collection of myths and legends, briefly told.

Stawell, F. M., Mayor, R., and **Marvin, F. S. The Story of the Iliad.** 214 pp. 1921 (latest impression; original date 1900). Dent. King's Treasury of Literature. 1*s*. 6*d*.

The Adventures of Odysseus. 221 pp. Dent. 1920 (original date, 1908). 1*s*. 6*d*.

By far the best of all the stories retold from Homer; simple and beautiful diction. Strongly recommended.

Tappan, E. M. The Story of the Greek People. 271 pp. Harrap. 1911. 2*s*. 6*d*.

A well-written general survey, useful to Senior Schools and to teachers of younger children.

Vaughan, D. M. The Mediterranean World in Greek and Roman Times. 247 pp. Longmans. 1927. 3*s*. 6*d*.

A very interesting and useful little book; the history of Greece and Rome told through a series of stories based on child life in each succeeding age, but containing a quantity of sound information about social conditions and great events.

D. ROME

Baikie, J. Ancient Rome. 92 pp. Black. 1917. 1*s*. 6*d*.

A good, graphic account of social conditions and the spirit of the people; gives a useful background for stories.

Burke, E. M. The Violet Crown and the Seven Hills. See Greek section above, p. 47. (The concluding volume, The Old Order and the New, is much more difficult.)

Church, A. J. See note in Greek section above. **Stories from Livy.** 277 pp. Seeley. 1883. 5*s*. **The Children's Aeneid.** 300 pp. Seeley. 1909. 5*s*.

Lamprey, L. Children of Rome. 224 pp. Harrap. 1923. 2*s*.

Quite a good and simple description of social conditions and everyday life, with a slight fictitious setting of child life.

Quennell, M. and C. Everyday Life in the Romano-British Age. 108 pp. Batsford. 1924. 5*s*. Illustrations very attractive to children.

Tappan, E. M. The Story of the Roman People. 256 pp. Harrap. 1912. 2*s*. 6*d*.

A well-written general survey, useful to Senior Schools and to teachers of younger children.

Vaughan, D. M. The Mediterranean World. See Greek section above.

Wilmot-Buxton, E. M. Stories from Roman History. 117 pp. Methuen. 1926 (original date, 1907). 2*s*.

A useful and well-written survey of Roman history through legendary and true stories. For Seniors.

4. MEDIEVAL TIMES

Andrews, J. C. Lords' Men of Littlebourne. 192 pp. Harrap. 1913. 1*s*. 9*d*.

Lively, sturdy sketches of the life of villeins and monks in the

fourteenth century. Has a fictitious setting, but gives a good idea of social life and work. Of special interest to the children of Kent, where the scene is laid.

Bowman, F. L. Britain in the Middle Ages. 103 pp. C.U.P. 1919. 2*s*. 6*d*.

An excellent book. Stories retold from chronicles. Good illustrations from medieval manuscripts.

Bowman, F. L. Craftsmen and Merchants. 152 pp. Black. 1925. 2*s*. 6*d*.

Contains much interesting material and good use of original sources.

Davis, M. O. Saints and Heroes of the Western World. 140 pp. O.U.P. 1921. 2*s*. 6*d*.

Medieval European History told in a series of biographies from Constantine the Great up to (and including) characters of the Renaissance and Reformation. Very useful in giving a background of medieval civilization, as the heroes chosen are all men of ideas as well as men of action. For Senior children or for re-telling by the teacher. Good contemporary illustrations.

Davis, M. O. Joan of Arc. 192 pp. Putnam's Sons. 1927. 2*s*. 6*d*.

A very sound sketch. Could be read only by the exceptional Senior School child, but most useful to the teacher.

Davis, H. S. Life in a Medieval Barony. 414 pp. Harper. 1923. 7*s*. 6*d*.

For the teacher; a delightful reconstruction.

Devas, E. H. Social Life in England to 1500. 94 pp. Methuen. 1921. 2*s*.

Interesting and useful little sketches illustrating different aspects of medieval life—work, food, clothes, amusements, education, etc. Excellent illustrations. For Senior Schools.

Edgar, M. C. The Boys' Froissart. 256 pp. Harrap. 1912. 2*s*. 6*d*. and 3*s*. 6*d*.

An attractive volume of selections.

Farjeon, E. Mighty Men. Vol. II. From Beowulf to Harold. 119 pp. Blackwell. 1925. 1*s*. 8*d*.

Charming stories for Juniors. See note on Vol. I under Ancient History, p. 45.

Finnemore, J. Famous Englishmen. Vol. I. Black. 3*s*.

A useful series of simply told biographies for top classes of Juniors and for Seniors. Old-fashioned illustrations.

Finnemore, J. A First English History Reader. 268 pp. Black. 1928 (latest issue). 2*s*. 6*d*.

Very readable, simple stories about the main events of medieval history. For Juniors. Illustrations generally poor.

Guest, G. English Social Reformers. Book I. Marshall. 1923. 2*s.*

Stories of Langton, de Montfort, Wyclif and Caxton, etc.

Guildford, N. The Pageant of Medieval England. 175 pp. Bell. 1923. 3*s.*

Contains excellent illustrative material on social history. For the teacher and for reference by older children. Good contemporary pictures.

Hartley, D. and **Elliot, M. The Life and Work of the People of England.** The Fourteenth Century. 1928. The Fifteenth Century. 1925. 32 pp. of text and 49 pp. of plates each. Batsford. 4*s.* 6*d.* and 5*s.* 6*d.* each.

Part of a series in progress. The pictures are of the greatest value, and would give children a vivid idea of the life of the time.

Holland, E. The Story of Mohammed. 191 pp. Harrap. 1914. 2*s.*

Very pleasantly told ; useful for the teacher's preparation and in some parts for children's reading.

Ireland, A. J. Episodes in the History of England, 55 B.C.–A.D. 1066. Longmans. 1926. 3*s.* 6*d.*

A series of vividly interesting episodes, with a certain fictitious element but giving the life and spirit of the period. Very useful for the teacher to re-tell or for private reading by the top class of a Senior School.

Jones, C. M. Duncan. The Candle of the North. 148 pp. Mowbray. 1924. 4*s.* 6*d.*

Charmingly told stories from Bede.

Keary, A. and **E. Stories of Asgard.** 80 pp. Collins. 1923. 7*d.*, 8*d.*

Simply told stories of Teutonic mythology for Juniors. Adapted for individual reading by H. Hayens.

Lamprey, L. In the Days of the Guilds. 256 pp. Harrap. 1927 (latest issue). 2*s.* 6*d.*

A book of descriptions of various crafts, illustrating methods, materials, organization, etc. Charmingly told in a fictitious setting. For telling to Juniors or reading by Seniors.

Lang, A. The Book of Romance. 384 pp. Longmans. 1902. 5*s.*

Contains well-told stories of early legendary history—Arthur, Grettir, Roland, etc.

Lees, B. A. (ed.). **History in Biography.** Vols. I (out of print) and II. Black. 1902. 3*s.* each.

Useful for supplementary reading. Biographies well chosen but sometimes dull. For Seniors.

McDougall's Educational Co. The Wars of the Cross. 80 pp. 1915. 10*d.*

A pleasant and readable little volume of crusading stories based on the chronicles. For Juniors (top classes) and Seniors.

Major, A. F. and **Speight, E. E. Stories from the Northern Sagas.** 284 pp. Marshall. 1905 (latest issue). 3*s.*

Well-told vivid stories.

Mowat, R. B. Makers of British History. Book I, 192 pp. Arnold. 1926. 2*s.* 6*d.*

A series of brief, clear informative summaries of the lives of outstanding characters. Useful for a teacher preparing a biographical scheme, or for older children to use for reference.

Newbolt, Sir Henry. Stories from Froissart. 284 pp. Wells, Gardiner. 1899.

A good selection, mostly of war stories.

Newbolt, Sir Henry. Froissart in Britain. 272 pp. Nisbet. 1900.

Newbolt, Sir Henry. The Book of the Happy Warrior. 284 pp. Longmans. 1917. 5*s.* or 2*s.* 6*d.*

Stories of medieval chivalry, told as closely as possible in accordance with original historical or legendary sources. Stories centre round Roland, Richard I, St. Louis, Robin Hood, Du Guesclin, Bayard. The chivalric code is idealized. Interesting for Seniors to read and for teachers to re-tell to young children.

Niemeyer, N. Stories for the History Hour. 253 pp. Harrap. 1917. 3*s.* 6*d.*

Very useful, since they are almost the only group of stories covering the period of the barbarian invasions in Europe. Stories vividly told with at times a fictitious setting of child life. For Seniors to read and for teacher to tell to younger children.

Niemeyer, N. Stories from History. I. Patrick to Dunstan. II. Henry III to Edward IV. Dent: King's Treasuries of Literature. 1*s.* 4*d.* each.

Charming little volumes of stories told from the chronicles.

Plunket, I. L. Stories from Medieval Spain. 214 pp. Sheldon Press. 1923. 6*s.*

Contain material not easily found elsewhere in a simple form. Stories of Spanish characters (e.g., the Cid) told in a popular style suited for re-telling by the teacher. Book list given.

Power, E. and **R. Boys and Girls of History.** Part I. 161 pp. C.U.P. 2*s.* 6*d.*

Excellent, vivid and well-founded reconstructions of the life of each period from the point of view of a child. At the end of the volume there is a short note on books which would be of great use to the teacher looking for story material. For the top class of Junior and for Senior Schools.

Quennell, M. and **C. B. Everyday Life in Anglo-Saxon, Viking and Norman Times.** 128 pp. Batsford. 1926. 5*s*.

History of Everyday Things in England. Vol. I. 201 pp. Batsford. 1925. 8*s*. 6*d*.

Reed, G. H. The Lives of Great Men. Vol. I. 96 pp. Black. 1926. 1*s*. or 1*s*. 3*d*.

Useful though rather dull biographies for reference and supplementary reading for the top classes of Junior and lower classes of Senior Schools. Contains maps and charts, exercises for individual work and pictures of varying value; some merely fanciful.

Seers, A. W. The Story of Early English Travel and Discovery. 239 pp. Harrap. 1923. 2*s*. 6*d*.

Tales of early adventure freely retold from the sources. Ends at the age of Elizabeth. Language rather hard.

Speight, E. E. Children of Odin. 166 pp. Marshall. 1903. 1*s*. 9*d*.

A delightful group of Norse stories for juniors. Does not overlap with the author's Stories from Northern Sagas.

Spence, H. D. M. Dreamland in History. 192 pp. Harrap. 1927. 1*s*. 6*d*.

Deals with the history of the Norman dukes from Rollo to William the Conqueror and with the abbey of Gloucester in Norman times. Interesting and valuable. For the top class of Senior Schools or for the teacher.

Stamp, A. Tales from the Chroniclers. 96 pp. Nelson. 1927. 10*d*.

Chosen stories from the time of Bede to Froissart. A very easy source book.

Stenton, D. M. William the Conqueror. 187 pp. Putnam's Sons. 1927. 2*s*. 6*d*.

Intended as a biography for children and young people, but the difficult language puts it out of the reach of most. Most useful for the teacher; describes not only the career of William but the influence of the Normans in England.

Stevinson, E. Pictures of Social Life. Harrap. 1*s*. 9*d*.

Gives short and charmingly told stories of children in different social settings from the earliest times to the fourteenth century. For Juniors.

Stuart, D. M. Chivalry and Social Life in the Middle Ages. 192 pp. Harrap. 1927. 1*s*. 6*d*.

A popularly written book which gives bright illustrative material on knights, arms and chivalry; commerce; monks, friars and pilgrims. Good illustrations. Language rather hard for reading by top class.

Tappan, E. M. Heroes of the Middle Ages. 252 pp. Harrap. 1926 (latest issue; original date, 1911). 2*s*. 6*d*.

Useful simple biographies covering a wide field; for private reading by Seniors.

Thomson, C. L. Adventures of Beowulf. Marshall. 1904. 1*s*. 9*d*.

Beautifully told.

Thomson, C. L. Selections from the Morte d'Arthur. 240 pp. Marshall. 1902. 2*s*. 6*d*.

Thomson, C. L. (ed.). **Tales of the Middle Ages.** 131 pp. Marshall. 1905. 1*s*. 9*d*.

Wilmot-Buxton, E. M. Britain Long Ago. 238 pp. Harrap. 1922 (original date, 1906). 2*s*. 6*d*.

Well and interestingly told stories, mainly of early medieval history. For Seniors. (Some of these stories have been reprinted separately under the titles of Tales of Early England and Old Celtic Tales.)

Wilmot-Buxton, E. M. Anselm. 191 pp. Harrap. 1915. 2*s*.

A very useful little biography, illustrating medieval education and monastic life as well as the career of Anselm. For older children and teachers.

Wilmot-Buxton, E. M. The Story of Jeanne d'Arc. 191 pp. Harrap. 1924. 2*s*.

An interestingly told story, making use of the evidence at the trial. For top class of Senior School. (See also under Historical Fiction, Mark Twain.)

Wilmot-Buxton, E. M. Told by the Northmen. 243 pp. Harrap. 1908. 2*s*. 6*d*.

Well-told stories from the Eddas and Sagas.

5. MODERN TIMES

A. THE TUDOR PERIOD

Bodilly, R. B. Fighting Merchantmen. 278 pp. Heath Cranton. 1927. 10*s*. 6*d*.

A spirited selection of tales retold from Hakluyt. Contains maps. Very good for Seniors or teacher.

Buchan, J. Sir Walter Raleigh. 188 pp. Nelson. 1927. 1*s*. 6*d*.

Eleven stories describing the life of Raleigh in gallant, adventurous style; not always easy for children.

Davis, M. O. Saints and Heroes of the Western World. (See p. 49.)

Contains stories of sixteenth-century religious thinkers.

Finnemore, J. Second English History Reader. Black. 2*s*. 6*d*. Simply told for Juniors.

Ford, H. R. The Story of Sir Francis Drake. 96 pp. O.U.P. 1*s*. Attractive little book for private reading by children.

Guest, G. Social Reformers. (See p. 50.) Book I.

Hartley, D. and **Elliot, M. Life and Work of the People of England : the Sixteenth Century.** 32 pp. of text and 49 of notes. Batsford. 1925. 4*s.* 6*d.* and 5*s.* 6*d.*

A valuable and vivid collection of contemporary pictures.

Home, G. The Period of the Renaissance and Reformation. 2 vols. Marshall. 1926. 2*s.* each.

A group of charmingly told short biographies, mainly European ; very useful material for lessons on such figures as Isabella of Spain, Lorenzo, Leonardo da Vinci, Luther, etc.

Lees, B. A. (ed.). **History in Biography.** (See above under Medieval.) Vol. III.

Mitton, G. E. Columbus. 100 pp. Black. 1927. 2*s.* 6*d.*

Pleasantly told ; for top class of Senior School or for teacher to re-tell.

Mowat, R. B. Makers of British History. (See above under Medieval.) Vol. I.

Plunket, I. L. Daily Life in Tudor Times. 96 pp. O.U.P. 1*s.*

Simple descriptions of social life. For private reading by Senior Schools.

Plunket, I. L. Queen Elizabeth. 224 pp. Putnam's Sons. 1927. 2*s.* 6*d.*

An account of the period as well as a biography. Intended for children, but rather difficult.

Ponsonby, A. and **D. Rebels and Reformers.** (See p. 41.)

Excellent graphic stories for the teacher to re-tell. Covers new ground in dealing with men of thought.

Power, R. The Age of Discovery. 190 pp. Putnam's Sons. 1927. 2*s.* 6*d.*

An ideal book for children, simple and vivid.

Quennell, M. and **C. H. B. A History of Everyday Things in England.** (See p. 43.) Vol. II.

Reed, G. H. The Lives of Great Men. (See p. 52.) Vol. II.

Roper, W. The Life of Sir Thomas More. A school edition is published by Blackie. 128 pp. 1924. 1*s.*

Tickner, F. W. Schools and Scholars in History. (See p. 43.)

Towle, G. Francis Drake. 255 pp. Harrap. 1920. 2*s.* 6*d.*

Excellent exciting narrative for Seniors. Based on contemporary writers. Language not always easy, but swaggering and suits the subject.

Wood, E. Famous Voyages of the Great Discoverers. 270 pp. Harrap. 1910. 2*s.* 6*d.*

A fairly comprehensive collection of the most famous sixteenth-century voyages of all nations.

B. THE STUART PERIOD

Birkhead, A. Peter the Great. 188 pp. Harrap. 1915. 2*s*.
Quite good short biography, including an account of Peter's stay in London. For top class of Senior Schools.

Guest, G. English Social Reformers. (See p. 50.) Vol. I.

Hall, C. J. School Edition of the Diary of Samuel Pepys. Black. 1928. 2*s*. 6*d*.
Collection of well-chosen extracts.

Hartley, D. and **Elliot, M. Life and Work of the People of England : the Seventeenth Century.** 32 pp. of text and 49 of plates. Batsford. 1928. 4*s*. 6*d*. and 5*s*. 6*d*.
A valuable and vivid collection of contemporary pictures.

Lees, B. A. History in Biography. (See p. 50.) Vol. IV.

Mowat, R. B. Makers of British History. (See p. 51.) Book II.

Ponsonby, A. and **D. Rebels and Reformers.** (See p. 41.)

Quennell, M. and **C. H. B. A History of Everyday Things in England.** (See p. 43.) Vol. II.

Reed, G. H. The Lives of Great Men. (See p. 52.) Vol. II.

Wilmot-Buxton, E. M. The Struggle with the Crown. 212 pp. Harrap. 1912. 2*s*. 3*d*.
A history of the period told with some realistic detail ; parts would be excellent for Senior children to use to supplement their text-books.

C. THE EIGHTEENTH CENTURY

Birkhead, A. The Story of the French Revolution. 236 pp. Harrap. 1913. 2*s*. 6*d*.
Quite a good and spirited account from which Senior children could read parts ; it gives a fair idea of the causes and describes the great scenes of the Revolution.

Cleare, C. R. Napoleon. 204 pp. Putnam's Sons. 1927. 2*s*. 6*d*.
A sound sketch ; but though it is written for juveniles the language is not easy. Interesting and valuable for those that can read it.

Fitchett, W. H. Fights for the Flag. Deeds that Won the Empire. Cheap editions published by Murray. 2*s*. 6*d*.
Dramatic stories of warfare. Black publishes a selection under the title of Great Deeds on Land and Sea. 6*d*. or 8*d*.

Fitzgerald, W. B. John Wesley : through England on Horseback in the Eighteenth Century. 156 pp. Kelly. 1913. 2*s*.

Simple and charming pictures of social life based on Wesley's Journals and centred round his work. Could be read by Seniors.

Gatty, R. Robert Clive. 206 pp. Putnam's Sons. 1927. 2*s.* 6*d.*

Contains good material for lessons; difficult for children's private reading.

Guest, G. English Social Reformers. (See p. 50.) Vols. I and II. Very useful.

Mitton, G. E. Captain Cook. 150 pp. Black. 1927. 2*s.* 6*d.*

Mowat, R. B. Makers of British History. (See p. 51.) Book II.

Newbolt, Sir Henry. The Book of the Blue Sea. xii + 307 pp. Longmans. 1914. 5*s.*

Spirited and well-told stories of sea life about the age of Nelson. For Seniors.

Quennell, M. and **C. H. B. A History of Everyday Things in England.** (See p. 43.) Vol. II.

Reed, G. H. The Lives of Great Men. (See p. 52.) Book II.

D. THE NINETEENTH AND TWENTIETH CENTURIES

Allsopp, H. The Change to Modern England. 236 pp. Nisbet. 1928. 3*s.*

An excellent survey of economic conditions from about 1750 for the teacher and for exceptional children in the top class of a Senior School.

Blackie. Rambles among our Industries Series. About 80 pp. each. 1*s.* 3*d.*

Most useful; includes a volume on almost every industry.

Browne, E. G. Queen Victoria. 189 pp. Harrap. 1915. 2*s.*

Describes the life of the queen and the social and political reforms of her day. Quite a good introduction for modern children, to whom Victoria is ancient history.

Buchan, J. and **Newbolt, Sir Henry. Days to Remember.** 200 pp. Nelson. 1923.

A short account of the Great War which retains much of the atmosphere of 1914–18. Language not always easy, but very fine and spirited. The war cannot yet be seen in its historical perspective.

Claxton, W. J. Our Country's Industrial History. 253 pp. Harrap. 1915. 2*s.* 6*d.*

A good sketch, dealing chiefly with the eighteenth and nineteenth centuries. Includes names and short accounts of the great inventors.

Cooke, A. O. Work and Workers. 2 vols. 96 pp. each. Nelson. 1927. 10*d*. each.

Very good simple studies of modern occupations, well illustrated. Contains questions and exercises. For the top class of Junior and for Senior Schools.

Guest, G. English Social Reformers. Book II. 1726–1865. 127 pp. Marshall. 1923. 2*s*.

Very useful; social history taught through biography. Illustrates nearly all the great movements of the century. For abler children to read, and for teacher to re-tell.

Horne, A. R. The Age of Machinery. 222 pp. Blackie. 1925 (latest issue; original date 1913). 2*s*. 9*d*.

A simple and interesting account of machines. For Seniors.

Jones, Dr. R. Since Waterloo. 333 pp. Constable. 1920. 7*s*. 6*d*.

A vigorous outline of European and Imperial affairs during the period. Preserves a sense of unity and continuity while giving the essential facts. Contains numerous maps, diagrams, list of historical fiction and useful index.

McDougall's Educational Co. How Italy became a Nation. 79 pp. 10*d*.

A simple, interesting little account for Seniors.

Mowat, R. B. Makers of British History. (See p. 51.) Book III.

Tabor, M. Pioneer Women. 2 vols. Sheldon Press. 1927. 2*s*. 6*d*. each.

Each life is also published separately at 6*d*. Good sketches, suited for girls of fourteen.

Tickner, F. W. A Hundred Years Ago: the Movement for Parliamentary Reform. 128 pp. Nelson. 1*s*.

A most useful little source book.

E. EXPLORATION AND EMPIRE

Bowman, F. L. The Story of the Empire. 251 pp. Oxford History Readers, Book IX. O.U.P. 2*s*. 4*d*.

Excellent general sketch from 1453 to 1910; sound and picturesque.

Bridges, T. C. The Book of Discovery. 288 pp. Harrap. 1926. 7*s*. 6*d*.

A comprehensive collection, containing most of the famous stories of all lands from the earliest times to Shackleton and Scott.

Buchan, J. The Last Secrets. 303 pp. Nelson. 1923. 2*s*.

The stories of modern exploration (at the South Pole, Mount Everest, etc.) nobly told. Excellent for the teacher and possibly the top class; the book is not written in a juvenile style, but is so good as to deserve an effort.

Stories from Hakluyt. 160 pp. Dent. 1927. 1*s.* 4*d.*
Consists of selections from Hakluyt. Excellent for top classes of Senior Schools.

Guest, G. An Imperial History of England. 192 pp. Bell. 1925. 2*s.* 6*d.*
A well-written and interesting little general survey. For top class of Juniors and lower classes of Senior Schools.

Hewitt, W. H. Mungo Park. 75 pp. Sheldon Press. 1923. 2*s.* 6*d.*
Useful as a book of reference for older children. Contains book list for teacher.

Johnston, Sir H. The Explorer Series. Includes **The Old Navigators, The Old Explorers, Nineteenth Century Explorers, Modern Travellers, Pathfinders of To-day,** and **Trading Companies.** Collins. 1*s.* 6*d.* each.

Keltie, Sir John Scott and **Gilmour, S. C. Adventures of Exploration.** I. Finding the Continents. 132 pp. 1*s.* 6*d.* II. Central and South America. 160 pp. 1*s.* 8*d.* III. Asia. 164 pp. 1*s.* 10*d.* IV. Africa. 184 pp. 2*s.* V. Australia and New Zealand. 208 pp. 2*s.* 3*d.* VI. N. America. 228 pp. 2*s.* 6*d.* Philip. 1925–8.
An excellent series, full of interest and information. Graded in difficulty. Very useful.

Ker, A. J. and **Cleaver, C. H. Heroes of Exploration.** 208 pp. Blackie. 1913. 2*s.* 9*d.*
Good straightforward concrete narratives of exploration from the time of Pizarro to to-day. Includes Cartier, Drake, Cook, Mungo Park, Livingstone, etc. Language rather hard. For top classes of Senior Schools and for teachers.

Matthews, Basil. Livingstone the Pathfinder. 215 pp. O.U.P. 1913. 2*s.* 6*d.*
A clear and spirited narrative, simply told. For Seniors.

Mitton, G. E., has written a number of good and interesting short biographies for top classes of Senior Schools and for the teacher. **Columbus. Vasco da Gama. Sir Humphrey Gilbert. Captain Cook. David Livingstone.** Black. 2*s.* 6*d.* each.

Newbolt, Sir Henry. The Book of the Long Trail. 312 pp. Longmans. 1919. 7*s.* 6*d.* or 5*s.* (2*s.* 6*d.* abridged).
An excellent volume of the stories of great explorers.

Palmer, H. W. Our Empire Overseas. 304 pp. Blackie. 1920. 3*s.*
A combination of history and geography. Deals with the age of discovery and then with each great section of the empire in turn. A useful reference book for the top classes of Senior Schools.

Power, R. and E. More Boys and Girls of History. 273 pp. C.U.P. 1928. In 2 parts. 2*s*. 6*d*. each.

Charming, attractive and well illustrated stories of adventure and discovery connected with the growth of the British Empire. Ideal for private reading in the top classes of Junior and in Senior Schools.

Synge, M. B. A Book of Discovery. 554 pp. Jack. 1912. 7*s*. 6*d*.

Stories of exploration most attractively told.

Williamson, J. A. Builders of the Empire. 298 pp. O.U.P. 1925. 3*s*. 6*d*. and 7*s*. 6*d*.

A fascinating book. A series of biographies of imperial pioneers from Cabot to Kitchener. Delightful pictures. For Senior Schools and the teacher.

Wilson, R. (ed.). **Children of the Seven Seas.** 288 pp. Macmillan. 1923 (latest issue). 2*s*. 6*d*.

A good and well-illustrated sketch of imperial history dealing with the development of the Empire in each period, rather than in separate regions. Contains some extracts from contemporary sources or great historians. Connects imperial affairs with the general thread of national history. For Senior Schools.

F. THE LEAGUE OF NATIONS

Jones, R. and **Sherman, S. S. The League of Nations School Book.** 120 pp. Macmillan. 1928. 1*s*. 3*d*. and 1*s*. 6*d*.

The best Senior School textbook on the subject. Deals in a lively and stimulating way with the origin, organisation and *raison d'être* of the League.

Spaull, H. The Fight for Peace. 119 pp. Bell. 1925. 2*s*.

The best introduction for Junior School children. Brings out various aspects of the League's work through brightly told stories of children's lives in other countries.

Spaull, H. Peeps at the League of Nations. vi + 89 pp. Black. 1927. 2*s*. 6*d*.

A good collection of simply told incidents illustrating the growth of the League ideal in history and the kind of work the League is doing to-day. For private reading.

Spaull, H. Champions of Peace. 112 pp. Allen and Unwin. 1926. 3*s*. 6*d*.

Simple biographies of men who have worked for the cause of peace—Wilson, Cecil, Nansen, etc.

Spaull, H. Women Peacemakers. 123 pp. Harrap. 1924. 1*s*. 6*d*. or 2*s*. 6*d*.

A companion volume of biographies of women.

IV

BOOK LISTS FOR TEACHERS

1. WORLD HISTORY

Bragg, Sir W. Old Trades and New Knowledge. xii + 266 pp. Bell. 1926. 8*s.* 6*d.*

Takes various industries and sets their development in the perspective of world history as well as describing their present condition. Extremely valuable illustrations.

Breasted, J. H. Ancient Times. 742 pp. Ginn. 1916. 10*s.* 6*d.*

It is impossible to recommend this book too highly to teachers of world history. The descriptions of the life and atmosphere of each age are vivid, clear, and based on scholarship. Wonderful illustrations.

Burns, C. Delisle. A Short History of International Intercourse. 159 pp. Allen & Unwin. 1924. 3*s.* 6*d.* or 5*s.*

Most useful and stimulating in suggesting new lines of approach to the teacher: deals with the peaceful co-operation by which the peoples of Europe since the fall of Rome have developed a common civilization.

Cunningham, W. An Essay on Western Civilization in its Economic Aspects. 2 vols. Ancient Times. 6*s.* Medieval and Modern Times. 8*s.* C.U.P. Valuable.

Day, Clive. History of Commerce. x + 676 pp. Longmans. 1922. 14*s.*

A valuable manual to the teacher. Sketches concisely but interestingly the history of ancient, medieval and modern commerce, with special emphasis on recent times. Many maps.

Grant, A. J. A History of Europe. xiv + 868 pp. Longmans. 1922. 15*s.*

An extremely useful text-book, sound yet not dull. Gives political outline of classical, medieval and modern times. Can be obtained in three parts.

Happold, F. C. The Adventure of Man: a Brief History of the World. 242 pp. Christophers. 1926. 3*s.*

A fascinating, simple yet accurate introduction for the teacher or older children.

Hattersley, A. F. Short History of Western Civilization. ix + 245 pp. C.U.P. 1927. (2nd ed.) 6*s*.

A brilliant essay on the development of social and political groups and ideas throughout world history: enlightens and stimulates the reader.

Hearnshaw, F. J. C. A First Book of World History. xx + 194 pp. Macmillan. 1924. 2*s*. 6*d*.

A highly compressed, yet marvellously clear survey: most useful to the teacher who wishes to scan the whole 'programme' of history.

Marvin, F. S. England and the World. 268 pp. O.U.P. 1925. 10*s*. 6*d*.

A series of essays by various authors, showing the part played by England in the great world story.

Robinson, J. H. Medieval and Modern Times. xii + 806 pp. Ginn. 1926. 10*s*. 6*d*.

The continuation of Breasted's Ancient Times (see p. 60).

Somervell, D. C. Studies in Statesmanship. xii + 427 pp. Bell. 1923. 15*s*.

Extremely interesting and useful to the teacher: world history grouped round the vividly told biographies of Pericles, Caesar, Charles the Great, Innocent III, Richelieu, Washington, Napoleon, Bismarck and Gladstone.

Somervell, D. C. A Short History of our Religion. xii + 356 pp. Bell. 1925. 5*s*. and 6*s*.

A fascinating and engrossing story: Part I deals with the preparation for Christianity and the Old Testament; Part II with early Christianity; Part III with the medieval Church and the Reformation; Part IV with Great Britain since the Reformation. There are short bibliographies to each section.

Somervell, D. C. A History for British Schools. Four Vols.: I. Foundations (Greek, Roman and early Medieval History). II. 1066–1714. III and IV. Modern Times. 3*s*. each Vol. Also an Outline for revision and prevision. 1*s*. 6*d*. Bell. 1925–8.

This is an attempt to tell the British story in a setting of general history for secondary schools. The teacher might often find himself in disagreement with the selection of material, and in any case he would have to simplify the work for elementary schools; but he would find it most useful and suggestive as a basis on which to work.

Stawell, F. M., and Marvin, F. S. The Making of the Western Mind. xiii + 353 pp. Methuen. 1923. 7*s*. 6*d*.

An interesting, vivid study of those elements in the civilization of each age which have had lasting influence on mankind. Suggestive and stimulating.

Thorndike, L. A Short History of Civilization. xiv + 619 pp. Crofts. 1926. 21*s*.

A valuable book of reference for all those aspects of life which political histories ignore—science, art and peaceful intercourse between nations. Has a wide range: deals with East as well as West.

Wells, H. G. The Outline of History. 767 pp. Cassell. 1925–6 (4th ed.). 30*s*.

It would be impossible to omit this book, which was the pioneer of world histories. But the teacher should recognize that while the book may be read for its stimulating and individual quality, it should not be relied on for accurate facts. See the reviews in History VIII, p. 246, XI, p. 44.

For the development of art in its relation to world history the teacher might use Creighton, U., *Music*, Blum, A. S., *A Short History of Art*, and Lethaby, W. R., *Architecture* (for full references, see the book list on the History of the Arts).

For other books, see the bibliography issued by the Historical Association, Leaflet No. 59 (1*s*. 1*d*. or 7*d*. to members).

2. PREHISTORIC TIMES

The teaching of prehistoric times has of late years become popular among teachers of very little children. There are arguments in favour of such a course: but teachers who are convinced by them should be warned against a too confiding use of those highly imaginative books where children of a twentieth-century type, thinly disguised under extraordinary monosyllabic names, disport themselves in an artificial 'primitive world' from which most of the terror (and with it, we must suppose, most of the reality) of primitive times is withdrawn. Such books are dangerous because they assume on the part of the author a completeness of knowledge which no one in the world possesses, and so weaken the effect of the knowledge which we do possess. It is suggested that teachers should take as their material the true romance of the tools and dwellings actually in existence, and that their starting-point should be, 'Here is a strange thing found in the earth. What can it have been used for? What sort of people can have made it?'

The following books will be found useful for teaching on such lines.

I. SHORT AND INTRODUCTORY BOOKS

Ault, N. Life in Ancient Britain. xiv + 260 pp. Longmans. 1920. 5*s*. or 6*s*.

Clear, simply and attractively written, and one of the best and most practical books for the beginner. Illustrated.

Boyle, M. E. Man Before History. 127 pp. Harrap. 1924. 2*s.* or 3*s.* 6*d.*

A charming and sound little book, which could be read by children of twelve and which would be useful to the teacher of younger children. Illustrated.

Boyle, M. E. In Search of our Ancestors. 287 pp. Harrap. 1927. 10*s.* 6*d.*

An ideal book for the non-specialist: readable, modern, ample yet clear and simple, and beautifully illustrated. Traces man's origin from later ages back to their beginnings.

British Museum publications:

Stone Age Antiquities. 204 pp. 1926. 2*s.* 6*d.*

A Guide to Antiquities of the Bronze Age. 187 pp. 1920. 2*s.* 6*d.*

A Guide to early Iron Age Antiquities. 175 pp. 1925. 2*s.* 6*d.*

Flints. 54 pp. 1926. 6*d.*

All excellent. 'Flints', which is a wonderful sixpennyworth, is the best possible practical introduction. Fully illustrated.

Burkitt, M. C. Our Forerunners. 227 pp. Home Univ. Library. 1924. 2*s.* 6*d.*

A brief but very useful and accurate introduction to the subject. Illustrated.

Davison, D. Our Prehistoric Ancestors. xiv + 208 pp. Methuen. 1926. 7*s.* 6*d.*

An explanation in simple language of recent theories of evolution and primitive development. Teachers would find Part II useful to them. Illustrated.

Fleure, H. J. and **Peake, H. The Corridors of Time.**

Vol. I. Apes and Men.
,, II. Hunters and Artists.
,, III. Peasants and Potters.
,, IV. Priests and Kings.
,, V. The Steppe and the Sown.

O.U.P. 1927–8. 5*s.* each.

A most valuable series: traces the development of man in times of prehistory and the primitive civilizations of Egypt, Mesopotamia, Crete, etc. Of special interest in showing the development of crafts and the connexion between man's progress and geography. Excellent illustrations.

Quennell, M. and **C. H. B. Everyday Life in the Old Stone Age.** 109 pp. Batsford. 1921. 5*s.*

Quennell, M. and **C. H. B. Everyday Life in the New Stone, Bronze and Early Iron Ages.** 109 pp. Batsford. 1922. 5*s.*

Picturesque and well-illustrated volumes.

Stonehenge. H.M. Stationery Office. 6*d*.
An up-to-date summary. Very helpful to the teacher.

II. FULLER AND MORE ADVANCED BOOKS

Burkitt, M. C. Prehistory. 438 pp. C.U.P. 1925.
A valuable work: contains some wonderful illustrations.

Crawford, O. G. S. Man and his Past. xvi + 227 pp. O.U.P. 1921.
A sound and interesting discussion of the general methods of this work and the ideas underlying it.

De Morgan, J. Prehistoric Man. xxiii + 304 pp. Kegan Paul. 1924.
A sound and admirable work, excellently illustrated: closely written.

Sollas, W. J. Ancient Hunters. xxxvi + 697 pp. Macmillan. 1924 (3rd ed.).
A magnificent book. Although it is one of the standard authorities on the subject, the non-specialist will find it fascinating reading. Fully illustrated.

Tyler, J. M. The New Stone Age in N. Europe. 310 pp. Bell. 1921.
Excellent for the Neolithic period and full of information and thought.

III. FOLK TALES AND OTHER STORIES ILLUSTRATING EARLY CIVILIZATIONS

Fleming, R. M. Ancient Tales from many Lands. 193 pp. Benn. 1922. (Out of print.)
A wonderful story book of the earliest history and myth: contains an appendix on the use of traditional stories in the teaching of geography and history.

Fleming, R. M. Round the World in Folk Tales. 49 pp. Batsford. 1924. 2*s*. or 3*s*.
Sixteen fascinating stories coming from all parts of the world.

Fleming, R. M. Stories from the Early World. 156 pp. Benn. 1922. 10*s*. 6*d*.
Well-told stories illustrating the earliest history of Egypt, Mesopotamia, N. America, China, etc., etc.

Hull, E. Folklore of the British Isles. 298 pp. Methuen. 1928.
Very useful for more advanced reading: contains much valuable compressed material.

Squire, C. Mythology of the British Islands. 418 pp. Blackie. 1910.
Contains a helpful and interesting introduction and a collection of well-chosen stories.

3. ANCIENT HISTORY

[This section has been edited by S. Ridout, M.A., Lecturer in History at Goldsmiths' College.]

As this list is primarily designed to help teachers in preparing their lessons, it has been divided into sections and graded according to the standard required. First, a considerable number of stories has been collected (see 'Sources for Stories' section, p. 155) and references attached to them, so that the teachers can read in English translations (see Bibliography A) the original accounts.

A number of books on different periods (see Bibliography B) is next added, which includes books useful to the non-specialist and selected on the basis that they are reasonably accurate and cheap, as well as other works of a more advanced or expensive type, which may be useful to teachers who wish to read more widely and have opportunities of visiting good public libraries.

A

Lang, A., Leaf, W. and **Myers, E.** **The Iliad.** (Translated.) Macmillan. 4*s.* 6*d.*

Butcher, S. H. and **Lang, A.** **The Odyssey.** (Translation.) Macmillan. 4*s.* 6*d.* Or O.U.P.

Macaulay, G. C. **Herodotus: Histories.** (Translation.) Macmillan. 1904. 15*s.* Or Dent: Everyman's Library. 2 vols. 2*s.* each.

Jowett, B. **Thucydides.** (Translation.) 2 vols. O.U.P. 18*s.*

Stewart, A. and **Long, G.** **Plutarch's Lives.** (Translation.) Bell. 4 vols. 2*s.* each. Or Dent: Everyman's Library. 3 vols. 2*s.* each.

Shuckburgh, E. S. **The Histories of Polybius.** (Translation.) Macmillan. 24*s.*

Foster, B. O. **Livy.** (Translation.) Heinemann. Or by W. M. Roberts. Dent: Everyman's Library. 6 vols. 2*s.* each.

Holmes, Rice. **Caesar's Gallic War.** (Translation.) Macmillan. 5*s.* 6*d.* Or by E. P. Long. O.U.P. 5*s.*

Ramsay, G. G. **Tacitus. Annals.** (Translation.) Murray. 2 vols. 18*s.* each. Or in Dent: Everyman's Library. 2*s.*

Fyfe, W. F. **Tacitus. Histories.** (Translation.) O.U.P. 2 vols. 5*s.* each, or 8*s.* 6*d.* together. Or by Ramsay, G. C. Murray. 18*s.*

Fyfe, W. H. **Tacitus. Agricola and Germania.** (Translation.) O.U.P. 5*s.*

B

1. GENERAL

Breasted, J. H. Ancient Times. Ginn & Co. 10*s*. 6*d*.
Far the best general outline: scholarly, yet simple: a wonderful picture of civilization. Numerous and beautiful illustrations.

Cambridge Ancient History.
Excellent for advanced work.

Childe, V. G. The Dawn of European Civilization. Kegan Paul. 16*s*. Very good work.

Myres, J. L. The Dawn of History. Home Univ. Library. 2*s*. 6*d*. A most fascinating treatment of a difficult subject.

2. THE EARLY EMPIRES

Breasted, J. H. A History of Egypt. Hodder & Stoughton. (2nd ed.) 42*s*.

Budge, E. A. T. W. Babylonian Life and History. R.T.S. (2nd ed.) 10*s*. 6*d*.
Useful and well-written.

Budge, E. A. T. W. Tutankamen. Hopkinson. 10*s*. 6*d*.
A good book for those specially interested.

Budge, E. A. T. W. A Short History of the Egyptian People. Dent. (2nd ed.) 5*s*.
Very useful.

Budge, E. A. T. W. The Literature of the Ancient Egyptians. Dent. 5*s*.

Budge, E. A. T. W. The Dwellers on the Nile. R.T.S. 10*s*. 6*d*.

Delaporte, L. Mesopotamia. Kegan Paul. 16*s*.
A very fascinating description of the social life of the inhabitants.

Hall, H. R. The Ancient History of the Near East. Methuen. (5th ed.) 21*s*.
A detailed work useful for the specialist on the period.

Hogarth, D. G. The Ancient East. Home Univ. Library. 2*s*. 6*d*.

Jones, M. E. Monckton. Ancient Egypt from the Records. Methuen. 7*s*. 6*d*.
Well-written popular book.

Kellett, E. E. A Short History of the Jews down to the Roman Period. Routledge. 7*s*. 6*d*.

Petrie, W. M. Flinders. (ed.) **History of Egypt.** 6 vols. Methuen. From 9*s*. to 12*s*. 6*d*. per vol.
A detailed work.

Petrie, W. M. Flinders. Social Life in Ancient Egypt. Constable. 6*s*.
A charming work written in popular style.

Petrie, W. M. Flinders. Arts and Crafts of Ancient Egypt. Foulis. 5*s*.
Beautiful pictures.

Quibell, A. A. Egyptian History and Art. S.P.C.K. 6*s*.
A good outline combining history and archaeology.

3. GREECE

Abbott, E. Pericles and the Golden Age of Athens. Putnam. 7*s*. 6*d*.

Baikie, J. The Sea-Kings of Crete. Black. 10*s*. 6*d*.
Interesting and instructive.

Burgh, W. G. de. The Legacy of the Ancient World. (2nd ed.) McDonald & Evans. 16*s*.
Good for both Greece and Rome.

Bury, J. B. History of Greece. Macmillan. (2nd ed.) 10*s*.
The standard one-volume history.

Bury, J. B., with Barber, E. A., Bevan, E. and Tarn, W. W. The Hellenistic Age. C.U.P. 6*s*.
Excellent work.

Cotterhill, H. B. Ancient Greece. In 'Great Nations' Series'. Harrap. 15*s*.
Well illustrated.

Dickinson, G. L. The Greek View of Life. Methuen. 5*s*.
Interesting supplement.

Ferguson, W. S. Greek Imperialism. Constable. 8*s*. 6*d*.
A good general account of the Hellenistic kingdoms.

Glover, T. R. From Pericles to Philip. Methuen. (3rd ed.) 12*s*. 6*d*.
Good for the special period.

Grote, G. History of Greece. A classic: should not be neglected. Dent: Everyman's Library. 12 vols. 2*s*. each. The same abridged (Solon to 403 B.C.) by Mitchell & Caspari. Routledge. 5*s*. Reproduces the valuable and important parts.

Grundy, G. B. A History of the Greek and Roman World. Methuen. 22*s*. 6*d*.
A really good handbook.

Hamilton, M. A. Greece: a Short History. O.U.P. 4*s*. 6*d*. and 2*s*. 6*d*.
Excellent introduction.

Hogarth, D. G. The Ancient East. Home University Library. 2*s*. 6*d*.
Shows the relationship between Greece and the East.

Hogarth, D. G. Philip and Alexander of Macedon. Murray. 16*s*.
Good essays in biography.

Hopkinson, L. W. Greek Leaders. Constable. 5*s*.
Good biographies of Greek generals and statesmen.

James, H. R. Our Hellenic Heritage. Macmillan. 2 vols. 5*s*. 6*d*. each.
As a popular work, worthy of commendation. Useful to the teacher.

Mahaffy, J. P. Alexander's Empire. Stories of the Nations series. Fisher Unwin. 7*s*. 6*d*.
A continuous history of Greece for the period after the death of Alexander.

Mahaffy, J. P. Social Life in Greece. Macmillan. 8*s*. 6*d*.
Interesting.

Marshall, F. H. The Second Athenian Confederacy. C.U.P. 5*s*.
A brilliant critical essay.

Myres, J. L. Greek Lands and the Greek People. O.U.P. 1*s*. 6*d*.
Good geographical sketch.

Robinson, C. E. The Days of Alcibiades. Arnold. 5*s*.
Sketches of social life. Good material for teaching. See Chapter 11 on the Olympic Games.

Rose, H. J. A Handbook of Greek Mythology. Methuen. 16*s*.
Scholarly work.

Tarn, W. W. Antigonus Gonatas. O.U.P. 14*s*.
A brilliant work.

Thomson, J. A. K. Greeks and Barbarians. Allen & Unwin. 7*s*. 6*d*.
A good series of essays especially with reference to the colonization period.

Ure, P. N. The Greek Renaissance. Methuen. 6*s*.
A very pleasing introduction to a detailed study of the civilization and politics of Greece.

Warde-Fowler, W. The City State of the Greeks and Romans. Macmillan. 6*s*.
Excellent discussion of democracies.

Wheeler, B. I. Alexander the Great. Putnam. 7*s*. 6*d*.

Wright, F. A. Greek Social Life. Dent. 5*s*.
Useful work.

Zimmern, A. E. The Greek Commonwealth. O.U.P. 16*s*.
Gives an excellent view of the city state to 431 B.C. Fascinating reading.

4. ROME

Abbott, F. Roman Politics. Harrap. 5*s*.
Interesting in that it compares ancient and modern problems of democracy.

Armytage, D. Christianity in the Roman World. Its rise and progress to the fall of the Western Empire. Bell. 5*s*.

Especially useful for older scholars, but capable of adaptation for younger ones.

Arnold, W. T. Roman Provincial Administration. Blackwell. *7s. 6d.*

Arnold, W. T. The Second Punic War. Macmillan. *8s. 6d.*

Bailey, G. The Legacy of Rome. O.U.P. *8s. 6d.*

Bryce, Viscount. The Ancient Roman Empire and the British Empire in India. O.U.P. *8s. 6d.*

Many excellent comparisons are suggested by this able work.

Charlesworth, M. P. Trade Routes and Commerce of the Roman Empire. C.U.P. *8s. 6d.*

Interesting on the special subject.

Cromer, Lord. Ancient and Modern Imperialism. Murray. *2s. 6d.*

Interesting and good for discussions.

Frank, Tenney. Roman Imperialism. Macmillan. *12s. 6d.*

A very stimulating work.

Gibbon, E. The Decline and Fall of the Roman Empire. (6 vols.). Dent: Everyman's Library. *2s.* per vol.

A great classic.

Giles, A. F. Roman Civilization. Nelson. *5s.*

Well illustrated. Popular account of Roman life in imperial times.

Jones, H. Stuart. The Roman Empire. Stories of the Nations. Fisher Unwin. *7s. 6d.*

Good brief sketch of the history of the Empire down to A.D. 476.

Marsh, F. B. The Founding of the Roman Empire. O.U.P. *10s. 6d.*

Very interesting book of considerable value.

Matheson, P. E. The Growth of Rome. O.U.P. *2s. 6d.*

Chief characteristics of Ancient Rome. Does not take the place of a textbook but supplements it.

Mommsen, T. The History of Rome. Dent: Everyman's Library. 4 vols. *2s.* each.

This still remains the great history of the Roman Republic.

Mommsen, T. The Provinces of the Roman Empire. (2nd ed.) Macmillan. Two Vols. *25s.* each.

Deals with Rome's organization of her provinces.

Myres, J. L. A History of Rome. Rivington. *6s.*

The best of the many short histories of the Roman Republic.

Nilsson, M. P. Imperial Rome. Bell. *21s.*

A thoroughly up-to-date summary.

Pelham, H. F. Outlines of Roman History. Rivington. *7s.*

Very good and fairly full outline.

Rogers, H. L. and **Harley, T. R. The Life of Rome.** O.U.P. *6s.*

Warde-Fowler, W. Social Life at Rome in the Age of Cicero. Macmillan. 12s. 6d.

Instructive and delightful.

See also the biographies in the Heroes of Nations Series (Putnam, 7s. 6d. each) of Caesar by Warde-Fowler, Cicero by Strachan Davidson, Augustus, and Constantine, both by J. B. Firth. The biographies in Plutarch's Lives [in Everyman's Library, Dent, 3 vols., 2s. each] are well worth reading by all students.

5. ROMAN BRITAIN

Codrington, T. Roman Roads in Britain. S.P.C.K. 10s.

Collingwood, R. G. Roman Britain. O.U.P. 2s. 6d.

With illustrations and maps. An excellent little manual.

Haverfield, F. The Romanization of Britain. O.U.P. 7s. 6d.

Probably the best short history of Roman influence in Britain.

Haverfield, F. The Roman Occupation of Britain. O.U.P. 18s.

Brilliant but advanced.

Holmes, T. Rice. Ancient Britain and Julius Caesar. O.U.P. 30s.

A mine of information.

Home, G. Roman Britain. Benn. 6d.

An excellent little summary.

Quennell, M. and C. H. B. Everyday Life in Roman Britain. Batsford. 5s.

Picturesquely written with many charming and useful illustrations.

Oman, Sir Charles. England Before the Norman Conquest. Methuen. 12s. 6d.

A valuable work containing a good account of the Roman occupation of Britain.

Source Book. **Chambers, R. W.** and **Cary, M. England Before the Norman Conquest.** Longmans. 1926. 10s. 6d.

4. GENERAL ENGLISH HISTORY

A. POLITICAL HISTORY

One of the first requisites of the non-specialist junior history teacher is that he should possess a good up-to-date textbook of English history. He should not use this simply with the aim of condensing it to suit his children's needs, for, as every practical teacher knows, such a book is at once too long and too short to form the basis of lessons to elementary school children. It is too long because it covers more ground and introduces more complications than the children can manage: and too short because it leaves out those details and explanations which make history real to them. For direct preparation of lessons the teacher requires at once fuller and simpler material. But the textbook is essential for reference, for a fairly comprehensive list of the political material from which the teacher must select his simpler outline, and above all for giving in a brief form the modern scholar's conclusions as to what actually happened. It is important, therefore, that the book should be of recent date. Among the best textbooks of the last few years are :—

Greenwood, A. D. History of the People of England.
Vol. I. 55 B.C.–A.D. 1485. xii + 388 pp. 1921.
,, II. 1485–1688. xii + 416 pp. 1923.
,, III. 1688–1834. xii + 336 pp. 1926.
,, IV. 1834–1910. 208 pp. 1929.
Sheldon Press. Bede Histories. Senior Series. First three vols., 7*s*. 6*d*. each. Vol. IV, 6*s*.

This is intended for the general reader. It is clear, full and interesting, and contains excellent pictures. Special emphasis is laid throughout on ecclesiastical history.

Mowat, R. B. A New History of Great Britain. xxviii + 776 pp. O.U.P. 1928. 10*s*. 6*d*.

A straightforward summary of political and social history, condensed yet interesting, and containing many extracts from sources. Good illustrations.

Somervell, D. C. A History for British Schools. 1152 pp. 4 Vols. I. Foundations. II. 1066–1714. III and IV. Modern Times. Also an Outline for general prevision and revision. Bell. 1925–8. 3*s*. each. Outline, 1*s*. 6*d*.

Interesting and individual. Describes English history in the setting of general history (see comment in world history section).

Warner, G. T. and **Marten, C. H. K. The Groundwork of British History.** xiv + 803 pp. Blackie. 1921. 8*s*.

A deservedly famous textbook, which not only outlines the great events of history but shows something of their significance.

Side by side with the textbook of political events may be placed the more literary histories which aim at interpreting events and showing the relations between them. The following will be found of interest :—

Green, J. R. (ed. Mrs. J. R. Green and K. Norgate). **A Short History of the English People.** Illustrated ed. 4 Vols. Newnes. 1907–8.

This book has appeared in Everyman's Library. 2 Vols. 1915. 2*s.* each.

A famous book, still valued for its high literary quality and interest: but in several places the facts have been superseded by later research, and therefore teachers should not rely on it as their only version.

Marvin, F. S. England and the World. 268 pp. O.U.P. 1925. 10*s.* 6*d.*

A series of essays by various authors showing the part played by England in the great world story.

Pollard, A. F. The History of England. 256 pp. Home University Library. 1912. 2*s.* 6*d.*

A brilliant sketch bringing out the continuity of English history.

Trevelyan, G. M. A History of England. xx + 723 pp. Longmans. 1926. 12*s.* 6*d.*

A valuable enlightening essay, based on the conclusions of modern research: has been termed 'the only true literary history of England since the days of Green'.

More detailed histories:—

Bigham, Hon. Charles Clive. The Chief Ministers of England. 920–1720. x + 422 pp. Murray. 1923. 10*s.* 6*d.* (cheaper ed.).

The Prime Ministers of Britain. 1721–1921. xiii + 384 pp. Murray. 1924 (4th ed.). 10*s.* 6*d.*

Interesting biographical sketches.

Fletcher, C. R. An Introductory History of England. 5 Vols. Murray. 1904–23. 9*s.* each volume.

A vivid though often prejudiced description of English history up to 1880. The earlier volumes, which include social as well as political history, are especially good.

Muir, J. Ramsay. A Short History of the British Commonwealth. Can be obtained in 6 parts:—To 1485, 4*s.* 6*d.* 1485–1660, 5*s.* 1660–1763, 6*s.* 1763–1815, 4*s.* 1815–1880, 6*s.* 1880–1919, 6*s.* Or in two parts:—Vol. I. The Islands and the First Empire (to 1763), 15*s.* Vol. II. The Modern Commonwealth (1763–1919), 15*s.* Philip. 1924.

As the reference shows, the main emphasis here is on the later ages and imperial aspects of English history. The aim of the book is to describe the traditions and development of 'the British Commonwealth of Nations'.

Wingfield-Stratford, Esmé. History of British Civilization. 2 Vols. 1332 pp. Routledge. 1928. 42*s.*

A fascinating treasure house for the teacher, who would find here excellent material for lessons.

There are several works or series of works from which the teacher could get detailed information. The chief are :—

A History of England in 7 Vols. Ed. **Oman, Sir C. W. C.** Methuen. 1904. 12*s*. 6*d*. each. See details given under each period.

This is perhaps the most useful series for the teacher.

The Political History of England in 12 Vols. Ed. **Hunt, W.** and **Poole, R. Lane**. Longmans. 1905. 12*s*. 6*d*. each.

The Dictionary of English History. Originally compiled by Low & Pulling : re-edited by Hearnshaw, Chew & Beales. x + 1154 pp. Cassell. 1928. 30*s*.

The Dictionary of National Biography. Smith, Elder & Co. 1885–1900. Now presented to the University of Oxford. The O.U.P. has published a new edition.

B. SOCIAL AND ECONOMIC HISTORY

i. SHORT AND INTRODUCTORY BOOKS

Cheyney, E. P. An Introduction to the Industrial and Social History of England. x + 317 pp. Macmillan. 1910. 10*s*. 6*d*.

A very useful straightforward survey, covering the whole ground. Illustrated.

Ditchfield, P. H. Old Village Life : or, Glimpses of Village Life through all Ages. xii + 253 pp. Methuen. 1920. 7*s*. 6*d*.

A picturesque delightful survey which illustrates the daily life of the village in successive periods from the earliest times to to-day and shows the continuity between them. Illustrated.

Gloag, J. and **Walker, C. T. Home Life in History.** 302 pp. Benn. 1927. 12*s*. 6*d*.

An entertaining popular description of the customs and atmosphere of everyday life in succeeding ages. Illustrated.

Guest, G. English Social Reformers. Book I. 1066–1740. Book II. 1726–1865. Horace Marshall. 1923. 2*s*. each.

Very useful : each great movement of social history grouped round the simply told biography of a great reformer.

Leathes, S. The People of England.

The People in the Making. xxiv + 289 pp. 1921. 3*s*. 6*d*.
The People in Adventure. xxiv + 303 pp. 1920. 3*s*. 6*d*.
The People on its trial. xxii + 471 pp. 1923. 6*s*. Heinemann.

A simple suggestive study of the development of English society, its adventures, its institutions, its learning and its everyday life. For the teacher and in parts for the older children. Very useful. Shows the relation between political history and the history of civilization.

Levett, E. English Economic History. Benn. 1928. 6*d.*
A very useful survey.

Spalding, E. H. (ed.). **The Piers Plowman Social and Economic Histories.** 7 vols.
Book I. Primeval Times to 1066. Bell, J. J. 244 pp. 3*s.*
,, II. 1066–1300. Snape, R. H. 244 pp. 3*s.*
,, III. 1300–1485. Niemeyer, N. 156 pp. 3*s.*
,, IV. 1485–1600. Niemeyer, N. and Wragge, P. 240 pp. 3*s.*
,, V. 1600–1760. Spalding, E. 216 pp. 3*s.* 6*d.*
,, VI. 1760–1830. Spalding, E. 224 pp. 3*s.* 6*d.*
,, VII. 1830–to-day. Spalding, E. and Taylor, J. R. 283 pp. 3*s.* 6*d.*
Philip. 1921–7.
An excellent series full of useful material for lessons. Illustrated.

Waters, C. M. A Short Economic History of England.
Part I. 1066–1750. xi + 310 pp. 1920. 4*s.*
Part II. 1750–1874. x + 310–604 pp. 1925. 4*s.* Or in 1 vol., 7*s.* 6*d.*
An excellent simply told survey: clear, interesting and contains much material in a readable form: good pictures.

ii. FULLER AND MORE ADVANCED BOOKS

Cunningham, W. The Growth of English Industry and Commerce. 2 Vols. C.U.P. 1922, 1921 (5th and 6th ed.)
The classical authority on the subject.

Meredith, H. O. Outlines of the Economic History of England. viii + 366 pp. Pitmans. 1908.
Useful and informative reference book.

Prothero, R. E. English Farming Past and Present. xvi + 506. Longmans. 1927 (4th ed.).
The standard authority for agricultural history.

Traill, H. D. and **Mann, J. S.** (ed.). **Social England.** 6 Vols.
1. From the earliest times to the accession of Edward I.
2. From Edward I to the death of Henry VII.
3. From Henry VIII to the death of Elizabeth.
4. From James I to the death of Anne.
5. From George I to Waterloo.
6. From Waterloo to 1885.

Cassell & Co. 1893–1898.
A series of detailed descriptions by various writers of the progress of the people in religion, learning, industry and commerce, &c.

Usher, A. P. An Introduction to the Industrial History of England. xxii + 529 pp. Harrap. 1921.

C. SPECIAL ASPECTS

i. CONSTITUTIONAL HISTORY

Constitutional History as such cannot, of course, be attempted in elementary schools. But it makes a good deal of difference to the teaching of such subjects as Magna Carta or the Civil War whether the teacher himself has a grasp of the subject. One clear up-to-date survey is therefore recommended for the teacher's reading :—

Hall, D. G. E. A Brief Survey of English Constitutional Development. 270 pp. Harrap. 1925. 5*s*.

A useful, lucid, and comprehensive study.

ii. NAVAL HISTORY

Callender, G. A. R. The Naval Side of British History. 305 pp. Christophers. 1924. 8*s*. 6*d*.

A gallant, vivid story. Illustrated.

For further books, see the Bibliography of Naval History by G. A. R. Callender, Historical Assoc. Leaflets 58, 61. (1*s*. 1*d*. each, or 7*d*. each to members.)

iii. RELIGIOUS HISTORY

There are two series of ecclesiastical histories covering the whole ground of English history. The shorter is in 6 volumes published by Methuen and edited by J. H. Burns. The longer is published by Macmillan and edited by W. R. W. Stephens and Hunt. Some details are given below under periods. A good and clear general narrative is :—

Wakeman, H. O. An Introduction to the History of the Church of England. From the Earliest Times to the Present Day. xxii + 519 pp. Rivingtons. 1914 (8th ed.). 7*s*. 6*d*.

For further books, see the Bibliography of Church History by J. P. Whitney, and that on the Early Church by N. H. Baynes. Historical Assoc. Leaflets, Nos. 55, 71. (1*s*. 1*d*. each, or 7*d*. each to members.)

D. SOURCE BOOKS

Adams, G. B. and **Stephens, H. M. Select Documents of English Constitutional History (1066-1885).** 555 pp. Macmillan. 1901. 12*s*. 6*d*.

For more advanced work. Teachers would find here an English text of practically every great constitutional document.

Bland, A. E., Brown, P. A. and **Tawney, R. English Economic History : Select Documents.** xx + 730 pp. Bell. 1914. 7*s*. 6*d*.

Essential to the serious study of economic history.

Cheyney, E. P. Readings in English History drawn from the Original Sources. xxxix + 849 pp. Ginn. 1922. 11*s*. 6*d*.

An extremely valuable manual. The variety and wide range of the extracts, which deal with social as well as political history, and the fact that it covers all the ground from Caesar's coming to our own day, make this the most useful volume for the personal possession of the teacher.

Innes, A. D. A Source Book of English History.

Vol. I. A.D. 597–1603. viii + 384 pp. 5*s*. 6*d*.
,, II. A.D. 1603–1815. viii + 282 pp. 4*s*. C.U.P.

Useful: deals with political and social history.

Keatinge, M. W. and **Frazer, N. L. Documents of British History.** A.D. 78–1900. 459 pp. [Or in 6 sections, 1*s*. 4*d*. each.] Black. 7*s*. 6*d*.

A very useful, comprehensive collection: covers the whole ground and includes social as well as political extracts. Next to Cheyney, this is probably the best collection for the teacher to possess.

Kendall, E. K. Source Book of English History. xxii + 482 pp. Macmillan. 1906. 7*s*.

Contains many extracts of a dramatic value: has aimed at giving fairly full accounts of selected episodes rather than covering the whole ground.

Jones, M. E. Monckton. A Source Book of English Social History. vii + 198 pp. Methuen. 1922. 4*s*. 6*d*.

Very useful to the teacher: contains extracts illustrating the social and economic history of each age from Saxon times to the eighteenth century, with introductory notes.

Johnson, R. B. Manners makyth Man. 377 pp. Philpot. 1927.

A pleasant anthology from great writers illustrating the history of manners and customs from Chaucer's time to the age of Trollope. Does not of course give much help with historical events, but illustrates the atmosphere of the age.

Morgan, R. B. Readings in English Social History. xxx + 585 pp. Or in 5 volumes, 4*s*. each. C.U.P. 1923. 16*s*.

Entertaining illustrative material.

Turral, J. A Select Source Book of British History. 320 pp. O.U.P. 1926. 2*s*. 6*d*.

This volume aims primarily at illustrating changes in the conditions of living from 55 B.C. to A.D. 1878.

Turral, J. Pages of Britain's Story. 325 pp. O.U.P. 1917. 2*s*. 6*d*.

Contains lively extracts giving colour to the great political events of English History.

Windsor, M. E. and **Turral, J. Lyra Historica.** Poems of British History. A.D. 61–A.D. 1910. 95 pp. O.U.P. 1911. 3*s*. In 3 parts, 1*s*. 3*d*., 1*s*. 3*d*., 1*s*. 6*d*.

This is a little anthology of verse illustrating episodes in English history. Teachers using it should be careful to distinguish between poems written at the time of the event (which have a historical value) and poems written later (which cannot have more than a picturesque and literary value).

There are several good series of source books issued by various publishers. Among these are :—

Bell's English History Source-books. Ed. by **Winbolt, S. E.** and **Bell, K.** Cover the ground from 449 to 1887 in 21 short volumes. 1*s*. 6*d*. each. Illustrate both political and social history.

Black. English History illustrated from Original Sources. Covers the ground from earliest times to 1815 in 9 vols. 3*s*. 6*d*. each. Mainly political.

Blackie. Readings in English History. Covers the ground from the Roman Invasion to William IV in 4 vols. 2*s*. 6*d*. each.

Mainly political. Simple : contains much that children could read individually.

Dent. The 'Englishman' Series. Ed. by Sir A. T. Quiller Couch. Contains at present :—

The Age of Chaucer. Sir A. T. Quiller Couch. 192 pp.
The Fifteenth Century. W. Hadley. 222 pp.
In the Days of Elizabeth. W. R. Macklin. 192 pp.
The Coming of the Stuarts. G. N. Pocock. 192 pp. 2*s*. each.
Pleasant illustrative extracts.

Longmans. University of London Intermediate Source Books. In progress. Generally 10*s*. 6*d*. each. Full particulars of volumes already issued are given under separate periods below.

Scholarly and full : deal with comparatively short periods and illustrate every aspect of its history.

Horace Marshall. Illustrative Histories. Cover the ground from 55 B.C. to the nineteenth century in 5 vols. 3*s*. 6*d*. each.

Much of this is suited to children's own reading. It should be noted that this series contains extracts from great secondary histories as well as from original sources, and that the children should know which they are reading.

Methuen. English Life in English Literature. Ed. by E. Power and A. W. Reed. In progress. 6*s*. each vol. Details of volumes already published are given below. Illustrations drawn from literary sources.

Pitman. An Elementary History Source Book. 208 pp. 3*s*. 6*d*. Scholars' Books in 3 parts, 1*s*., 8*d*. and 8*d*. A handy, inexpensive little collection.

5. GENERAL EUROPEAN HISTORY

A. BOOKS COVERING ALL THE GROUND

Burns, C. Delisle. A Short History of International Intercourse. 159 pp. Allen & Unwin. 1924. 5*s.* or 3*s.* 6*d.*

Excellent; gives material and suggestions for the treatment of international affairs from the point of view of co-operation and progress rather than from the point of view of rivalry and war.

Cunningham, W. An Essay on Western Civilization in its Economic Aspects. Medieval and Modern Times. xii + 300 pp. C.U.P. 1898–1900. 8*s.*

Valuable.

Grant, A. J. History of Europe. xiv + 868 pp. Longmans. 1922. 15*s.*

A useful and well-written textbook. Can be obtained in three parts.

Hassall, A. European History chronologically arranged. ix + 439 pp. 1920. Macmillan. 12*s.*

Very useful for reference; covers the ground from A.D. 476–1920.

Lawrence, D. H. Movements in European History. 399 pp. O.U.P. 1926. 4*s.* 6*d.* and 8*s.* 6*d.*

A vivid and skilful popular treatment of history, giving a connected series of pictures of great movements from the time of Rome to the time of Bismarck. Teachers would find this useful for general background and introduction.

Mowat, R. B. A History of Europe 476–1925. 80 pp. Benn. 1928. 6*d.*

A compact survey of the whole programme.

Robinson, J. H. Medieval and Modern Times. xii + 806 pp. Ginn. 1926. 10*s.* 6*d.*

A very good general introduction, well illustrated, and dealing in a simple way with the story of civilization as well as political relations. Gives an excellent background to the English story, which is briefly included.

Robinson, J. H. Readings in European History. xxxiv + 573 pp. Ginn. 1906. 10*s.* 6*d.* Or in two much fuller volumes, 10*s.* 6*d.* each.

A good source book.

Webster, H. Readings in Early European History. xii + 544 pp. Heath. 1926. 6*s.*

Readings in Modern European History. xi + 554 pp. Heath. 1926. 6*s.*

Source Books.

A series of brief clear studies under the title of **Special Periods of History,** ed. by **D. C. Somervell,** is being published by Bell. 2*s*. Full particulars given below under periods.

There are several series covering the whole period. They are arranged here in order of difficulty.

Oxford Text Books of European History. Bell, K. 1095–1254. 269 pp.
Mowat, R. B. 1254–1494. 339 pp. 1917.
Tanner, E. N. 1494–1610. xii + 307 pp. 1908.
Sacret, J. H. 1610–1715. vi + 324 pp. 1914.
Guedalla, P. 1715–1815. vii + 311 pp. 1914.
Plunket, I. L. 1763–1815. iv + 248 pp. 1909.
Jane, L. Cecil. 1815–1878. 288 pp. 1910.
O.U.P. 4*s*. 6*d*. each.

Six Ages of European History.
The Dawn of Medieval Europe. Masterman, J. H. B.
The Central Period of the Middle Ages. Lees, B. A.
The End of the Middle Ages. Lodge, E. C.
Europe in Renaissance and Reformation. Hollings, M. A.
The Age of the Enlightened Despot. Johnson, A. H.
The Remaking of Modern Europe. Marriott, Sir J. A. R.
Europe and Beyond. (A supplementary volume dealing with 1870–1914.) Marriott, Sir J. A. R.
Methuen. 1909–27. 4*s*. and 5*s*. each.

Periods of European History.
The Dark Ages. Oman, Sir Charles.
The Empire and the Papacy. Tout, E. F.
The Close of the Middle Ages. Lodge, R.
Europe in the Sixteenth Century. Johnson, A. H.
The Ascendency of France. Wakeman, H. O.
The Balance of Power. Hassall, A.
Revolutionary Europe. Stephens, H. Morse.
Modern Europe (to 1899). Philipps, W. Alison.
Various dates. A rather old, but still useful series. Rivingtons. 8*s*. 6*d*. each.

Cambridge Medieval History. Ed. Gwatkin, H. M. and **Whitney, J. P.** C.U.P. 1911, &c. In progress.

Cambridge Modern History. Ed. **Ward, A. W., Prothero, G. W.** and **Leathes, S.** 13 Vols. C.U.P. 1902–11.
Extremely useful: deals with literature and thought as well as politics.

B. MEDIEVAL

Adams, G. B. Civilization during the Middle Ages. vi + 455 pp. Scribner. 1922. Revised edition. 12*s*. 6*d*.
A most valuable and suggestive work which has breadth of outlook.

Brown, W. E. The Achievement of the Middle Ages. 240 pp. Sands & Co. 1928. 5*s.*

A series of selected essays which would help the teacher to enter into the character of medieval civilization ; deals with the Roman tradition, the development of a rule of law, of city life and of general culture. Emphasizes the part played by the Church.

Coulton, G. G. A Medieval Garner. vi + 727 pp. Constable. 1910. 30*s.*

A most delightful collection of extracts from sources. Contains much illustrative social material that would enliven lessons. This is being re-edited by the C.U.P. 1928 in 4 volumes under the general title '**Life in the Middle Ages**', 1. Religion, Folklore and Superstition. 2. Chronicles, Science and Art. 3. Men and Manners. 4. Monks, Friars and Nuns.

Crump, G. G. and **Jacob, E. F.** (editors). **The Legacy of the Middle Ages.** xii + 549 pp. O.U.P. 1926. 10*s.*

The most advanced and valuable book in the section ; full of learning, but not difficult to read. Describes the contributions made by medieval civilizations to art, literature and thought.

Cunningham, W. Western Civilization in its Economic Aspects. Medieval and Modern Times. xii + 300 pp. C.U.P. 1904. 8*s.*

Deals with the development of economic life and trade.

Davis, H. W. C. Medieval Europe. 256 pp. Home University Library. 1911. 2*s.* 6*d.*

A brief, brilliant sketch, analysing all the main movements of the age.

Dymond, D. An Introduction to Medieval History. Methuen. 1929. 6*s.*

Intended as a guide to non-specialists ; contains descriptions of the great political, social and religious movements, together with a full book list on each topic.

Henderson, E. F. Select Historical Documents of the Middle Ages. ix + 477 pp. Bell. 1907. 6*s.*

Contains documents essential to the serious study of general medieval history.

Knight, M. M. Economic History of Europe to the End of the Middle Ages. x + 260 pp. Allen & Unwin. 1926. 12*s.*

A sound and stimulating book. Most valuable to the teacher who wishes to take the international standpoint, since it contains material as to the manor, trade, industry, &c., in Europe as a whole, and this kind of material is very hard to find in English. Covers the whole ground of economic history from Roman times.

Power, E. Medieval People. ix + 216 pp. Methuen. 1925. 6*s*.

A group of charming sketches of typical medieval figures.

Robinson, J. H. Readings in European History. Vol. I. Ginn. 1904. 10*s*. 6*d*.

A useful source book for political and social history.

Thorndike, L. Medieval Europe. xviii + 665 pp. Harrap. 1920. 8*s*. 6*d*.

Illustrates the general development of medieval civilization.

These books have been chosen to give the teacher a background of European civilization as a whole. The teacher who wishes to enter on the more detailed study of political history should consult the Cambridge Medieval History (in progress: 5 volumes published) for full detail and book lists, and should use one of the following textbooks: **Previté-Orton. Outlines of Medieval History.** 603 pp. C.U.P. 1921. **Six Ages of European History.** Methuen (first three volumes). **Periods of European History.** Rivington (first three volumes).

C. MODERN

Gooch, G. P. Annals of Politics and Culture. 1492–1899. ix + 530 pp. C.U.P. 1901. 10*s*. 6*d*.

A reference book giving under each year its main literary, social and scientific events. Useful for reference and for making charts.

Hoyland, J. S. Modern European History. 1494–1914. viii + 331 pp. Bell. 1924. 5*s*.

A clear, useful, straightforward text book, which includes a sketch of English history.

Knight, M. M. Economic History of Europe in Modern Times. vii + 808 pp. Allen & Unwin. 1928. 15*s*.

Valuable to the teacher who wishes to work from the international standpoint, since it surveys the whole field of economic history in other lands as well as our own.

Muir, J. R. B. The Expansion of Europe. xvi + 365 pp. Constable. 1922. (3rd ed.) 12*s*.

Very useful in setting the story of British imperialism in the context of general history. The story of world politics from the time of Columbus told from an imperialist standpoint.

Ogg, F. A. and **Sharp, W. R. Economic Development of Modern Europe.** xvi + 861 pp. Macmillan. 1926. 16*s*.

A useful manual for reference: gives a compact account of economic history, mainly from the the eighteenth century onwards, in all the chief European countries including England.

Renard, G. Life and Work in Modern Europe (fifteenth to eighteenth centuries) (trans.). xvi + 395 pp. Kegan Paul. 1925. 16*s.*

Deals with agriculture, industry and trade in England, France, Spain, &c. Full of matter but interesting to read.

Schevill, F. A History of Europe from the Reformation to our own Day. v + 728 pp. Harrap. 1926. 10*s.* 6*d.*

A useful introduction to the modern history of European civilization. Deals with social and intellectual as well as political development.

Tickner, F. W. Schools and Scholars in History from the Renaissance to the Nineteenth Century. A useful source book. Nelson. 1*s.*

6. MEDIEVAL ENGLISH AND EUROPEAN HISTORY

A. ENGLISH HISTORY: BOOKS COVERING THE WHOLE PERIOD

1. POLITICAL HISTORY

Fletcher, C. R. An Introductory History of England. Vol. I. xvii + 397 pp. Murray. 1904. 9*s.*

A vivid, lively story: valuable accounts of social changes given in the history of an imaginary village called Tubney.

Greenwood, A. History of the People of England. Vol. I. 55 B.C.– A.D. 1066. Sheldon Press. 1921. 7*s.* 6*d.*

Extremely useful to the teacher; accurate yet interesting, and deals with social as well as political affairs. Gives special emphasis to ecclesiastical history.

Hall, D. G. E. Brief Survey of English Constitutional History. 269 pp. Harrap. 1925. 5*s.* Chapters I to VII.

A good outline which supplies the teacher with the necessary background of constitutional development.

Smith, A. G. Short History of Medieval England. xi + 451 pp. Burns & Oates. 1925. 6*s.*

An excellent textbook, written from the Roman Catholic point of view. Full of interest and significance. Useful to teacher who wishes to get a general grasp of the period.

For more advanced work on constitutional history the teacher could have recourse to **Maitland's Constitutional History,** xxviii + 547 pp., C.U.P., 1909, a standard authority of great interest, or to **White, A. B., The Making of the English Constitution,** xxxiii + 461 pp. Putnam. 1925. 12*s.* 6*d.* For more advanced work on political history consult the first three volumes of the **Political History of England,** published by Methuen, the first four volumes of the **Political History of England**, published by Longmans, and **Ramsay, J. H., The Scholars' History of England**, published in eight volumes by the O.U.P.

2. SOCIAL AND ECONOMIC HISTORY

Barnard, re-ed. by **Davis, H. W. C. Medieval England.** xxi + 632 pp. O.U.P. 1924.

A mine of information on social life and institutions; deals with architecture, war, costume, art, education, town and country life, commerce, monks and friars, &c.

Cutts, E. L. Scenes and Characters of the Middle Ages. viii + 552 pp. Daniel O'Connor. 1922 (4th ed.).

A full interesting description of various social classes or types —monks, hermits, pilgrims, priests, minstrels, knights, merchants.

Leach, A. F. The Schools of Medieval England. xv + 349 pp. Methuen. 1915.

Included because children are always interested in school life of other days. A stimulating though rather sceptical account.

Lipson, E. An Introduction to the Economic History of England: the Middle Ages. viii + 552 pp. A. & C. Black. 1926 (4th ed.).

Recommended as the best and most up-to-date account for serious reading; deals with the rise and fall of the manor, the growth of towns, gilds and the development of the wool trade and trade abroad.

Salzman, L. F. English Life in the Middle Ages. 288 pp. O.U.P. 1926. 7*s.* 6*d.*

Excellent for illustrative material: bright, interesting, and gives just the sort of detail that children like.

Salzman, L. F. English Industries of the Middle Ages. xx + 360 pp. O.U.P. 1923. 10*s.*

Picturesque, yet sound and valuable.

Traill, H. D. and **Mann, J. S. Social England.** See section on general English History.

3. RELIGIOUS HISTORY

Thompson, A. Hamilton. English Monasteries. 158 pp. C.U.P. 1923 (2nd ed.) 3*s.* 6*d.*

A very sound and useful outline.

Thompson, A. Hamilton. The Historical Growth of the English Parish Church. xi + 142 pp. C.U.P. 1911. 2*s.* 6*d.*

See also the series noted under English history: General.

4. SOURCE BOOKS

Coulton, G. G. Social Life in Britain from the Conquest to the Reformation. xvi + 540 pp. C.U.P. 1918. 24*s*.

An entertaining and varied collection of extracts illustrating child life and education, the church, chivalry, town and country life, &c.

Davies, R. T. Documents illustrating the History of Civilization in Medieval England (1066–1500). x + 413 pp. Methuen. 1926. 10*s*. 6*d*.

A collection of documents illustrating medieval government and social and economic life.

For more advanced work on constitutional documents use the volume by **G. B. Adams** and **H. M. Stephens** (see p. 75).

For source books covering the whole course of History, see the section on English History: General. Source books illustrating only one special period of medieval history are given below.

For general books on medieval European History, see Europe: General, p. 78.

B. ENGLISH MEDIEVAL HISTORY A.D. 400–1066

1. POLITICAL

Greenwood, A. (See p. 82.)

Ireland, A. J. Episodes in the History of England. 55 B.C. to 1066. xxxviii + 263 pp. Longmans. 1926. 3*s*. 6*d*. and 6*s*.

A convenient book for the quick preparation of lessons; tells the story of each great movement vividly and in detail; marred by some fanciful illustrations.

Oman, Sir C. W. C. England before the Norman Conquest. xx + 679 pp. Methuen. 1921 (5th ed.).

An excellent full political narrative.

The story of the Saxon invasions is surrounded by much historical controversy; if the teacher wishes to find out what this controversy is about, he should begin by tackling **Chadwick, H. M. Origin of the English Nation.** vi + 351 pp. C.U.P. 1907, and **Leeds, E. Thurloe. The Archæology of the Anglo-Saxon Settlements.** 144 pp. O.U.P. 1913. For the age of the Danish invasions see **Collingwood, W. G. Scandinavian Britain.** 272 pp. Sheldon Press. 1908. 3*s*. 6*d*., which gives an account of the background of the Viking invaders, their fleets and their methods, followed by a concise account of their attacks on Great Britain. See also the books on this topic in the European section.

See also in the biography section **important** lives of Alfred the Great and Canute.

2. SOCIAL AND ECONOMIC

Bell, J. J. Piers Plowman Social and Economic Histories. Book I. Primeval Times to 1066 A.D. xi + 244 pp. Philip. 1922. 3*s*.

A useful outline, full of good illustrative material.

Quennell, M. & C. Everyday Life in Anglo-Saxon, Viking and Norman Times. 115 pp. Batsford. 1926. 5*s*.

A picturesque volume; sometimes ekes out material with imagination.

Brown, G. Baldwin. The Arts in Early England. Vol. I. xxiii + 388 pp. Murray. 1926.

Most valuable to the teacher who wishes to make the life of the age real to children: deals with the life of Saxon England in its relation to art, particularly the art of architecture, showing how the history of England is illustrated by the history of the church, the castle and the monastery.

Dodd, A. F. Early English Social History from the Chronicles. vi + 211 pp. Bell. 1913. 2*s*. 6*d*.

Aims at giving the teacher the background needed for intelligent story telling. Contains many extracts from sources.

Teachers who wish to do more advanced work should read besides **Lipson** (see above, p. 83) **Vinogradoff, Sir P. The Growth of the Manor.** x + 384 pp. Allen. 1911, and **English Society in the Eleventh Century.** xii + 599 pp. O.U.P. 1908. The work of **Maitland, F. W. Domesday Book and Beyond.** C.U.P. 1907, is of the highest literary as well as academic quality. They should not use Stubbs for this period.

3. RELIGIOUS

Cruttwell, C. T. The Saxon Church and the Norman Conquest, 800–1135. xvi + 268 pp. Methuen. 1909.

Hunt, W. The English Church, A.D. 597–1066. xix + 444 pp. Macmillan. 1899.

A full narrative.

Maude, J. H. The Foundations of the English Church (to about 800). xi + 231 pp. Methuen. 1909.

See also in the biography section, lives of Gregory the Great, Dunstan.

4. SOURCES AND SOURCE BOOKS

(*a*) Original Sources

Anglo-Saxon Chronicle. viii + 301 pp. Dent. Everyman's Library. No. 624. 2*s*. For the Danish invasions.

Asser. Life of Alfred. lix + 163 pp. Chatto and Windus. 1908. 5*s*.

Bede. Ecclesiastical History. xxxiv + 370 pp. Dent. Everyman. 2*s*. Essential for the conversion of the Saxons and early monasticism.

Eddius Stephanus. Life of Bishop Wilfred. 192 pp. C.U.P. 1927. 12*s*. 6*d*.

(*b*) Books of Extracts from Sources

Chambers, R. W. England before the Norman Conquest. xxvi + 334 pp. Longmans. Intermediate source books. 1926. 10*s*. 6*d*. Includes extracts illustrating each century of English history from 410 to 1066.

Wallis, J. E. W. The Welding of the Race. vi + 120 pp. Bell. English History Source Book Series. 1924. 1*s*. 6*d*. A useful short collection.

Kea tinge and Frazer (see p. 76).

C. THE EUROPEAN BACKGROUND, A.D. 410–1066

The vital factors in history here are the breakup of the orderly Roman world by barbarian invaders, the settlement of the barbarians, and their conversion, through Roman influences, to Christianity. It is essential for the children to realize that these are European and not merely English movements. The important European topics are, therefore, the story of the Goths, told side by side with the story of Saxon invasions: the story of Justinian, to explain the continuance of the Roman Empire [later called the Eastern or Byzantine Empire] at Constantinople: the stories of Benedict and Gregory I in Italy as a necessary preliminary to the story of Augustine in England; the story of Charles the Great, to explain (what is otherwise a complete puzzle to children) the existence of a barbarian 'Roman Empire', and to show how the barbarians in Europe became civilized and tried to restore order as Alfred was shortly to do in England: and stories of the Norse invasions, showing how Charles' Empire broke up, how feudalism developed, and how the imperial power was transferred to Germany while a national monarchy began to develop in France. The story of Mahomet should also be included in its proper place, to prepare the children to understand the part played by Islam in world history.

1. GENERAL HISTORY AND THE BARBARIAN INVASIONS

Bradley, H. The Goths. xx + 376 pp. Fisher Unwin. Stories of the Nations. 1891.

A good and picturesque general survey. Illustrated.

Church, R. W. The Beginning of the Middle Ages. xxii + 216 pp. Longmans. 1877.

An old but still valuable introduction to political history.

Fletcher, C. R. L. The Making of Western Europe. 2 vols. Murray. 1912–14.

Gives a full vivid narrative of the barbarians' invasions and settlement and of their development down to 1190.

The 'big books' on this period are **Gibbon's Decline and Fall of the Roman Empire** (Bury's edition), **Hodgkin, T., Italy and her Invaders** (O.U.P.) and **Bury, J. B., A History of the Later Roman Empire** (Macmillan). These are too detailed to be useful to the general teacher; but any teacher who wants to find some particular story told in full would do well to search in them.

See also in the biography section, lives of Theodoric and Justinian.

2. THE CONVERSION OF THE BARBARIANS AND RELIGIOUS CHANGES

Deanesly, M. A History of the Medieval Church, A.D. 590–1500. viii + 280 pp. Methuen. 1925.

A sound concise study of ecclesiastical history in Europe and England; valuable to the keen teacher for reference and information.

Robinson, C. H. How the Gospel Spread through Europe. 184 pp. The Sheldon Press. 1919.

A brief, clear summary for reference.

See also in the biography section, lives of Gregory I (including an account of Benedict) and Mahomet.

The Rule of S. Benedict (trans. Gasquet). Chatto & Windus. 1909.

3. THE BARBARIAN EMPIRE

Funck-Brentano, F. The Earliest Times. 431 pp. Heinemann. 1927. Valuable for the early development of the Franks and for the Empire of Charles the Great.

The standard work on the imperial idea is still **Bryce, J., The Holy Roman Empire** (Macmillan). This is an essay of high literary quality, valuable for understanding the political theories of the Middle Ages. Material directly suited to teaching will be found in Fletcher (as above) and in the contemporary and modern lives of Charles the Great given in the biography section.

4. THE NORSE INVASIONS

Du Chaillu, P. B. The Viking Age. 2 vols. 591, 562 pp. Murray. 1889.

A storehouse of stories and information as to Viking religion, adventures, and civilization. Magnificent illustrations.

Haskins, C. H. The Normans in European History. viii + 258 pp. Constable. 1916.

A well-written and suggestive description of the whole Viking movement from the times of the early raids to the conquests of North France, England and Sicily.

Keary, C. F. The Vikings in Western Christendom. xv + 511 pp. Fisher Unwin. 1891.

A full account of the Viking religion, character and warfare, from which the teacher could draw splendid or entertaining detail for use in lessons.

Mawer, A. The Vikings. 150 pp. C.U.P. 1913. 2*s.* 6*d.*

A useful concise survey of the whole field, with a description of Viking civilization and influence.

5. THE DEVELOPMENT OF FRANCE

Funck-Brentano, F. The Earliest Times. [See p. 87.]

Funck-Brentano, F. The Middle Ages. vii + 356 pp. Heinemann. 1922.

A most valuable and vivid account of French social and political history from 996 to the end of the Middle Ages. The teacher who uses this will be able to make history real to the children.

Masson, G. Medieval France. xliv + 354 pp. Fisher Unwin. Stories of the Nations. 1888.

A pleasant readable account of French history from the accession of Hugh Capet (987) to about 1500.

Moreton Macdonald, J. R. History of France. Vol. I. xiv + 366 pp. Methuen. 1915.

The best and most interesting general textbook of French history.

D. ENGLISH MEDIEVAL HISTORY, A.D. 1066–1272

1. POLITICAL

Douglas, D. C. The Norman Conquest. Historical Association pamphlet. 1928. 1*s.* 1*d.* (7*d.* to members).

Greenwood, etc. (see p. 82).

Davis, H. W. C. England under the Normans and Angevins. xix + 577 pp. Methuen. 1915 (4th ed.). 12*s.* 6*d.*

Recommended as the best full political narrative.

Stubbs, W. The Early Plantagenets. vii + 286 pp. Longmans. Epochs of modern history. 1889.

Gives a narrative of political events from 1135 to 1327. A small book full of matter and learning.

Norgate, K. Richard the Lion Heart. viii + 349 pp. Macmillan. 1924.

A most vivid, striking narrative, from which the teacher could prepare lessons at once sound and picturesque.

Norgate, K. John Lackland. vi + 303 pp. Macmillan. 1902. (See comment above.)

See also in the biography section, lives of William I, Henry II.

2. SOCIAL AND ECONOMIC

Bateson, M. Medieval England. xvii + 448 pp. Fisher Unwin. Stories of Nations. 1905. 7*s*. 6*d*.

A most useful, well-illustrated account of social and economic history in town and village.

Ballard, A. The Domesday Inquest. xvi + 283 pp. Methuen. 1906. 10*s*. 6*d*.

This contains much material that is outside the scope of the non-specialist, but it is the ideal book of reference to the teacher who wishes to illustrate the working of the great survey: see especially p. 11, on methods of compilation, ch. xi on eleventh-century farming and ch. xv on a typical village.

Hone, N. J. The Manor and Manorial Records. xiv + 411 pp. Methuen. 1912 (2nd ed.).

Part I deals with the origin of the manor, its inhabitants and its working. Contains much useful illustrative material.

Quennell, M. and C. A History of Everyday Things in England. Part I, 1066–1499. xiv + 208 pp. Batsford. 1918. 8*s*. 6*d*.

Has a place as illustrating picturesquely those details of common life which appeal to children.

Snape, R. H. Piers Plowman Social and Economic Histories. Book II. 1066–1300. xi + 244 pp. Philip. 1922. 3*s*.

Excellent outline.

3. RELIGIOUS

Cranage, D. H. S. The Home of the Monk. xi + 123 pp. C.U.P. 1926. 6*s*.

Most useful for vivid description of monastic life. The book centres round the monastic building itself, and the monks' daily life in each part of the monastery is illustrated; in conclusion there are brief sketches of the various orders and the dissolution.

Gasquet, F. R. English Monastic Life. xix + 326 pp. Methuen. 1904.

Excellent in giving the atmosphere of monastic life.

Hutton, E. The Franciscans in England. 326 pp. Constable. 1926.

Describes the landing of the friars, their settlements in England, their great men (such as Roger Bacon) and their decline.

Jennings, A. C. The Medieval Church and the Papacy. xiv + 277 pp. Methuen. 1909. 5*s.*

Jessop, A. The Coming of the Friars. 344 pp. Fisher Unwin. 1890.

Contains accounts of the friars, village life, life in a monastery, &c.

Stephens, W. R. W. The English Church, 1066–1272. xiii + 351 pp. Macmillan.

A full general ecclesiastical history for reference.

See also in the biographical section, lives of Lanfranc, Anselm (Church's life contains many details of eleventh-century monasticism), Becket, Langton.

4. SOURCES AND SOURCE BOOKS

(*a*) ORIGINAL SOURCES

Chronicle of Jocelyn of Brakelond. xliv + 285 pp. Chatto & Windus. 1903.

A vivid contemporary picture of monastic life at Bury St. Edmund's in the time of Henry II and his sons.

Thomas of Eccleston (trans. E. Gurney Salter). **The Coming of the Friars Minor to England.** 198 pp. Dent. 1926.

(*b*) BOOKS OF EXTRACTS FROM SOURCES

Bland, A. E. The Normans in England. viii + 117 pp. Bell. 1921. 1*s.* 6*d.*

Hennings, M. A. England under Henry III. xiii + 281 pp. Longmans. Intermediate Source Books. 1924. 10*s.* 6*d.*

A detailed volume, covering every side of the life of the time.

Keatinge and Fraser. [See p. 76.]

Robieson, W. D. The Growth of Parliament and the War with Scotland. 1216–1307. viii + 120 pp. Bell. 1920. 1*s.* 6*d.*

Toyne, S. M. The Angevins and the Charter. 1154–1216. ix + 116 pp. Bell. 1913. 1*s.* 6*d.*

E. THE EUROPEAN BACKGROUND. A.D. 1066–1272.

The important point here again is for the child to realize that medieval institutions were cosmopolitan, not national, and that there was more common feeling, for instance, between an English and French knight than between an

English knight and villein. It is therefore essential that the great institutions of the period—feudalism, monasticism, the friars, the papacy and the crusades—should be approached from the European point of view. Feudalism abroad might be introduced by the story of William the Conqueror's early life and by the description of a French feudal village as he knew it, side by side with the description of the manors and vils that he found in England. The long war against feudalism of such English kings as William, Henry I and Henry II can be connected with the similar war in France under kings like Louis VI, Philip Augustus and St. Louis. Monasticism can be described through the stories of Lanfranc, Anselm, and St. Bernard; it should be made clear to the children that Lanfranc and Anselm are bringing European ideas of reform and architecture into England, and that the Cistercian monasteries in England take their name from Bernard's first spiritual home. The story of the friars is primarily the story of St. Francis in Italy. The power of the medieval papacy and its war with the empire for world supremacy is the dominant factor of this period of history, and it is too often ignored completely in English schools. The story of Hildebrand (Gregory VII) in Europe leads naturally on to the stories of Anselm and Becket in England, which lead in their turn to the climax of papal power under Innocent III and his quarrel with John. Finally, the crusades should not be introduced as a bright idea suddenly conceived by Richard I, but should begin in their proper place with the fall of Jerusalem to the Turks, the appeal to Constantinople for help, the council of Clermont and the first crusade; though naturally a special emphasis will be placed on the third crusade because it affected England so directly. The following books will be found useful:—

1. FEUDALISM IN EUROPE

Coulton, G. G. The Medieval Village. xxx + 603 pp. C.U.P. 1925.

Contains a wealth of illustrative material on life in feudal England, and would furnish material for vivid descriptions. The teacher must be careful to notice the dates of the various episodes, and not use, for instance, a fifteenth-century quotation to illustrate life on a Domesday Manor.

Luchaire, A. (trans.). **Social France at the time of Philip Augustus.** viii + 441 pp. Murray. 1912.

Interesting.

The social side of French history is dealt with in Funck-Brentano and Moreton Macdonald (as above under section C). There are also two difficult but extremely valuable chapters in the Cambridge Medieval History (vol. II, chap. XX, vol. III, chap. XVIII) on the origins and character of feudalism, containing a description of a typical manor. These do not, of course, contain material directly suited to teaching children; but small and old-fashioned history books so often contain wrong conclusions on the origin of feudalism —such as, for instance, that William I 'introduced the feudal system into England'—that history teachers would greatly benefit by having grasped a really good account.

2. FRANCE

Masson, Funck-Brentano and **Moreton Macdonald** as above under section C.

Knox, W. The Court of a Saint. 367 pp. Methuen. 1909.

A picturesque account of the age of St. Louis in France.

See also in the biography section a life of Philip II, and one modern and one very charming contemporary life of St. Louis.

3. MONASTICISM

Illustrative material from two different points of view can be drawn from—

Gasquet, F. A. English Monastic Life in the Middle Ages. xix + 326 pp. Methuen. 1904.

Coulton, G. G. Five Centuries of Religion. Vol. I, 1000–1200. xliii + 578 pp. 1923. Vol. II, 1200–1400. xxx + 703 pp. 1927. C.U.P.

This is a work on a monumental scale; but it contains a wealth of illustrative detail into which the teacher can dip. The author's general attitude to monasticism has been criticized. (See reviews in History.)

Workman, H. B. The Evolution of the Monastic Ideal. xii + 368 pp. Kelly. 1913.

Gives a clear account of the movement as a whole.

See also in the biography section the very useful and interesting life of St. Bernard, which includes descriptions of Cistercian monasticism.

4. THE FRIARS

The important material here is to be found in lives of St. Francis and Dominic (see section on biography). The life of the friars in Europe can also be illustrated by—

The Little Flowers of the Glorious St. Francis (trans.) and **The Mirror of Perfection** (trans.). xxii + 397 pp. Dent. Everyman Library. No. 488.

A collection of Franciscan stories.

Coulton, G. G. From St. Francis to Dante. vi + 364 pp. Nutt. 1906.

Contains many extracts from the racy chronicle of a Franciscan friar.

Thomas of Celano (trans.). **Lives of S. Francis.** xxiv + 360 pp. Methuen. 1908.

A contemporary authority.

5. THE PAPACY AND THE EMPIRE

Barry, W. The Papal Monarchy. A.D. 590–1303. xxviii + 435 pp. Fisher Unwin. Stories of Nations. 1902.

Contains a good and readable general account.

Greenwood, A. Empire and Papacy in the Middle Ages. vi + 227 pp. Macmillan. 1902.

A clear and interesting sketch of the relations between Church and State.

Jacob, E. F. The Holy Roman Empire. 79 pp. Benn. 1928. 6*d*.

A brilliant concise summary.

The teacher who wants to go more thoroughly into the war of Church and State should read Bryce and Deanesly (as above under section C) and **Smith, A. L., 'Church and State in the Middle Ages'.** (O.U.P.)

6. THE CRUSADES

For an understanding of the Byzantine Empire and its position use—

Baynes, N. H. The Byzantine Empire. 256 pp. Home University Library. 1925. 2*s*. 6*d*.

A brilliant sketch containing a bibliography.

Oman, Sir C. W. C. The Byzantine Empire. xviii + 364 pp. Fisher Unwin. Stories of the Nations. 1902.

A very readable general survey.

For the crusades themselves use—

Archer, T. A. and **Kingsford, C. L. The Crusades.** xxx + 467 pp. Fisher Unwin. Stories of Nations. 1899. 7*s*. 6*d*.

A readable and interesting general account in which the teacher will find useful material for lessons. Rather over-emphasizes the effects of the crusades (compare Davis' 'Medieval Europe' and Barker).

Archer, T. A. The Crusade of Richard I. xi + 388 pp. Nutt. 1887.

A collection of extracts from sources illustrating the third crusade.

Barker, E. The Crusades. 112 pp. O.U.P. 1923. 2*s*. 6*d*.

A valuable succinct account, full of information. Reprinted from the 'Encyclopedia Britannica'. See also in the biography section, lives of Richard I and Saladin.

F. ENGLISH MEDIEVAL HISTORY. A.D. 1272–1485

1. POLITICAL

Greenwood, etc. (see p. 82).

Vickers, K. H. England in the Later Middle Ages. xv + 542 pp. Methuen.

Full political narrative.

Trevelyan, G. M. England in the Age of Wycliffe. xvi + 380 pp. Longmans. 1909.

Gives a detailed narrative of the years *c.* 1370–1400, together with a 'general picture of English society, politics and religion' at that time; useful for lessons on Wycliffe and on the Peasants' Revolt.

For advanced work an important and controversial recent work is—

Pollard, A. F. Evolution of Parliament. xi + 459 pp. Longmans. 1926.

Although the greater part of **Stubbs' Constitutional History** is outside the scope of the non-specialist, the political chapters in Vol. III (viii + 652 pp. O.U.P. 1903 (5th ed.)) are extremely valuable to the teacher.

See also in the biography section, lives of Edward I, John of Gaunt, Henry V, Warwick the King Maker, Caxton.

2. SOCIAL AND ECONOMIC

Abram, A. Social England in the Fifteenth Century. xv + 243 pp. Routledge. 1909.

Describes the economic changes of the fifteenth century and their effect on social life. Full of illustrative material.

Bennett, H. S. The Pastons and their England. xvii + 289 pp. C.U.P. 1922.

A book illustrating everyday life in the fifteenth century; deals with the story of the Paston family, telling of love and marriage, women and children, houses and furniture, travel, religion, etc. Specially interesting from the domestic point of view.

Chadwick, D. Social Life in the Days of Piers Plowman. xiii + 125 pp. C.U.P. 1922.

This is a summary of the descriptions of clergy, government, chivalry, town and country life and the position of women given in Langland's poem 'Piers Plowman'. It would be very useful to the teachers who wish to use this source.

Coulton, G. G. Chaucer and his England. xii + 321 pp. Methuen. 1908. 12*s.* 6*d*.

A full and entertaining picture of the poet's life and of social conditions in his day; ideal for the teacher who is telling the Canterbury Tales.

Hartley, D. and **Elliot, M. M. Life and Work of the People of England.** The Fourteenth Century. The Fifteenth Century. 81 pp. each. Batsford. 1925. 4*s*. 6*d*. each.
A delightful pictorial record.

Jusserand, J. J. (trans.). **English Wayfaring Life in the Middle Ages.** 464 pp. Fisher Unwin. 1920.
Full of information of everyday life ; deals with English roads and the people who pass along them—minstrels, pedlars, workmen, friars, pilgrims, etc.

Niemeyer, N. Piers Plowman Social and Economic Histories. Book III, 1300–1485. viii + 160 pp. Philip. 1924. 3*s*.
An excellent general survey, full of illustrative material.

3. RELIGIOUS

Capes, W. W. The English Church in the Fourteenth and Fifteenth Centuries. xi + 391 pp. Macmillan. 1900.
A full narrative of ecclesiastical history, useful for reference.

Manning, B. H. The People's Faith in the Time of Wycliffe. xvi + 191 pp. C.U.P. 1919.

Poole, R. L. Wycliffe and Movements of Reform. xi + 204 pp. Longmans. 1909.
The best short work on the decline of the Church in England and Europe.

4. SOURCES AND SOURCE BOOKS

(*a*) Original Sources

Chaucer. Canterbury Tales. Dent. Everyman's Library. No. 307. 2*s*.

Langland. The Vision of Piers Plowman. xxix + 151 pp. Chatto & Windus. King's Classics. 1905. 5*s*. Or Everyman's Library, No. 571. 2*s*.

Paston Letters. The best edition is the big one by **Gairdner, J.** There is a cheap edition in Dent, Everyman, Nos. 752, 753, 2*s*. each, and selections have been published by Greenwood (Bell, 1920. 15*s*.), and Jones, M. D. (C.U.P. 1922. 1*s*. 9*d*.).

Froissart (trans. and abridged). **Chronicles.** Dent. Everyman's Library, No. 57.

(*b*) Books of Extracts from Sources

Bennett, H. S. England from Chaucer to Caxton. xii + 246 pp. Methuen. 1928. 6*s*.
Extracts from the literature of the period illustrating home, village, town, church, and foreign life. The old spelling is generally kept.

Fleming, J. England under the Lancastrians. xxi + 301 pp. Longmans. Intermediate Source Book. 1921. 10*s.* 6*d.* Detailed.

Hughes, D. Illustrations of Chaucer's England. xiv + 302 pp. Longmans. Intermediate Source Books. 1924. 10*s.* 6*d.* See comment above.

Jones, W. G. York and Lancaster. 1399–1485. viii + 130 pp. Bell. English History Source Books. 1920. 1*s.* 6*d.*

Kingsford, C. L. English History in Contemporary Poetry. Lancaster and York. Bell. 1913. 1*s.* 6*d.*

Keatinge and **Fraser** (see p. 76).

Locke, A. A. War and Misrule 1307–1399. vi + 120 pp. Bell. English History Source Books. 1920. 1*s.* 6*d.*

Thornley, I. D. England under the Yorkists. xx + 280 pp. Longmans. Intermediate Source Books. 1920. 10*s.* 6*d.* Detailed.

G. THE EUROPEAN BACKGROUND. A.D. 1272–1492

This period is to see the decline of the great medieval institutions. Feudalism, monasticism, the crusading movement, papal authority, the idea of unity in Christendom, all suffer change and lose importance ; and again it is the business of the teacher to show that these changes are universal. With the story of the Peasants' Revolt in England can be told the story of the Jacquerie in France ; the reform movement led by Wycliffe can be connected with the story of Hus and the failure of the Conciliar idea at Constance ; the fall of Constantinople to the Turks can be represented as the natural sequel to the failure of the crusades.

At the same time, other great movements and institutions are beginning to appear. The development of trade, industry and town life is a great feature of this period. It should be studied, not only from the point of view of town life and gilds in England, but from the point of view of world commerce between East and West, resulting largely from the crusades, and passing along great trade routes which help to bind the world together. The work of Italian and German merchants should be described, and children should know the stories of Venice, Marco Polo, or the Hanseatic League as well as the story of Dick Whittington. The brilliance of Italian city life in the fourteenth and fifteenth centuries, and especially the age of Lorenzo de' Medici in Florence, is an essential preface to the English Renaissance of Tudor times.

The second outstanding feature of this period is the development of nationality. The children will study this most fully, of course, in connexion with England. But the Hundred Years' War can lead them to realize it in connexion with France also, and the story of Joan of Arc can be followed by the story of how the French monarchy revived under Louis XI. The tale of Swiss independence can be included; if William Tell is a myth, Arnulf von Winkelried is a historical figure. The victory of Spain over the Moors and her rise to national greatness can be introduced by the story of Ferdinand and Isabella, and will prepare the way for understanding the causes of the Armada.

Finally, the children learn in their English history of the rise and growth of Parliament. It would be interesting for them to discover, from the stories of Philip IV and the States-General, Etienne Marcel, and Louis XI, how a similar institution rose in France at the same time and did not grow quite so well; for this difference in early development will prepare them to understand something of the differences between English and French constitutional progress at a later date.

1. TOWN LIFE AND TRADE

See **Day, C. History of Commerce** (see p. 60) and **Knight** and **Cunningham** above under General European History (p. 80).

Brinton, S. The Golden Age of the Medici. xiv + 234 pp. Methuen. 1925.

A picture of art, learning and politics in Florence in the fifteenth century.

Federn, C. Dante and his Time. xviii + 306 pp. Heinemann. 1902.

A life of Dante containing a picture of Italian politics in the late thirteenth and early fourteenth centuries.

Newton, A. P. Travel and Travellers of the Middle Ages. ix + 223 pp. Kegan Paul. 1926.

Tells of world communications as carried on by pilgrims, raiders, Arab merchants, European merchants and explorers.

Roper, E. Florentine Life in the Thirteenth and Fourteenth Centuries. 59 pp., *and* **Florentine Life in the Fifteenth Century.** 64 pp. Sheldon Press. 1920. Two books of extracts from sources. 1*s*. each or 2*s*. together.

Sichel, E. The Renaissance. 256 pp. Home University Library. 1914. 2*s*. 6*d*. Brilliant sketch.

Marco Polo's Travels. Dent. Everyman's Library. No. 306. 2*s*.

The wonderful narrative of the great Venetian traveller. His story is well retold in E. Power's Medieval People.

Oliphant, Mrs. Makers of Florence. xx + 422 pp. Macmillan. 1881 *and* **Makers of Venice.** xii + 390 pp. Macmillan. 1887. Popular readable accounts.

Pirenne, H. Medieval Cities: their Origins and the Revival of Trade. 249 pp. Princeton University Press. 1925. Valuable.

Zimmern, H. The Hansa Towns. xvii + 389 pp. Fisher Unwin. Stories of the Nations. 1889.

A pleasant and interesting description of German trade and the life of the Hanseatic merchants.

Dent's Medieval Towns Series contain good short narratives of individual towns. (5*s.* 6*d.* each, illustrated.)

See also the section on biography, Lorenzo de' Medici.

2. HISTORIES OF OTHER NATIONS

(*a*) FRANCE

Masson, Funck-Brentano, Moreton Macdonald, as above under section C, pp. 87–8.

Lang, A. The Maid of France. xv + 352 pp. Longmans. 1922. 7*s.* 6*d.*

See also the section on biography for life of Charles the Bold.

(*b*) SWITZERLAND

Hug and **Stead, R. Switzerland.** xxiii + 430 pp. Fisher Unwin. Stories of the Nations. 1890.

A pleasant narrative.

(*c*) SPAIN

Poole, S. L. The Moors in Spain. xvii + 286 pp. Fisher Unwin. Stories of the Nations. 1890.

Watts, W. E. Spain. xxviii + 315 pp. Fisher Unwin. Stories of the Nations. 1893.

See also the section on biography for lives of the Cid and Isabel of Castile.

7. MODERN ENGLISH AND EUROPEAN HISTORY

A. THE SIXTEENTH CENTURY

1. POLITICAL ENGLISH HISTORY

(*a*) BOOKS COVERING ALL THE PERIOD

1. *Brief Outline*

Feiling, K. England under the Tudors and Stuarts. v + 256 pp. Home University Library. 1927. 2*s.* 6*d.*

A good brief analysis of the main movements of the period: comprehensive but readable.

2. Fuller Accounts

Fletcher, C. R. L. An Introductory History of England. Vol. II (from Henry VII to the Restoration), xv + 583 pp. Murray. 1907. 9*s*.

A lively story, which tells the political narrative in an entertaining style and illustrates social effects by the story of the imaginary village of Tubney.

Greenwood, A. D. History of the People of England, vol. II, 1485–1688. xii + 416 pp. Sheldon Press. 1923. 7*s*. 6*d*.

An excellent clear account which gives the essential facts comprehensively, but also retains interest by well-chosen detail and comment.

Hall, D. G. E. A Brief Survey of English Constitutional History (see p. 75). Chapter VII gives a good outline of Tudor government.

Innes, A. D. England under the Tudors. xviii + 481 pp. Methuen. 1905. 12*s*. 6*d*.

A full but rather dull political narrative with maps and book lists.

Innes, A. D. Ten Tudor Statesmen. xii + 402 pp. Nash. 1906.

A most useful group of studies, covering all the period: deals with Henry VII, Wolsey, More, Cromwell, Henry VIII, Somerset, Cranmer, Cecil, Walsingham, Raleigh.

Pollard, A. F. Factors in Modern History. xii + 325 pp. Constable. 1926.

Stimulating lectures which bring out the significance of sixteenth and seventeenth century history in its relation to history as a whole. Contains a lecture on the value of history in education.

A still fuller and extremely interesting political narrative is given in the excellent volumes on this period by **Fisher, H. A. L.**, and **Pollard, A. F.**, in Longman's **Political History.**

(*b*) Special Topics

For the reigns of Henry VII and Henry VIII see in the biographical section, lives of Henry VII, Henry VIII, Wolsey, More, Cromwell.

For the reigns of Edward VI and Mary see in the biographical section, lives of Somerset, Lady Jane Grey, Mary Tudor.

Pollard, A. F. England under the Protector Somerset, gives a full account.

For the age of Elizabeth and for sea power use **Froude, J. A. English Seamen in the Sixteenth Century.** xv + 164 pp. Longmans. 1923. 2*s*.

A handy reprint of a famous work, which tells a vigorous and fascinating tale, but which is strongly prejudiced against Catholicism.

Corbett, Sir J. S. Drake and the Tudor Navy. 2 vols. xii + 415 pp. viii + 462 pp. Longmans. 1899.

The standard authority. Contains a valuable introduction on the development of ships in this period.

Creighton, M. The Age of Elizabeth. 236 pp. Longmans. Epochs of Modern History. 1906.

Valuable and useful: deals with the whole Reformation drama in Europe and England.

See also in the biographical sections, lives of Elizabeth, Drake, Hawkins, Raleigh.

2. SOCIAL AND ECONOMIC ENGLISH HISTORY

(*a*) Books Covering the Whole Period of Social History

Hartley, D. and **Elliot, M. M. Life and Work of the People of England in the Sixteenth Century.** 81 pp. Batsford. 1925. 4*s*. 6*d*.

A 'pictorial record' of social life from contemporary illustrations.

Niemeyer, N. Piers Plowman Social and Economic Histories, vol. IV (1484–1600). xi + 240 pp. Philip. 1922. 3*s*.

An excellent survey, containing much illustrative material useful in teaching.

Quennell, M. and **C. A History of Everyday Things in England.** Part II. xi + 208 pp. Batsford. 1919. 8*s*. 6*d*.

A picturesque volume.

Salzman, L. F. England in Tudor Times. 143 pp. Batsford. 1926. 7*s*. 6*d*.

A delightful and most useful book, admirably illustrated and containing the sort of detail that makes the daily life of another age real to children.

Traill, H. D. and **Mann, J. S. Social England.** Vol. III, 1509–1603. liv + 800 pp. Cassell. 1902.

A mine of useful information and good pictures.

(*b*) Books on Special Topics or Periods of Social History

Byrne, M. St. Claire. Elizabethan Life in Town and Country. viii + 294 pp. Methuen. 1925. 7*s*. 6*d*.

A valuable account of everyday life drawn mainly from literary sources.

Raleigh, Sir W. (ed.). **Shakespeare's England.** 2 vols. xxiv + 546 and x + 610 pp. O.U.P. 1917.

A wonderful treasure house for the teacher: deals with every aspect of the Elizabethan age—religion, travel, commerce, education, art, dress, home life, etc.; full of interesting detail and good pictures.

For the serious study of economic history use :—

Cunningham, W. The Growth of English Industry and Commerce. Modern Times. Part I. 609 pp. C.U.P. 1921 (6th ed.).

Tawney, R. H. The Agrarian Policy in the Sixteenth Century. xii + 464 pp. Longmans. 1912.

Tawney, R. H. and Power, E. Tudor Economic Documents. 3 vols. Longmans. University of London Historical Series, No. 4. 1924.

Unwin, G. Industrial Organization in the Sixteenth and Seventeenth Centuries. viii + 277 pp. O.U.P. 1924.

3. RELIGIOUS AND INTELLECTUAL ENGLISH HISTORY

(*a*) The Renaissance

Einstein, L. The Italian Renaissance in England. xvii + 420 pp. Columbia Univ. Press. 1902.

Lee, Sidney. Great Englishmen of the Sixteenth Century. 327 pp. Harrap. 1925. 3*s*. 6*d*. and 7*s*. 6*d*.

An interesting group of biographies connecting history with literature: includes More, Sidney, Raleigh, Spenser, Bacon, Shakespeare.

Seebohm, F. Oxford Reformers. xi + 331 pp. Dent. Everyman's Library. 1914. 2*s*.

The classical work on the Renaissance scholars of Henry VII's reign—More, Erasmus and Colet.

Full of most valuable and interesting information. Every teacher of history should read this stimulating story.

Watson, Foster. The English Grammar Schools to 1660 : their curriculum and practice. ix + 548 pp. C.U.P. 1908.

A delightful hunting-ground for the teacher who wishes to make school life in another age real to the children.

(*b*) The Reformation

Creighton, M. The Age of Elizabeth.
(See p. 100.)

Gairdner, J. The English Church in the Sixteenth Century. xv + 430 pp. Macmillan. 1902.

A full and interesting account based on wide scholarship.

Gasquet. Henry VIII and the English Monasteries. xlvi + 495 pp. Bell. 1920. (7th ed.)

Gives full illustrative material for the teacher who wishes to describe the progress and consequences of the Dissolution. From the Catholic standpoint.

Innes, A. D. Cranmer and the English Reformation. xix + 199 pp. Clark. 1900.

A valuable book for the teacher, since it sets the English story in its proper relation to the story of Luther and the Continental movement. Ends with the death of Mary.

Wakeman, H. O. An Introduction to the Church of England. 507 pp. Rivington. 1914. (8th ed.) Chapters 10–16.

See also in the biographical section, lives of More, Cranmer, Luther.

4. SOURCE BOOKS AND CONTEMPORARY WRITERS ON ENGLISH HISTORY

(*a*) *Contemporary Writers*

Cavendish, G. The Life of Cardinal Wolsey. Ed. M. Tout. 114 pp. Macmillan. 1908. 1*s.* 3*d.* and 1*s.* 6*d.*

A wonderful story.

Drake, Sir Francis. The World Encompassed. 128 pp. Blackie's English School Texts. 1905. 10*d.*

The story of Drake's famous voyage round the world.

Hakluyt's Voyages. 8 vols. Dent. Everyman's Library. 2*s.* each.

The great collection made by an Elizabethan geographer of English voyages from the earliest times. One of the finest sources for adventurous stories available to any teacher in any language. Blackie has published an extract on The Spanish Armada for 10*d.*

Hawkins, R. Voyage into the South Seas. 1593. 128 pp. Blackie's English School Texts. 10*d.*

Irving, L. Hakluyt's Voyages: a selection. xxiv + 294 pp. Heinemann. 1926. 10*s.* 6*d.*

An admirable selection, edited in such a way as to retain the spirit (and spelling) of the age. Contains dramatic black and white illustrations.

Raleigh, Sir W. The Discovery of Guiana. 111 pp. Blackie's English Texts. 10*d.*

Roper, W. The Life of Sir Thomas More. 192 pp. Moring. King's Classics. 1908.

More's life beautifully told by his son-in-law.

(*b*) *Books of Collected Extracts from Sources*

Bewsher, F. W. The Reformation and the Renaissance. 1485–1547. viii + 118 pp. Bell. English History Source Book Series. Vol. VII. 1924. 1*s.* 6*d.*

A book of extracts illustrating political and social history.

Bland, A. E., Brown, P. A. and **Tawney, R. English Economic History.** Select Documents. xx + 730 pp. Bell. 1914. 7*s.* 6*d.*

Contains most valuable extracts for the serious study of economic history.

Esdaile, A. The Age of Elizabeth. 1547–1603. viii + 120 pp. Bell. English History Source Book Series. Vol. VIII. 1924. 1*s.* 6*d.*

A book of extracts illustrating political and social history.

Keatinge, M. and **Frazer, N. L.**

(See p. 76.)

A useful collection of extracts illustrating political and social history.

Tanner, J. R. Tudor Constitutional Documents. 1485–1603. 636 pp. C.U.P. 1922. 37*s.* 6*d.*

A valuable collection of constitutional, social and religious documents with excellent commentaries.

Tawney, R. and **Power, E. Tudor Economic Documents.** 3 vols. Longmans. 1924. For advanced work.

Williams, C. H. England under the Early Tudors. 1485–1529. 281 pp. Longmans. Intermediate Source Books. 1925. 9*s.* 6*d.*

A full collection, illustrating every aspect of the life of the period.

Wilson, J. Dover. Life in Shakespeare's England. xvi + 292 pp. C.U.P. 1913. 7*s.* and 5*s.*

A delightful book of extracts from Elizabethan prose, chosen to illustrate the life of the time.

5. ENGLAND, EUROPE AND THE WORLD IN THE SIXTEENTH CENTURY

It would be a misnomer to speak of a 'European background' to the history of sixteenth-century England. Renaissance Europe is young and vigorous, and so far from being kept in the background it insists on the middle of the stage. The general principle of this century's history is that tremendous intellectual and political movements—the Renaissance, Exploration, the development of the New Monarchy and the Reformation—begin in Europe and pass towards England, there to meet with an instant response and to be deflected to new paths. This principle is generally acknowledged and acted on by teachers. We tell the story of Luther before we enter on Henry VIII's religious policy, and of Columbus before we speak of Drake.

The story of the Renaissance in England must begin by

reviving memories of Gutenberg and his printing in Germany and of Lorenzo de' Medici and all the bright godlike strength of Renaissance life in fifteenth-century Italy. These movements form the necessary prelude to the first great group of English Renaissance scholars whom we generally call the Oxford Reformers—More, Colet, Grocyn and Erasmus: and from them we pass to the tragic figure of Cranmer and on to the age of Elizabeth, most brilliant child of the Renaissance, with her glorious crowd of poets and scholars. The philosophical and intellectual ideas of the Renaissance are far beyond children's ken: but they are generally quick to feel its spell if it is introduced to them through such concrete instances as a picture, a biography, or an account of changes in school life.

The story of Exploration emphatically must begin with the fall of Constantinople to the Turks in 1453, which, by erecting a barrier across all the old trade routes between East and West, made the discovery of new roads necessary. This explains the motive of all the early explorers, Da Gama and Columbus and the rest, who were trying to reach the precious drugs and spices of the East by sailing round Africa, or by the North-West passage, or by circumnavigating the globe. A great sequel follows each line of exploration. The African route does really lead to the East, and along it pass the pioneers of the East India Companies. The North-West route was unproductive. But the Western route opened the door to a new world. England enters into the story of this new world by the voyage of Cabot, and France by the voyage of Cartier; but the Spanish Empire is the dominant feature of the Western tale, and the adventures of Cortes and Pizarro prepare the way for the trade voyages of Hawkins and the pirate raids of Drake and at last for the crisis of the great Armada.

The story of Exploration is straightforward and interesting to teach. But the story of the Reformation bristles with difficulties, nor can the impartial teacher hope to satisfy anybody. It is clearly best to begin with the tale of Luther and his revolt against the abuses that did undoubtedly exist in the Church of his time. But when the story passes on to Henry VIII and the English quarrel with the Pope, the political aspect of the Reformation can be stressed, and it can be pointed out that Henry was able to dominate religious affairs, as he dominated political government, because a war-weary people was ready to submit to the rule of an efficient king. The vicissitudes of the English Reformation form a good illustration of the bewildered gropings of a nation in a time of religious turmoil, and this should be made as lifelike as possible to the child by connecting it with the changes that took place in his own district and parish church. The Elizabethan settlement gives a breathing space. But it is not too difficult for children to realize that the question of how far the Reformation should go in England has been deferred rather than solved, and they are thus prepared for the struggle with Puritanism in the next century. Finally, it is very unfair to leave children (as is often done) with no further reference to Catholicism in history after the break with Luther. They should realize that the abuses of which Luther complained were at last remedied by the Church herself from within, and through biographies of such men as Ignatius Loyola and François Xavier they should have some understanding of the aims of the post-Reformation Church.

This religious question is linked with political quarrels of outstanding importance. Spain in the sixteenth century stands for Catholicism, absolutism, and European domination. She is opposed by the Protestant spirit in England and in the Netherlands. The story of this conflict forms one of the most heroic and significant episodes of modern history.

(*a*) Short and Introductory Books

Creighton, M. The Age of Elizabeth. See comment above, p. 100.

Dark, S. The Renaissance. 191 pp. Hodder & Stoughton. 1923. 2*s*. 6*d*.

A simply and freshly written popular introduction which deals with Renaissance politics, literature and art, with the Reformation and with social conditions.

Happold, F. C. European History 1515–1598. vi + 152 pp. Bell. 1927. 2*s*.

A very handy little outline, which manages to compress the facts without being dull.

Home, G. The Period of the Renaissance and Reformation. 2 parts. 108 and 100 pp. Horace Marshall. 1923. 2*s*. each part.

An extremely useful book to the general teacher; a group of charmingly told short biographies, mainly European, some of which could be read by the children. Includes the stories of Lorenzo de' Medici, Isabella of Spain, Leonardo da Vinci, Luther, etc.

Hudson, W. H. The Story of the Renaissance. 268 pp. Harrap. 1924. 2*s.* 6*d.*

A description of the Renaissance spirit as it affected every nation and every department of life; deals with discovery and invention, learning and science, the Reformation, education, art and literature. A useful general introduction.

Ogg, D. The Reformation. 80 pp. Benn. 1927. 6*d.*

A good summary.

Seebohm, F. The Era of the Protestant Revolution. xv + 236 pp. Longmans. Epochs of Modern History. 1915. 4*s.*

By far the best short account of the Reformation for the general reader. Gives the European and English stories: fascinating to read.

Sichel, E. The Renaissance. 256 pp. Home University Library. 1914. 2*s.* 6*d.*

A brilliant sketch.

(*b*) Fuller or More Advanced Books

Benians, S. From Renaissance to Revolution 1500—1789. 203 pp. Methuen. 7*s.* 6*d.*

Excellent for the teacher who has already some knowledge of the period and who wishes to take the international standpoint. The history of civilization is told in a series of stimulating and philosophical essays grouped round such great movements as the Renaissance, Reformation, Expansion of Renaissance States, etc.

Gardiner, K. M. Anglo-European History 1492–1660. xi + 244 pp. Methuen. 1924. 6*s.*

A valuable account of international history, stimulating and full of insight. Teachers would find useful the chapters on such general topics as the Renaissance, Reformation and economic change; the chapters on international relations are perhaps rather allusive for the general reader.

Hearnshaw, F. J. C. (ed.). **The Social and Political Ideas of some Great Thinkers of the Renaissance and Reformation.** 216 pp. Harrap. 1925.

A series of lectures by various authors; includes lectures on Machiavelli, Erasmus, More, Luther, Calvin.

Hollings, M. A. Europe in Renaissance and Reformation, 1453–1659. xxv + 275 pp. Methuen. 1912. (3rd ed.) 4*s.*

A useful straightforward text-book.

B. THE SEVENTEENTH CENTURY

1. POLITICAL ENGLISH HISTORY

(a) Books Covering all the Century

1. Brief Outlines

Buchan, J. (ed.). **The Teaching of History Series.** Nelson.
Commonwealth and Restoration. 1649–1688. Turberville, A. S. 255 pp. 1928. 2*s.*
The Age of Anne. 1688–1714. Wood, A. C. 255 pp. 1928. 2*s.*
Good outlines which act as introductions to further reading; references are given throughout the text to bigger books to which the reader can refer on each topic.

Feiling, K. England under the Tudors and Stuarts. v + 256 pp. Home Univ. Library. 1927. 2*s.* 6*d.*

Wrong, E. M. A History of England, 1688–1815. 250 pp. Home Univ. Library. 1927. 2*s.* 6*d.*
These little volumes are very useful in giving the teacher a general grasp of the period; they are condensed and do not contain much material directly suited to teaching children, but they are most interesting to read, and point out the real significance of events.

2. Fuller Accounts

Fletcher, C. R. L. An Introductory History of England. Vol. II (from Henry VII to the Restoration), xv + 583 pp. 1907. Vol. III (1660–1792), x + 372 pp. 1909. Murray. 9*s.* each vol.
A vivid, spirited and prejudiced narrative, giving much attention to military affairs.

Gooch, G. P. Political Thought in England: from Bacon to Halifax. 256 pp. Home Univ. Library. 1915. 2*s.* 6*d.*
Recommended highly to the general teacher who wishes to understand the atmosphere of the period, since it deals simply and briefly but brilliantly with the political ideas underlying each phase of the great struggle.

Greenwood, A. D. History of the People of England. Vol. II. 1485–1688. xii + 416 pp. 1923. Vol. III. 1688–1834. xii + 336 pp. 1926. The Bede Histories. Sheldon Press. 7*s.* 6*d.* each vol.
A clear, interesting narrative, dealing with social and economic as well as political history, and laying special emphasis on the history of the Church.

Hall, D. G. E. A brief Survey of Constitutional History (see p. 75). Chapter VIII gives a good outline of the constitutional struggle.

Pollard, A. F. Factors in Modern History (see p. 99).

Trevelyan, G. M. England under the Stuarts. xvi + 566 pp. Methuen. 1925. *12s. 6d.*

Highly recommended to the teacher, especially before 1660; a full, interesting history of political development with a background of social and intellectual life. The first two chapters have been published separately by Methuen, under the title **English Life Three Hundred Years Ago.** *2s.*

A still more detailed but admirable account is given in the volumes by **Lodge** and **Leadham** in Longmans' **Political History.** Those who are interested in the political ideas underlying the century will find **Tanner, J. R., English Constitutional Conflicts of the Seventeenth Century** (C.U.P., 1928) most valuable for advanced reading.

(*b*) Special Topics

For the causes of the Civil War, see in the biographical section, lives of Eliot, Laud, Strafford.

The classic authority on this subject is **Gardiner, S. R., History of England, 1603–1642.** 10 vols. Longmans. 1883–5. From the point of view of the general teacher these volumes form a fascinating hunting-ground in which to find details of stirring debates or full material for the stories of outstanding episodes. The chapter headings are very full, and the reader who has decided beforehand what event he wants to study in detail will have little difficulty in finding it. Gardiner has also written a valuable concise study. **The First Two Stuarts and the Puritan Revolution 1603–1660.** xxi + 215 pp. Longmans. Epochs of Modern History. 1907.

For the Civil War, see in the biographical section, lives of Cromwell, Rupert.

Firth, C. H. Cromwell's Army. xx + 444 pp. Methuen. 1921 (3rd ed.).

Deals with the organization, discipline, weapons and social conditions of the army. Full of material for describing the methods and spirit of the Ironsides.

Gardiner's great work is continued as **'History of the Great Civil War'** (4 vols.). Longmans. 1904.

For the Commonwealth, an outstanding authority is **Carlyle's 'Letters and Speeches of Oliver Cromwell'.** The best edition is by Mrs. Lomas, 1904, but the most convenient is Dent's Everyman's edition in 3 vols., 1908.

A biography, but containing much contemporary material. Vivid, vigorous, and biased in Cromwell's favour.

Gardiner's History is continued as '**History of the Commonwealth and Protectorate**' (4 vols.). Longmans. 1903. It was left unfinished at his death, and the story was taken up by **Firth, C. H. The Last Years of the Protectorate.** 2 vols. Longmans. 1909.

Gardiner has also written a sketch, '**Cromwell's Place in English History**'. 120 pp. Longmans. 1897. Valuable as setting out in a brief and simple form some of the general conclusions of this great writer.

See also in the biographical section lives of Cromwell.

For the Restoration, see Airy's excellent life of Charles II and lives of Shaftesbury and Halifax (Biographical section).

Airy, O. The English Restoration and Louis XIV. xii + 282 pp. Longmans. Epochs of Modern History. 1907. Useful and informative.

For the Revolution, **Macaulay, T. B.** (ed. Firth, C. H.). **The History of England from the accession of James II.** 6 vols. Macmillan. 1913–15, is the great classical authority which, like Gardiner, may be used by the general teacher to find full details for stories. The work has a Whig bias.

See also biographies of James II and William III.

For the French Wars and the reign of Anne, see **Lecky, W. E. H. History of the Eighteenth Century.** Vol. I. Longmans. 1892.

A famous literary history: full, leisurely, and eminently readable. The sketch of Anne's reign given in the opening chapter is the best existing short account.

See also in the biographical section lives of Marlborough.

2. SOCIAL AND ECONOMIC ENGLISH HISTORY

(*a*) BOOKS COVERING THE WHOLE PERIOD OF SOCIAL HISTORY

Coate, M. Social Life in Stuart England. xii + 188 pp. Methuen. 1924. 6*s*.

A charming picturesque volume which gives just the kind of illustrative detail needed for a lesson.

Hartley, D. and **Elliot, M. M. Life and Work of the People of England: The Seventeenth Century.** 81 pp. Batsford. 1928. 4*s*. 6*d*. and 5*s*. 6*d*.

A valuable pictorial record.

Quennell, M. and **C. A History of Everyday Things in England.** Part II. xi + 208 pp. Batsford. 8*s*. 6*d*. 1919.

Spalding, E. H. Piers Plowman Social and Economic Histories, vol. V (1600–1760). xi + 215 pp. Philip. 1921. 3*s*. 6*d*.

An excellent volume.

Traill, H. D. and **Mann, J. S. Social England,** Vol. IV. 1603–1714. lv + 864 pp. Cassell. 1903.
A mine of useful information and good pictures.

(*b*) BOOKS ON SPECIAL TOPICS OF SOCIAL HISTORY

Clark, A. The Working Life of Women in the Seventeenth Century. vi + 328 pp. Routledge. 1919.
Describes from the sources the part taken by women in agriculture, industry, business and the professions, etc.

Jusserand, J. A French Ambassador at the Court of Charles II. 259 pp. Fisher Unwin. 1892.
A lively humorous description of the etiquette, splendours and gossip of court life.

Parkes, J. Travel in England in the Seventeenth Century. xvi + 354 pp. O.U.P. 1925.
Sound, entertaining, full of illustrative material and contains very good and numerous pictures. Deals with centres of population, roads, inns, means of transport, security, etc.

Tanner, J. H. Mr. Pepys : an Introduction to the Diary, together with a sketch of his later life. xv + 308 pp. Bell. 1925.
A life based on the Diary, and containing much illustrative material on manners and customs.

Trotter, E. Seventeenth Century Life in a Country Parish. xiv + 242 pp. C.U.P. 1919.

For the serious study of economic history use :—

Cunningham, W. The Growth of English Industry and Commerce. Modern Times. Part I. 609 pp. C.U.P. 1921. (6th ed.)

Unwin, G. Industrial Organization in the Sixteenth and Seventeenth Centuries. vii + 277 pp. O.U.P. 1904.

3. ECCLESIASTICAL ENGLISH HISTORY

Frere, W. H. The English Church in the Reigns of Elizabeth and James I (1558–1625). xiii + 413 pp. Macmillan. 1904.
A full narrative.

Hutton, W. H. The English Church from the accession of Charles I to the death of Anne. ix + 368 pp. Macmillan. 1903.
Continues Frere's narrative on the same scale.

Overton, H. Life in the English Church. 1660–1714. xiv + 376 pp. Longmans. 1885.
Gives interesting detail as to the Church and social life, with many brief sketches of outstanding clergy and laity (both men and women) of the period.

See also in the biographical section, lives of Laud (for the Anglican point of view) and Baxter, Bunyan and Milton (for the Puritan).

4. SOURCE BOOKS AND CONTEMPORARY WRITERS ON ENGLISH HISTORY

(a) *Contemporary Writers*

Evelyn, J. Diary. A good edition of this charming contemporary work is Dobson's. 3 vols. Macmillan. 1906. The most convenient edition is in Dent's Everyman's Library. 2 vols. 1907. 2*s*. each.

Hutchinson, Mrs. (ed. Firth). **Memoirs of the Life of Colonel Hutchinson.** 2 vols. London Library. 1906. Also published in Dent's Everyman's Library. 1908. 2*s*.

Useful for illustrating Puritan ideals and showing how the war affected everyday life.

Osborne, Dorothy. Letters. x + 320 pp. Dent. Everyman's Library. 1914. 2*s*.

Most natural, human and charming letters.

Pepys' Diary. The standard edition of this famous diary is Wheatley's. It is also published in Dent's Everyman's Library.

Verney, F. P. and **M. H. Memoirs of the Verney Family.** 2 vols. Longmans. 1925.

Illustrate the Civil War from within.

(b) *Books of Collected Extracts*

Bell, K. Puritanism and Liberty. viii + 120 pp. Bell's English History Source Books. Vol. ix. 1912. 1*s*. 6*d*.

Extracts illustrating history from 1603–1660.

Bland, A. E., Brown, P. A. and **Tawney, R. H. English Economic History. Select documents.** xx + 730 pp. Bell. 1914. 7*s*. 6*d*.

Contains most valuable extracts for the serious study of economic history.

Keatinge, M. and **Frazer, N. L.** (See p. 76.)

Perrett, G. B. A Constitution in Making. viii + 120 pp. Bell's English History Source Books. Vol. x. 1920. 1*s*. 6*d*.

Extracts from sources illustrating the period 1660–1714.

Pocock, Guy. The Coming of the Stuarts. 192 pp. Dent. 1927. 2*s*.

Smith, D. N. Characters from the Histories and Memoirs of the Seventeenth Century. lii + 331 pp. O.U.P. 1918. 6*s*.

Most interesting collection of contemporary character sketches.

Stone, T. England under the Restoration. xix + 260 pp. Longmans. Intermediate Source Books. 1923. 10*s.* 6*d.*

Extracts illustrating every aspect of life in Restoration times —political, social, religious and constitutional.

5. ENGLAND, EUROPE AND THE WORLD IN THE SEVENTEENTH CENTURY

English history is so absorbing during this period that foreign history tends to be crowded out: and it is true that much of the complicated international history, for instance in the period of the Thirty Years' War, cannot be touched even in the simplest way in a general course. But the century contains at least two great movements that must not be ignored.

The first of these is the expansion of Europe in America and India. The development of trade, trade routes and trade organization, as well as the development of colonies and their connexion with religious history at home, form an essential link between the heroic pioneer work of the sixteenth century and the great commercial wars and economic progress of the eighteenth. This work can be taken most easily and intelligently if it is centred round maps.

Secondly, the dominant feature of European history proper is the rise of France under Richelieu and Louis XIV. This can never be seen by children in its proper light if Louis XIV is introduced to them for the first time in 1689 as some one for England to fight against—a wicked old man whose country gets beaten as it deserves. They should first understand a little of how Richelieu prepared the way for French greatness: and then they should find out something of what this greatness meant—how Versailles was the centre of learning and poetry and science in Europe as well as the centre of diplomacy—how kings from far away sent their sons to learn in Paris what was meant by good manners and civilization—how one of the most brilliant ages that ever adorned history claims the Great Monarch, if not as its inspiration, at least as its figurehead. The children can thus realize that for Louis XIV the cause of civilization seemed to be bound up with the principle of monarchy and authority, so that he stood for absolute government in politics and Catholicism in religion: and this will help them to understand the history of England under Charles II and James II, cousins and devout followers of Louis XIV.

From this the class goes on to consider the ambition of Louis to extend the boundaries of France. The problem of the Franco-German frontier is one that they *must* grasp, since it has influenced the whole of European history since the break-up of Charles the Great's Empire (see the introduction to medieval European history) and is unfortunately still with us to-day. They will quickly recognize from a physical map how tempting the idea of a Rhine frontier must have appeared to Louis: and they can then contrast the physical and political maps and realize that this geographical tidiness could be obtained only at the expense of the freedom of non-French Rhineland peoples. This brings them naturally to Holland, the figure of William, and his gallant defiance of France: and when in 1688 he accepts the English invitation to supplant James II, he steps on the shore at Torbay, no longer as a puppet suddenly produced out of a conjurer's box, but as the embodiment of a political idea. In choosing him, England has decided for Protestantism and a constitutional monarchy in contrast to the absolute monarchy and Catholicism of Louis and James II.

Finally, it is during this period that the interdependence of nations begins to take the shape that we knew in 1914. This interdependence is based on increased commercial and intellectual intercourse: it is officially recognized in each country by an apparatus of diplomacy, treaties and international law: it is intermittently broken by wars. There is no part of history where clear thinking is more important to the teacher, whose pupils may witness in their own lifetimes a great advance in the delicate business of reconciling the independence of each nation with the interdependence of all nations. He should first try, by emphasizing the commercial and peaceful intercourse of peoples, to maintain a right proportion in history and to show that war, after all, is the exception and not the rule. To too many children of the past European nations have never existed in history at all except when they were at war with England. And secondly, the war when it does come may be approached with a sympathetic inquiry into its causes and revealed as the attempt of some generation of people to cut through a

Gordian knot that was tied long before their own day and that they had not yet found means to unravel. Simply though this must be put, it cannot be neglected if history teaching is to give the children any real preparation for understanding the world in which they live.

(*a*) Short and Introductory Books

Innes, A. D. European History, 1598–1715. 172 pp. Bell. 1926. 2*s*.

A very handy political outline.

Mowat, R. B. The European States System. 96 pp. O.U.P. 1923. 2*s*. 6*d*.

An excellent little book which exactly meets the need of the teacher who wants to explain the development of international organization and law. Traces briefly and in simple language the international significance of each great war and treaty beginning with the Thirty Years' War and ending with the establishment of the League of Nations as representing 'the permanent effort of mankind towards international law and order'.

See also in the biographical section, lives of Richelieu, Louis XIV.

(*b*) Fuller and More Advanced Books

Benians, S. From Renaissance to Revolution. (See p. 106.)

Gardiner, K. M. Anglo-European History, 1492–1660. (See p. 106.)

Gardiner, J. R. The Thirty Years' War. xxv + 233 pp. Longmans. 1874.

Best short account.

Hollings, M. A. Europe in Renaissance and Reformation. 1453–1659. (See p. 106.)

Johnson, A. H. The Age of the Enlightened Despot. 1660–1789. xxiii + 278 pp. Methuen. 1927 (13th ed.) 4*s*.

A useful text-book, continuing Hollings' narrative.

Ogg, David. Europe in the Seventeenth Century. x + 579 pp. Black. 1925.

For more advanced work. Substantial and interesting. Teachers would find useful for political history the chapters on Richelieu, Louis XIV and the Dutch Republic, and for general background the first and last chapters of the book, which deal with seventeenth-century institutions, science and thought.

Seeley, Sir J. R. The Growth of British Policy. 2 vols. C.U.P. 1903.

Wakeman, H. O. The Ascendancy of France. xi + 394 pp. Rivingtons. 1901.

An excellent full text-book of European History 1598–1715.

For advanced work on the interrelation of English and European politics the teacher should consult A. W. Ward's Cambridge History of British Foreign Politics (3 vols. C.U.P. 1922). The introductory chapter will be found specially useful.

C. THE EIGHTEENTH CENTURY

1. POLITICAL ENGLISH HISTORY

(*a*) Books Covering all the Century

1. *Brief Outlines*

Hall, D. G. E. Brief Survey of English Constitutional History (see p. 75). Chapter IX gives a good summary of constitutional development from 1688 to about 1800.

Hearnshaw, F. J. C. British Prime Ministers of the Eighteenth Century. 80 pp. Benn. 1928. 6*d*.

A useful terse account of the constitutional situation in the early eighteenth century, and the work of each prime minister from Walpole to Pitt.

Wrong, E. M. A History of England. 1688–1815. 250 pp. Home University Library. 1927. 2*s*. 6*d*.

See section on seventeenth-century history.

2. *Fuller Accounts*

Bigham, C. Prime Ministers of England. xiii + 384 pp. Murray. 1924.

Useful, bright biographical sketches.

Fletcher, C. R. L. An Introductory History of England. Vol. III (1660–1792). See p. 107. 9*s*.

Greenwood, A. D. History of the People of England. 1688–1834. xiv + 336 pp. The Bede Histories. Sheldon Press. 1926. See p. 107. 7*s*. 6*d*.

Lecky, W. E. H. History of England in the Eighteenth Century. 8 vols. Longmans. 1892.

The classical work on the period: deals in full detail with the politics, society and wars of the eighteenth century. Useful to the teacher who wishes to find the full details of some story, or a picture of the social life of some particular class. Not at all difficult to read—a leisured literary history.

Macaulay's Essays on Chatham, Clive, etc., are of great value. Published in Everyman's Library, Nos. 225, 226. 2*s*. each.

Muir, J. Ramsay. History of the British Commonwealth. Vol. II. Specially useful for India. (See p. 72.)

Robertson, C. Grant. England under the Hanoverians. xix + 555 pp. Methuen. 1912 (2nd ed.).

A substantial narrative of political history with a chapter on the industrial revolution.

The teacher who wishes to enter into the ideas underlying the period would find Leslie Stephens' **History of English Thought in the Eighteenth Century** (2 vols. Smith Elder. 1902) valuable for advanced reading. See especially Chap. X on political theories.

(*b*) Special Topics

For the Jacobite Risings, see **Terry, C. S. The Jacobites and the Union.** xii + 274 pp. C.U.P. 1922 and **The Rising of Forty-five.** xii + 208 pp. C.U.P. 1922.

Contemporary records are combined into one dramatic and fully detailed narrative.

For the development of constitutional government under the early Hanoverians, see in the biographical section, Morley's life of Walpole.

For the Anglo-French Wars, see **Bradley, A. G. The Fight with France for North America.** ix + 392 pp. Constable. 1908, which gives a full account of the military history of the fight for Canada. See also in the biographical section, lives of Chatham, Wolfe and Clive.

For the American Revolution, see **Egerton, H. E. The Causes and Character of the American Revolution.** vi + 207 pp. O.U.P. 1923.

An analysis of the causes and principles of the revolution; gives more difficult material than could be included in lessons, but would make a great difference to the background of the teaching.

A great classic on this subject is **Trevelyan, Sir G. O. The American Revolution.** 6 vols. Longmans. 1905–16. In sympathy with the Whig point of view.

There are also full chapters in Lecky's History (see p. 115).

For the Revolutionary and Napoleonic period, see **Fitchett, W. H. How England saved Europe.** 1792–1815. 4 vols. Smith Elder. 1899–90.

The story of the wars: dramatic, detailed and fascinating to read.

See also the section on European history below, and in the biographical section, lives of Pitt, Nelson.

Chapter I of **Mahan's 'Influence of Sea Power on History'** gives an excellent introduction to the naval history of the period.

2. SOCIAL AND ECONOMIC ENGLISH HISTORY

(*a*) BOOKS COVERING THE WHOLE PERIOD OF SOCIAL HISTORY

Quennell, M. and **C. A History of Everyday Things in England.** Part II, 1500–1799. xi + 208 pp. Batsford. 1919. 8*s*. 6*d*.

A picturesque illustrative volume.

Spalding, E. H. Piers Plowman Social and Economic Histories. Book V. 1600–1760. xi + 224 pp., and VI. 1760–1830. xii + 216 pp. Philip. 1921. 3*s*. 6*d*. each.

Excellent and interesting volumes, full of useful material for lessons.

Sydney, W. C. England and the English in the Eighteenth Century. 2 vols. Grant. 1891.

Illustrates the social atmosphere of the period; deals with dress, travel, education, the spirit of politics and literature, etc.

Traill, H. D. and **Mann, J. S. Social England.** Vol. V. 1714–1815. liii + 864 pp. Cassell. 1904.

A mine of information on every aspect of social life.

Turberville, A. S. English Men and Manners in the Eighteenth Century. xxiii + 531 pp. O.U.P. 1926. 10*s*.

A most fascinating and useful book; depicts the civilization of the age by short vivid biographies of its leaders.

(*b*) BOOKS ON SPECIAL TOPICS OF SOCIAL HISTORY

Bailey, J. Dr. Johnson and his Circle. 256 pp. Home Univ. Library. 1913. 2*s*. 6*d*.

An interesting, human picture.

George, M. D. London Life in the Eighteenth Century. x + 452 pp. Kegan Paul. 1925.

Contains a mass of material about the life of the poor—population, housing conditions, trade, etc.

Greenwood, A. D. Horace Walpole's World. xi + 257 pp. Bell. 1913.

A delightful leisurely account of the life of the rich in the eighteenth century: a companion picture to Miss George's book.

Marshall, D. The English Poor in the Eighteenth Century. 292 pp. Routledge. 1926.

An interesting study of poor-law administration.

Masefield, J. Sea Life in Nelson's Time. x + 218 pp. Methuen. 1905.

A lively, popular account of ships, guns, officers and organization, sailors and their manner of life.

Woodforde, J., ed. by Beresford, J. **The Diary of a Country Parson.** 3 vols. O.U.P. 1924.

Charming homely stuff.

For the Agricultural Revolution use :—

Curtler, W. H. R. A History of English Agriculture. viii + 371 pp. O.U.P. 1909.

A good short history with plenty of illustrative material useful in teaching.

Hammond, J. L. and **B. The Village Labourer.** 1760–1830. xii + 339 pp. Longmans. 1927.

Tells the story of enclosures from the labourer's point of view ; very useful.

Prothero, R. E. English Farming, Past and Present. xvi + 506 pp. Longmans. 1927 (4th ed.).

The classical work on the subject ; very valuable and interesting.

For the Industrial Revolution use :—

Cunningham, W. The Growth of English Industry and Commerce. Modern Times. Part II. 609–1039 pp. C.U.P. 1921 (6th ed.).

Hammond, J. L. and **B. The Rise of Modern Industry.** xi + 280 pp. Methuen. 1927.

Valuable. Part I deals with the causes of the Revolution, Part II with monographs on various aspects (e.g., the steam engine), Part III with effects.

Hammond, J. L. and **B. The Skilled Labourer, 1760–1832.** ix + 397 pp., and **The Town Labourer, 1760–1832.** ix + 342 pp. Longmans. 1919 and 1925.

Interesting accounts of the effects of the Revolution on particular classes. Full of illustrative material.

Toynbee, A. The Industrial Revolution. xxxv + 282 pp. Longmans. 1908 (new ed.).

One of the earliest works on the subject, which still holds its own as a classic ; should be read subsequently to a more modern book.

3. ECCLESIASTICAL ENGLISH HISTORY

Tyerman, L. The Life and Times of John Wesley. 3 vols. Hodder & Stoughton. 1871.

Old, but still the best authority for a full picture of Wesley's work and its effect on his age. By using the index of this book or of Wesley's Journal the teacher could quickly find an account of any connexion that existed between Wesley and the school district. For general reading there is a good short life of Wesley by Hutton (see biographical section).

Wesley, J. Journal. There is a handy abridged edition edited by Parker. xxxii + 512 pp. Pitman. 1905.

Contains a charming little appreciation by Birrell.

There is also an edition published by Dent. Everyman's Library. 4 vols. 1906.

The chapters on religious history in **Lecky** are very good. The Wesleyan movement should be connected with the humanitarian movement, which can be studied in the lives of Howard, Wilberforce and Fry.

4. SOURCE BOOKS AND CONTEMPORARY WRITERS ON ENGLISH HISTORY

(*a*) *Contemporary Writers*

Cobbett, W. Rural Rides. 2 vols. Dent. Everyman's Library. 1912. There is also a short selection published in Blackie's English School Texts. 127 pp. 1923.

Montagu, Lady Mary Wortley. Letters. xiii + 551 pp. Dent. Everyman's Library. 1906. 2*s.*

Delightful spirited gossip about Court life in England and abroad; the letters of a famous ambassador's wife.

Walpole, Horace. Letters (selected). xvi + 535 pp. Dent. Everyman's Library. 1926. 2*s.*

The charming gossiping letters of a man of fashion.

(*b*) *Books of Collected Extracts from Sources*

Bland, A. E., Brown, P. A. and **Tawney, R. English Economic History. Select Documents.** See comment above under seventeenth century.

Esdaile, K. A. Walpole and Chatham. 1714–1760. viii + 120 pp. Bell. English History Source Book Series. 1925. 1*s.* 6*d.*

A collection of extracts on political and social history.

George, M. D. England in Johnson's Day. xvi + 239 pp. Methuen. 1928. 6*s.*

Interesting lively extracts illustrating the history of everyday life.

George, M. D. English Social Life in the Eighteenth Century. vii + 125 pp. Sheldon Press: Texts for Students. 1923. 3*s.* 6*d.* Or in two parts, 1*s.* 6*d.* each.

Extracts illustrating the social and economic problems of the age: useful in containing extracts from the long contemporary works like Arthur Young's which teachers would not have time to explore.

Thomson, J. P. The Jacobite Rebellions. 1689–1746. viii + 120 pp. Bell. English History Source Book Series. 1914. 1*s.* 6*d.*
Extracts illustrating the rebellions.

Winbolt, S. E. American Independence and the French Revolution. 1760–1801. viii + 120 pp. Bell. English History Source Book Series. 1925. 1*s.* 6*d.*
Continues Esdaile, above.

5. ENGLAND, EUROPE AND THE WORLD IN THE EIGHTEENTH CENTURY

During the first part of the century the main interest on the Continent is the development of certain nations in the North-East, and as these nations have been important in European politics ever since, the children should certainly be introduced to them. Sweden under Charles XII (1697–1718), Russia under Peter the Great (1698–1725) and Catherine, and Prussia under Frederick the Great (1740–1786) can all be approached by children through biographies of their heroic leaders, and the difficulty of settling frontiers between these vigorous new forces can be represented as a real geographical problem, not simply as a piece of self-seeking worldliness on the part of individual monarchs. Nothing can be less sound, either politically or ethically, than to try to simplify the causes of a frontier war by saying, 'So you see Frederick wants to get Silesia. So what will he do? Come along, that's not very difficult! . . . That's right! *of course* he'll go to war!' Nothing but children's fatalistic readiness to accept lesson periods as water-tight compartments of knowledge can save the teacher from the unspoken comment, 'You didn't talk like that in Scripture twenty minutes ago!' There is no doubt that Frederick was ambitious and no reason to hide that he was: but his desire 'to get myself talked about' need not be represented as the commonsense motive of the normal person. The children can see for themselves from the map that Prussia has no obvious snug geographical frontiers, and that all sorts of temptations and difficulties will arise from that fact. They can go on from this to understand the position of Poland as a middle kingdom between Germany and Russia, to realize the crime of partitioning it, and to be prepared for its reappearance on the map in 1919. The story of the long complicated wars need not be touched: what should be included is the simple account of international relations, centred round outstanding biographies and the map.

Closely connected with Frederick's European wars—so closely that the two stories can be easily combined—is the war of expansion between France and England. Here the foundation of the whole subject is to make the development of trade and colonization real to the children by means of maps and illustrative detail, and then to let them discover why the problem of rivalry between France and England appeared in India, in America and by sea. The great events of the war may be grouped round the figures of Chatham and Clive, Wolfe and Hawke; but the essential point is that the children should understand the story of the map and see how and why the political divisions of the world differed in 1700 and 1763. During this period the 'old colonial theory' may be explained to them in preparation for the story of the American Revolution: and finally when the Revolution itself is reached they are ready to see both sides of the question and to agree that if Canada and other lands are to remain in union with England another 'colonial theory' must be found.

Towards the end of the century there breaks on Europe that tremendous storm of intellectual, political and military energy which we call the Revolutionary and Napoleonic era. It is the right of every English child to hear something of this story, not only because it forms one of the most heroic portions of all human history, but also because it provided the whole world with a stock of democratic ideas which alarmed England very much at the time, but much of which she put into practice at her leisure during the course of the nineteenth century. It is important, therefore, that the children should find out (if possible from extracts from sources such as Arthur Young's Travels) what France had to complain of before the Revolution: that they should next get some idea of Revolutionary history from the stories of Mirabeau, Louis XVI, Danton and Robespierre: that they should understand how Napoleon's power grew out of the Revolution and how he gave some good gifts as well as evil ones to France and Europe: and finally that during the tale of the Napoleonic wars they may experience at once a sense of resistance to tyranny and a sense of tragic pity for the ruined tyrant.

The following books will be found useful:—

(*a*) Short and Introductory Books

Belloc, H. The French Revolution. 256 pp. Home University Library. 1911. 2*s.* 6*d.*

A vigorous, brief sketch, which perhaps expresses the personality of the writer rather than the atmosphere of the age.

Fisher, H. A. L. Napoleon. 256 pp. Home University Library. 1913. 2*s.* 6*d.*

Brilliant.

Happold, F. C. (ed.). **Modern Historians of the French Revolution.** xiv + 200 pp. Nelson. 1928. 1*s.* 9*d.*

From these well-chosen extracts the teacher can gather the names and standing of historians of this great period and can make a choice for further reading.

Higgs-Walker, J. A. European History 1789–1815. viii + 184 pp. Bell. 1924. 2*s.*

A handy outline; brief but interesting.

Johnson, A. H. The Age of the Enlightened Despot. (See p. 114.)

Mowat, R. B. The European States System.
(See p. 114.)

(*b*) Fuller and More Advanced Books

Carlyle, T. The French Revolution. 2 vols. Everyman's Library, Nos. 31, 32.

Unrivalled for vivid scenes, but the facts have been modified by later research.

Benians, S. From Renaissance to Revolution.
(See p. 106.)

Fitchett, W. H. How England saved Europe. 1792–1815. 4 vols. Smith Elder. 1899–1900.

The story of the war period: dramatic, detailed, fascinating to read.

Longman, F. W. Frederick the Great and the Seven Years' War. xii + 252 pp. Longmans. Epochs of Modern History. 1881.

A good succinct account of the military events of the period and of the personalities concerned in them.

Madelin, L. (trans.). **The French Revolution.** xiii + 662 pp. Heinemann. 1916. 12*s.* 6*d.*

A dramatic and lucid narrative, containing the results of recent research. Far the best book on the Revolution for the general reader.

See also in the biographical section, lives of Elizabeth Farnese, Peter the Great of Russia, Frederick the Great, Mirabeau, Danton, Napoleon.

D. THE NINETEENTH CENTURY

1. ENGLISH POLITICAL HISTORY

(a) Books Covering all the Period

Butler, J. R. M. A History of England 1815-1918. 252 pp. Home University Library. 1928. 2s. 6d.

A useful general survey of the main economic and political forces that transformed England in the nineteenth century.

Marvin, F. S. The Century of Hope. v + 358 pp. O.U.P. 1919 (2nd ed.). 6s.

A short history of progress in the nineteenth century.

Rayner, R. M. Nineteenth Century England. xv + 411 pp. Longmans. 1927. 6s.

A valuable all-round survey, fresh and interesting, dealing with social and religious as well as political and foreign affairs. Would be very useful to the teacher: contains both the essential facts and some good illustrative material.

Somervell, D. C. British History 1815-74. x + 168 pp. Bell. 1924. 2s.

and

Somervell, D. C. British History 1874–1914. viii + 168 pp. Bell. 1924. 2s.

Good outlines.

Trevelyan, G. H. British History in the Nineteenth Century. 1782–1901. xvi + 445 pp. Longmans. 1922. 12s. 6d.

An enlightened and stimulating work. Teachers would find the social and industrial chapters of special value.

[N.B.—The fourth volume of **A. D. Greenwood's 'History of the People of England'** (Bede Histories: Sheldon Press) is in progress.]

The classical work on the nineteenth century in England is by **Halévy, E. 'History of the English People.'**

(b) Politics and Parliament

Bigham, Clive. The Prime Ministers of England. 1721–1924. xiii + 384 pp. Murray. 1924. 10s. 6d.

Covers the ground in biographical form. Most helpful to teachers who use a biographical syllabus, and contains lively incidents as well as sound facts.

Hall, D. G. E. Brief Survey of English Constitutional History. (See p. 75.) Chapter X outlines the constitutional changes of the nineteenth century.

Hearnshaw, F. J. C. (ed.). **The Political Principles of some Notable Prime Ministers of the Nineteenth Century.** 300 pp. Macmillan. 1926. 12s. 6d.

Very useful: contains sketches of the ideas and personalities of the great premiers from Canning to Salisbury. For Senior School teachers.

Ilbert, Courtnay. Parliament. 254 pp. Home University Library. 1911. 2*s.* 6*d.*

Extremely good, clear and useful.

Rose, J. H. The Rise of Democracy. viii + 256 pp. Blackie. 1912. 3*s.* 6*d.*

A succinct and useful account of the development of government in England from the French Revolution to 1911.

2. ENGLISH SOCIAL AND ECONOMIC HISTORY

(*a*) Books Covering the Whole Period of Social History

i. *Short and Introductory Books*

Allsopp, H. The Change to Modern England. 240 pp. Nisbet. 1928. 3*s.*

A most delightfully lively, simple yet sound account of social and industrial history from 1750 to to-day. Includes good short accounts of Trade Unionism, Chartism, etc. Many extracts from sources are set in the text.

Guest, G. English Social Reformers. Book II. 1726–1865. 127 pp. Horace Marshall. 1923, etc. 2*s.*

Extremely useful: social history taught through biography.

Spalding, E. H. Piers Plowman Social and Economic Histories.

Book VI. 1760–1830. 224 pp.

Book VII. 1830 to to-day. 284 pp. Philip. 1927. 3*s.* 6*d.* each.

An excellent series. Well illustrated.

Rees, J. F. A Social and Industrial History of England from 1815 to the Present Day. vii + 197 pp. Methuen. 1923 (3rd ed.). 5*s.*

A sound, clear and valuable account.

ii. *Fuller and More Advanced Books*

Cole, G. D. H. A Short History of the British Working Class Movement.

Vol. I. 1789–1848. vi + 192 pp.

Vol. II. 1848–1900. viii + 196 pp. Allen & Unwin and Labour Publishing Co. 1925.

Full of matter, solid, readable.

Fay, C. R. Life and Labour in the Nineteenth Century. viii + 319 pp. C.U.P. 1920.

A wonderful book: concise, yet detailed and sparkling.

Fay, C. R. Great Britain from Adam Smith to the Present Day. xii + 458 pp. Longmans. 1928.

A valuable summary of development in many branches of industrial life: the teacher would be almost certain to find here information about his local industry.

Hammond, J. L. and B. The Rise of Modern Industry. xi + 280 pp. Methuen. 1927. 10*s.* 6*d.*

A most useful book. Part III deals with the social effects of the Industrial Revolution.

Slater, G. The Making of Modern England. xi + 303 pp. Constable. 1919 (latest ed.).

Gives very useful material on social progress of every kind—trade unions, public health, municipal reform, education, etc.

Traill, H. D. and **Mann, J. S. Social England.** Vol. VI. 1815–1885. lvi + 948 pp. Cassell. 1904.

Full of interesting illustrative material.

For fuller study the reader should consult the works of **J. H. Clapham** and **Dr. Lilian Knowles.**

(*b*) Books on Special Topics of Social History

N.B.—These are almost entirely for more advanced work.

Chartism

Hovell, M., ed. Tout, T. F. **The Chartist Movement.** 327 pp. Manchester Univ. Press. 1925. Cheap edition. 6*s.*

Rather stiff, but the best book on the subject.

Factory Acts

Hutchins, B. L. and **Harrison, A. A History of Factory Legislation.** xvi + 298 pp. P. S. King & Son. 1926. 3rd edition.

See also in the biography section the life of Shaftesbury.

Free Trade

See in the biography section, lives of Peel and Cobden.

Poor Law

Webb, S. and **B. English Local Government: English Poor Law History.** Part I. The Old Poor Law. x + 447 pp. Longmans. 1927.

There is a good brief summary of the Poor Law question published by H.M.S.O. Reconstruction Problem Pamphlets. 2*d.*

Trade Unionism

Appleton, W. A. Trade Unions: their past, present and future. 183 pp. Allan. 1925.

An introductory account.

Cole, G. D. H. Organized Labour: an introduction to Trade Unionism. 182 pp. Allen & Unwin and the Labour Publishing Co. 1924. 6*s*.

Mainly on modern Trade Unionism, but has a historical introduction: succinct and scholarly.

Selley, E. Village Trade Unionism in Two Centuries. 183 pp. Allen & Unwin. 1919.

Has a definite bias in favour of unionism, but gives some biographical material that would be hard to get elsewhere. Brief and simply written.

Webb, S. and **B. The History of Trade Unionism.** xviii + 784 pp. Longmans. 1920.

The great standard authority.

See also in the biography section, lives of Francis Place and Joseph Arch.

3. SOURCE BOOKS OF ENGLISH HISTORY

Edwards, A. C. W. Peace and Reform 1815-37. viii + 117 pp. Bell. 1913. 1*s*. 6*d*.

Gretton, R. H. Commercial Politics. 1837–56. viii + 119 pp. Bell. 1914. 1*s*. 6*d*.

Gretton, R. H. Imperialism and Mr. Gladstone. 1876–87. viii + 120 pp. Bell. 1923. 1*s*. 6*d*.

Harding, E. From Palmerston to Disraeli. 1856–1876. viii + 120 pp. Bell. 1913. 1*s*. 6*d*.

Keatinge, M. E. and **Frazer, N. L. Documents of British History. A.D. 1815–1900.** Black. 1*s*. 4*d*. (See p. 76.)

Winbolt, S. E. England and Napoleon. 1801–15. viii + 120 pp. Bell. 1912. 1*s*. 6*d*.

A Hundred Years Ago: the Movement for Parliamentary Reform. 1815–1845. Nelson. 1*s*.

Illustrative readings from famous novels.

4. ENGLAND, EUROPE AND THE WORLD

The nineteenth century is to the teacher the most difficult and important of all centuries. No other age has such practical value in explaining the background of our own lives: and few others are so rich in great events, so advanced in every kind of specialized knowledge, so progressive, so extraordinarily complex. It is this very richness and complexity of human life that harasses the teacher, who feels that whatever he includes in his syllabus something essential is left out. For it is almost impossible to subdivide nineteenth-century history satisfactorily. In proportion as our civilization becomes more complex, it becomes also more united. Every European nation has its individual story; but at the same time the bond of international relations develops and strengthens so that no national story can stand alone. The development of British and other empires takes a different form in every part of the globe: yet the stories of every one are linked together by the idea that Ramsay Muir has christened 'the Europeanization of the world'. The coming of machinery and the subdivision of labour revolutionize the whole social life of England and form in themselves a titanic story of human enterprise, progress and suffering: yet this very development, by its dependence on commerce, reveals the interconnexion of the world and makes it impossible for the factory worker in England to ignore the factory worker in China or Japan. It seems as impossible for us intelligently to isolate some part of history for the children's study as it is impossible for them to grasp the whole.

This is a gloomy and terrifying preface. But it is so intentionally. We must approach such a problem with reverence. Only the teacher who is conscious of the spirit of unity in nineteenth-century civilization can hope to import that spirit into the teaching of selected parts. It might even be said that if such a spirit is present, the particular selection of facts is not of vital importance. The selection suggested here is one of many that could be made.

As regards the *history of other European nations*, in the first place, there are certain events of outstanding importance which must find place in the scheme. These are, the war of Italian independence, the second empire and republic in France, the rise of Prussia and the American Civil War. The stories are kind enough to lend themselves readily to simple biographical treatment. Lives of Mazzini or Cavour or (above all) Garibaldi illustrate the making of Italy. The career of Napoleon III not only forms a link with the Napoleonic wars, but makes it possible to describe in a simple way the vicissitudes that produced modern France. Bismarck stands for Prussia, and Lincoln for the American Civil War.

But beside the dramas of individual nations, it is of the utmost importance to describe simply *the interdependence of all nations* by tracing on the one hand the story of Europe in war—the development of opposing alliances after 1870 with their dangerous, delicate balance of political forces and their race for armaments leading to the Great War and the treaties that concluded it: and on the other hand the story of peace—the dawn of arbitration before the war and the establishment of the League of Nations as one of its main results. This story is told with admirable simplicity and directness in Jones and Sherman: The League of Nations: from Idea to Reality (see book-list on the League of Nations). The last four chapters of Delisle Burns: Short History of International Intercourse (see book-list on general European history) will be found of great value to the teacher.

Finally, the English teacher is in less danger than any other to ignore the *world outside Europe*. He cannot help going far afield: Imperial history takes him there. He has first to consider the development of the colonies, their self-government under the 'new colonial theory' and the ties that bind them to England: secondly, he has to deal with the dependencies, especially India and Egypt, and prepare the way for an adult understanding of their problems: thirdly, he has to explain the position and character of the mandated territories. And finally, throughout the course he has to show that the key to all these movements is the development of rapid transport—forging new routes through land, sea and air, bringing the world together, and driving out mankind from the self-contained and self-supporting political groups of the past.

The following books will be found useful:—

N.B.—For a fuller list, see the bibliography of Modern European History by H. W. V. Temperley and L. M. Penson. Historical Assoc. leaflet No. 68, 1*s.* 1*d.*, or 7*d.* to members.

1. POLITICAL

(*a*) General

Flenly, R. Makers of Nineteenth-Century Europe. xiii + 272 pp. Dent. 1927. 6*s.*

The story of nineteenth-century European history told in short biographies.

Grant, A. J. and **Temperley, H. Europe in the Nineteenth Century (1789-1914).** xix + 569 pp. Longmans. 1927. 12*s.* 6*d.*

An extremely valuable book. A clear, stimulating and readable account of European History, dealing with international relationships and with movements affecting the whole continent.

Hearnshaw, F. J. C. Main Currents of European History. 1815–1915. x + 367 pp. Macmillan. 1917. 7*s*. 6*d*.
A useful sketch, emphasizing the dominant idea of each successive era, and giving a book-list.

Levett, E. Europe since Napoleon (to 1919). vii + 400 pp. Blackie. 1926. 5*s*.
A brief but lucid and comprehensive survey. Deals with the histories of individual nations, and therefore serves as a complement to Grant and Temperley. Contains national bibliographies.

Marriott, J. A. R. Europe and Beyond : a preliminary survey of World Politics in the last half-century, 1870-1920. viii + 325 pp. Methuen. 1921. 6*s*.
A useful reference book.

(*b*) Special Topics

i. *France in the nineteenth century.*
See in biography section, life of Napoleon III.

ii. *Italy in the nineteenth century.*
See in biography section, lives of Cavour.

Trevelyan, G. M. Garibaldi and the Making of Italy. xix + 390 pp. Longmans. 1911. Cheap edition. 320 pp. Nelson. 1920. (Without notes or illustrations.)

Trevelyan, G. M. Garibaldi's Defence of the Roman Republic. xv + 387 pp. Longmans. 1907. Cheap edition. 314 pp. Nelson. 1920.

Trevelyan, G. M. Garibaldi and the Thousand. xv + 395 pp. Longmans. 1909. Cheap edition. 316 pp. Nelson. 1920.
Dramatic, graphic, fascinating volumes.

iii. *America in the nineteenth century.*
See in the biography section, life of Abraham Lincoln.

iv. *Germany in the nineteenth century.*
See in the biography section, lives of Bismarck and Wilhelm II.

v. *The War and After.*

Marten, C. H. K. The Groundwork of the War. 48 pp. Blackie. 1921. 1*s*. 6*d*.

Pollard, A. F. A Short History of the Great War. vi + 411 pp. Methuen. 1920. 10*s*. 6*d*.
A clear summary.

Gooch, G. P. History of Modern Europe, 1878–1919. 728 pp. Cassell. 1923. A standard authority.

Burns, C. Delisle. 1918–1928 : A Short History of the World. 447 pp. Gollancz. 1928.
Contains useful summaries of world affairs since the war, and stimulating comments upon them.

9

The Peace Handbooks issued by the Historical Section of the Foreign Office (over 100 volumes) contain much condensed information on foreign affairs.

Benn is bringing out a series of books on the present condition of various nations under the general title of The World of To-day.

2. SOCIAL

Gibbins, H. de B. Economic and Industrial Progress of the Century. xxx + 524 pp. Chambers. 1901.

Old, but useful in giving the progress of the Industrial Revolution outside England.

Knight, M. M. Economic History of Europe. Part II. vii + 808 pp. Allen and Unwin. 1928.

Contains material that would be hard to get elsewhere in a short form.

8. IMPERIAL HISTORY

The book-list that follows is necessarily a short one. For further information, particularly on the individual parts of the empire, the teacher should consult the admirable *Select List of Books relating to the History of the British Empire Overseas* drawn up by A. P. Newton (32 pp., Historical Association Leaflet No. 46). Most valuable suggestions for study and reading are given in A. P. Newton's *The Study of Colonial History* (Sheldon Press : Helps for Students Series. 9*d*.).

A. GENERAL

1. SHORT AND INTRODUCTORY BOOKS

Bulkeley, J. P. The British Empire : a Short History. x + 260 pp. O.U.P. 1926. 2*s*. 6*d*.

A stimulating introduction. Connects history with geography. Contains useful short book-lists and subjects for discussion.

Dodd, A. F. A Short History of the British Empire. 276 pp. Dent. 1925. 6*s*.

A very useful summary : gives the essential facts clearly; a handy reference book.

Higham, C. S. S. History of the British Empire. x + 276 pp. Longmans. 1927 (latest ed.). 5*s*.

A useful summary, containing much matter in little space. Deals with social and economic as well as political development.

Kermach, W. R. Expansion of Britain from the Age of Discoveries. 112 pp. O.U.P. 1922. 2*s*. 6*d*.

A good short geographical history, useful to the teacher who wishes to take a combined course.

Lucas, Sir Charles. The Story of the Empire. 286 pp. Collins. 1924. 6*s.*

A chronological narrative of British expansion as a whole from the earliest times to the present day. Sound in matter and graphically written : makes delightful reading. Very useful.

Muir, J. Ramsay. A Short History of the British Commonwealth. Vol. I. The Islands and the First Empire (to 1763). xvi + 824 pp. 1920. Vol. II. The Modern Commonwealth (1763–1919). xvi + 814 pp. 1922. Philip. 15*s.* each.

A history of war, politics and empire.

Newton, A. P. and **Ewing, J. The British Empire since 1783.** 280 pp. Methuen. 1929. 5*s.*

Invaluable to teachers in search of material on the modern period.

Williamson, J. A. Builders of the Empire. xii + 297 pp. O.U.P. 1925. 7*s.* 6*d.* and 3*s.* 6*d.*

Perhaps the most useful of all books to the teacher in the direct preparation of stories and oral lessons. A series of attractively told biographies of imperial pioneers from Cabot to Kitchener. Delightful pictures.

Williamson, J. A. Europe Overseas. 144 pp. O.U.P. 1925. 2*s.* 6*d.*

An excellent brief survey of the whole history of European expansion (i.e., Spanish, Dutch, French, etc., as well as English). A valuable companion to a purely British history.

Williamson, J. A. The Foundation and Growth of the British Empire. xii + 318 pp. Macmillan. 1923. 2*s.* 6*d.*

An excellent, clear outline, primarily intended as a secondary school text-book. Gives lists of important dates.

Woodward, W. H. A. A Short History of the Expansion of the British Empire. viii + 363 pp. C.U.P. 1924 (5th ed.). 3*s.* 6*d.*

A good narrative, containing the essential facts and also some interesting illustrative detail. Most useful.

Zimmern, A. The Third British Empire. x + 162 pp. O.U.P. 1927 (2nd ed.). 6*s.*

Most interesting and stimulating lectures on the present position of the Empire—her character, problems and future.

2. FULLER AND MORE ADVANCED BOOKS

Demageon, A. The British Empire : a Study in Colonial Geography. 299 pp. Harrap. 1925.

A translation from the French. An interesting, lucid and detached description of the development of the Empire. Fascinating to read and provokes thought.

Egerton, H. E. Short History of British Colonial Policy. xv + 579 pp. Methuen. 1913 (4th ed.). 10*s*. 6*d*.

Egerton, H. E. British Colonial Policy in the Twentieth Century. ix + 259 pp. Methuen. 1922. 10*s*. 6*d*.

Egerton, H. E. The Origin and Growth of Greater Britain. vi + 241 pp. O.U.P. 1920. 3*s*. 6*d*.

A general introduction to the study of colonial development, emphasizing the constitutional and economic side. An introduction to Sir Charles Lucas' Historical Geography (see below).

Knowles, L. The Economic Development of the British Overseas Empire. xv + 555 pp. Routledge. 1924. 10*s*. 6*d*.

Lucas, Sir Charles. A Historical Geography of the British Colonies. 7 vols. O.U.P. 1905–20.

Muir, J. Ramsay. The Expansion of Europe. xii + 380 pp. Constable. 1926 (latest ed.). 12*s*.

Williamson, J. A. A Short History of British Expansion. xxv + 647 pp. Macmillan. 1922. 25*s*.

The standard work for those who wish to enter on a serious study of imperial history.

B. BOOKS ON THE INDIVIDUAL PARTS OF THE EMPIRE

One or two introductory books or text-books on each of the greatest component parts of the Empire are given.

Africa. **Johnston, Sir H. H. The Colonization of Africa.** xv + 505 pp. C.U.P. 1913.

Scully, W. C. A History of South Africa from the Earliest Days to Union. xv + 327 pp. Longmans. 1915.

A useful, concise introductory narrative.

Australia. **Scott, E. Short History of Australia.** xxviii + 392 pp. O.U.P. 1927 (5th ed.).

A useful and interesting narrative.

Swinburne, G. H. Australian History Source Book. viii + 211 pp. Bell. 1919.

Canada. **Bradley, A. G. Canada.** 256 pp. Home University Library. 1912. 2*s*. 6*d*.

A graphic sketch.

Bryce, G. A Short History of the Canadian People. xii + 621 pp. Low. 1914.

A good popular narrative, giving the social and human detail that interests children.

Munro, J. A Source Book of Canadian History. viii + 120 pp. Bell. 1913. 2*s*.

Far East. **Douglas, R. K. Europe and the Far East 1506-1912.** vii + 487 pp. C.U.P. 1913.

India. **Hunter, Sir William Wilson** (ed.). **Rulers of India Series.** 27 volumes.
A very useful series of biographies, giving lives of Akbar, Dupleix, Clive, Warren Hastings, &c.

Muir, J. Ramsay. The Making of British India. xiv + 398 pp. Manchester Univ. Press. 1915.
A valuable collection of documents, with introduction and notes. For serious study.

Smith, V. V. A. The Oxford History of India. xxiv + 814 pp. O.U.P. 1923.
An excellent condensed narrative, bringing the story down to 1921.

Ireland. **Maxwell, C. A Short History of Ireland.** 155 pp. Dublin Talbot Press. 1925.
An excellent outline.

Gwynn, S. The Students' History of Ireland. 322 pp. Longmans. 1925.
A readable interesting survey, bringing the story down to the Treaty of 1921.

New Zealand. **Reeves, W. P. The Long White Cloud.** 390 pp. Allen and Unwin. 1924 (3rd ed.). 16*s.*
A good readable narrative, full of interesting detail.

Scotland. **Terry, C. S. A Short History of Scotland.** xv + 266 pp. C.U.P. 1921.
An excellent introduction which paves the way for further reading.

Wales. **Edwards, O. M. Wales.** xxiv + 431 pp. Fisher Unwin. Stories of Nations Series. 1925 (2nd ed.).
A readable general survey.

9. THE LEAGUE OF NATIONS

1. SHORT AND INTRODUCTORY BOOKS

Baker, W. P. Noel. The League of Nations at Work. xvi + 139 pp. Nisbet. 3*s.* 6*d.*
Very useful to the teacher: a clear, picturesque, stimulating account of the machinery and work of the League of Nations. Attractive yet sound. Illustrated.

Bradfield, B. A Little Book of the League of Nations. 106 pp. King. 1927. 2*s.*
A group of reprinted articles from the Children's Newspaper. Gives in a popular way the facts about the League's organization and some examples of its work in connexion with trade and health and the settlement of international disputes.

Innes, K. The League of Nations and the World's Workers. 48 pp. Hogarth Press. 1927. 1*s.* 6*d.*
An introduction to the work of the International Labour

Organization. Describes simply the buildings, organization and *raison d'être* of the I.L.O. and gives some examples of its work. Could be connected with lessons on factory reform in England : shows the need for similar reforms in the East.

Garnett, Maxwell. Organizing Peace. 72 pp. League of Nations Union Pamphlets No. 179. 2*d*.

A most valuable brief clear account of the League for beginners ; the best introduction for the teacher who has not yet entered into the subject at all. Illustrated.

Handbook of Suggestions for Teachers in Elementary Schools. H.M.S.O. 1927. 2*s*.

Has a valuable appendix on the place of the League of Nations in education.

Jones, R. and **Sherman, S. The League of Nations : from Idea to Reality.** xiv + 213 pp. Pitman. 1927. 5*s*.

Far the most useful, attractive and stimulating book for the practical teacher. Deals with the development of the idea of the League in History, with the causes and treaties of the Great War and the establishment of the League, with its organization, work and hopes for the future.

Marvin, F. S. and **Unwin, J. F. The Study and Teaching of International Relations.** 20 pp. League of Nations Union pamphlet. 3*d*.

The reports of two interesting addresses which emphasize the importance of teaching about international co-operation.

Secretariat of the League of Nations. The Aim and Organisation of the League of Nations. 90 pp. Geneva. 1929. 9*d*. or 2*s*.

An official book of reference for teachers.

Teachers and World Peace. 36 pp. League of Nations pamphlet No. 114. 3*d*.

A very useful pamphlet describing the importance of League of Nations teaching in the schools, the best methods of approach, and some programmes and experiments undertaken by particular schools.

Whelan, F. The Covenant Explained. 91 pp. League of Nations pamphlet No. 34. 9*d*.

Very useful ; gives the text of the Covenant with a clear explanation of the force of each clause.

2. LONGER AND MORE ADVANCED BOOKS

Butler, Sir G. A Handbook to the League of Nations. xvi + 239 pp. Longmans. 1928. (2nd ed.)

An excellent manual, placing the League in its proper historical perspective, and describing its machinery, achievements and obligations. Contains a useful chronological summary of the League's achievements.

Ellis, C. Howard. The Origin, Structure and Working of the League of Nations. 528 pp. Allen and Unwin. 1928.

The standard authority.

Wilson, F. The Origins of the League Covenant. xvi + 260 pp. Hogarth Press. 1928.

Gives a full record of the discussions on each article of the Covenant, showing what interpretation was intended by the men who drew it up.

The proceedings of the Geneva Institute of International Relations are being published annually under the title 'Problems of Peace' by the Oxford University Press. They contain most valuable lectures by international experts.

10. LOCAL HISTORY

It is not possible, of course, to give here any help for the study of particular districts. This list aims simply at putting teachers on the track of the particular material they may need.

A. BIBLIOGRAPHIES AND HELPS ON METHODS OF LOCAL ENQUIRY

Cox, J. C. How to write the History of a Parish. 216 pp. Allen. 1909. (2nd ed.) 4*s.* 6*d.*

Of the greatest value to the teacher who wishes to undertake the serious study of local history. Full of information and suggestion. A new edition including books published since 1909 would be very welcome.

Gross, C. Sources and Literature of English History from the Earliest Times to about 1485. xxiii + 820 pp. Longmans. 1915. (2nd ed.)

Contains full book lists on local history (arranged under counties) in the Middle Ages.

Gross, C. Bibliography of British Municipal History. xxxiv + 461 pp. Longmans. 1897.

Excellent up to that date.

Helps for Students of History Series ; published by the Sheldon Press.

This scholarly and helpful little series contains several volumes useful for local history.

Humphreys, A. L. A Handbook to County Bibliography. x + 501 pp. London. 1917.

Thompson, A. Hamilton. Parish History and Records. Historical Association Leaflet No. 66. 1926. **A Short Bibliography of Local History.** Hist. Ass. Leaflet No. 72. 1928. 7*d.* to members, 1*s.* 1*d.* to non-members. Both invaluable to the teacher.

Wake, Joan. How to compile a History and Present Day Record of Village Life. 64 pp. Kettering; T. Beaty Hart. 1925. 1*s*.

Deals with history of Northamptonshire but gives information and suggestions useful for other areas. Recommended in the Board's Suggestions to Teachers.

B. SOME USEFUL SERIES AND GENERAL INTRODUCTIONS

County Churches Series. Published by Allen and Unwin.

Borough Histories. A series of short and simple introductions to the history of various London boroughs. Pub. by Sampson, Low & Marshall. 2*s*. each.

Home, G., is editing a good series of books on cathedrals, abbeys and famous churches. Pub. by Dent. 2*s*. 6*d*. each.

Mawer, A. Placenames and History. 38 pp. Liverpool Univ. Press. 1922. 1*s*.

A useful introduction.

Melton, F. E. Local Lore. 224 pp. Nelson. 1926. 2*s*. 6*d*.

A very pleasant and readable little book which would suggest to teachers many ways of making history more real to the children by local illustration.

Methuen's Series of Little Guides contains volumes excellent within their limits. 4*s*. to 6*s*. each.

Royal Commission on Historical Monuments. The reports of this commission, large, exhaustive and beautifully illustrated, are invaluable to the teacher. Herts, Bucks, Essex and Huntingdon are finished. London and Hereford in progress.

Survey of English Place Names. C.U.P. Published by the Place Name Society. 1924. A valuable general introduction to the series of county volumes which are in progress.

Story of English Towns Series. Published by Sheldon Press. 4*s*. each.

An attractive series; contains among others 'Hastings' by L. F. Salzman.

Story Series. Pub. by Pitman. Simple popular little introductions to the history of various towns; could be used by the children. 2*s*. 6*d*. each.

Thompson, A. Hamilton. The Ground Plan of the English Parish Church. 138 pp. **The Historical Growth of the English Parish Church.** 142 pp. C.U.P. 2*s*. 6*d*. each.

Extremely valuable.

Victoria History of the Counties of England. Ed. W. Page and others. Begun 1900. In progress. This monumental series is the best material for the teacher when it covers his particular field.

II. THE HISTORY OF ART AND SCIENCE

A. THE HISTORY OF ART

I. ARCHITECTURE

i. Short and Introductory Books

Barman, C. Architecture. 80 pp. Benn. 1928. *6d.*
A most suggestive, interesting sketch which relates the development of architecture to the development of world history.

Budden, C. W. English Gothic Churches. ix + 145 pp. Batsford. *7s. 6d.*
A useful little handbook intended to act as a guide to the amateur visitor of Gothic churches : gives a list of the finest churches in each county and briefly describes their styles. Illustrated.

Ditchfield, P. H. The Charm of the English Village. 167 pp. Batsford. 1908. *12s.*
A picturesque, attractive book, specially suited for country school teachers ; deals with the architecture of the church, manor and farm houses, cottages, inns, etc. Illustrated.

Ditchfield, P. H. Handbook of Gothic Architecture. 130 pp. Dent. 1904. Temple Primers. *1s. 9d.*
Very useful to teachers—e.g., gives list of main architectural terms of the period with illustrative sketches.

Lethaby, W. R. Architecture. v + 256 pp. Home Univ. Library. *2s. 6d.*
A fascinating and enlightening introduction : deals with ancient as well as modern architecture : specially valuable to teachers of world history.

Quennell, M. and **C. H. B. A History of Everyday Things in England, 1066–1799.** 2 Vols. Batsford. 1918–9. *8s. 6d.* each.
Supplies picturesque illustrations.

Thompson, A. H. The Historical Growth of the English Parish Church. xi + 142 pp. C.U.P. 1911. *2s. 6d.*
An excellent guide ; invaluable to the school that can centre ecclesiastical history round its own parish church. Illustrated.

Thompson, A. H. The Cathedral Churches of England. xvi + 235 pp. Sheldon Press. 1925. *8s. 6d.*
Excellent ; beautiful illustrations.
Dent is publishing a good series of books on cathedrals, abbeys and famous churches edited by G. Home. *2s. 6d.* each.

ii. Fuller and More Advanced Books

N.B.—All the books in this section are illustrated.

Addy, S. O. The Evolution of the English House. xxviii + 223 pp. Sonnenschein. 1905 (2nd ed.).

Bond, F. Gothic Architecture in England. xxii + 782 pp. Batsford. 1905.

Deals with ecclesiastical architecture from 1066 to the dissolution of the monasteries.

Fletcher, Sir Banister. A History of Architecture on the Comparative Method. xxxvi + 929 pp. Batsford. 1924 (8th ed.).

The standard authority for advanced work.

Gardner, S. A Guide to English Gothic Architecture. xii + 228 pp. C.U.P. 1925.

Gotch, J. A. The Growth of the English House from Early Feudal Times to the Close of the Eighteenth Century. viii + 214 pp. Batsford. 1928 (2nd ed.).

An invaluable book for the teacher; traces the development of domestic architecture with a wide range of illustration.

Statham, H. H. A Short Critical History of Architecture. xvi + 563 pp. Batsford. 1927 (2nd ed.).

An excellent manual for general reference.

Thompson, A. Hamilton. Military Architecture in England during the Middle Ages. xxi + 384 pp. O.U.P. 1912.

For books on modern domestic architecture the teacher should consult the book list on Housing in the section on The Teaching of Present Day History.

A fuller bibliography on architecture is drawn up by A. Stratton and published by the Historical Association, 1923. Leaflet No. 54, price 1*s.* 1*d.* to non-members and 7*d.* to members.

2. MUSIC

Creighton, Ursula. Music. xi + 256 pp. Chatto and Windus. 1928. 7*s.* 6*d.*

A charming, suggestive introduction, which describes simply the work of great composers and connects each with the general history of his period. Excellent pictures.

White, R. T. Music and its Story. viii + 184 pp. C.U.P. 1924. 7*s.* 6*d.* and 5*s.*

A most pleasant introduction to a detailed study of the History of Music, well illustrated both pictorially and musically, and possessing practical suggestions invaluable to students and teachers.

See also in biographical section, lives of Bach and Beethoven.

3. PAINTING

Blum, A. S. (trans. by Tatlock, R. R.). **A Short History of Art.** xiv + 291 pp. Batsford. 1926. 21*s.*

A valuable manual for reference, specially useful to the teacher of world history; the author deals with the history of art in prehistoric and modern times, bringing his sketch down to the present day.

Bulley, M. H. A Simple Guide to Pictures and Painting. xvi + 240 pp. Chatto & Windus. 1927. 7*s*. 6*d*.

An introduction to the appreciation of pictures, followed by a simple and interesting outline of the history of painting. Brings the subject up to the Post Impressionism of modern times.

Cartwright, J. The Painters of Florence. xi + 373 pp. Murray. 1910. 6*s*.

Contains twenty-four illustrated studies of individual artists from the age of Giotto to the Renaissance.

Lethaby, W. R. Medieval Art. xvii + 315 pp. Duckworth. 1904. 7*s*. 6*d*.

Deals with architecture and sculpture. Enlightening and scholarly.

Smith, S. C. Kaines. An Outline History of Painting in Europe. xvi + 274 pp. The Medici Society. 1927. 6*s*.

Recommended as the most useful general outline.

Tabor, M. E. The National Gallery for the Young. viii + 115 pp. Methuen. 1924. 5*s*.

An admirable, suggestive introduction. Specially valuable to London teachers who know that their children on school visits find most pictures quite unintelligible without some preliminary help.

Tabor, M. E. The Other London Galleries. x + 116 pp. Methuen. 1926. 5*s*.

See comment above.

Tabor, M. E. Round the British Museum. xiv + 112 pp. Methuen. 1927.

See comment above.

B. THE HISTORY OF MATHEMATICS AND SCIENCE

(The preparation of this section has been undertaken by Dr. Curzon, Lecturer in Mathematics at Goldsmiths' College.)

1. GENERAL AND BIOGRAPHICAL

Brodetsky, S. Sir Isaac Newton. xii + 161 pp. Methuen. 1927. 5*s*.

Excellent. Written with gusto.

Bryant, W. W. Galileo. 64 pp. Sheldon Press. 1918. 1*s*. or 2*s*.

Darwin, Sir Francis. The Life and Letters of Charles Darwin. 3 vols. Murray. 1887.

[An abridged ed. published in 1892.]

Hobson, E. W. John Napier and the Invention of Logarithms. 48 pp. C.U.P. 1914. 2*s*. 6*d*.

Gibson, C. R. Heroes of the Scientific World. 343 pp. Seeley. 1913. 6*s.* net.

Excellent. Should be in every school library. An interesting and detailed account of endeavour from Pythagoras to Darwin.

Gibson, R. J. Harvey. The Master Thinkers. 240 pp. Nelson. 1928. 2*s.* 6*d.*

A series of biographical studies, simply told. Perhaps the best of the books of this type.

Heath, Sir T. L. Archimedes. 58 pp. Sheldon Press. 1920. 1*s.* or 2*s.*

Murray, R. H. Science and Scientists in the Nineteenth Century. xvi + 450 pp. Sheldon Press. 1925. 12*s.* 6*d.*

An excellent vacation book for the teacher. Contains an exhaustive bibliography.

Thompson, S. P. Michael Faraday: his Life and Work. ix + 308 pp. Century Science Series. 1898.

Thorndike, L. A Short History of Civilization. xiv + 619 pp. Crofts. 1926. 21*s.*

2. MATHEMATICS

i. General

All the general histories are based upon 'Vorlesungen über Geschichte der Mathematik', by Moritz Cantor, which is in four large volumes. The latest edition is 1922.

Cajori, F. History of Elementary Mathematics with Hints on Teaching. 304 pp. Macmillan. 1896. 10*s.* 6*d.*

Contains just the matter important for teachers and is attractively written.

Miller, G. A. Historical Introduction to Mathematical Literature. xiii + 302 pp. Macmillan. 1916. 10*s.*

Good for recent advances.

Rouse Ball, W. W. A Short Account of the History of Mathematics. 527 pp. Macmillan. 1908. 12*s.* 6*d.*

Interesting, but less detailed than Smith and not as concerned with teaching as Cajori.

Smith, D. E. History of Mathematics. 2 vols. Ginn. 1923–5. 21*s.* each.

Very good; profusely illustrated, pleasant to read. Better in dealing with personalities than with problems. Likely to appeal to teachers.

ii. Special Aspects

Heiberg, J. L. Mathematics and Physical Science in Classical Antiquity. 110 pp. O.U.P. 1922. 2*s.* 6*d.*

Excellent.

Kaye, G. R. Indian Mathematics. 73 pp. Thatcher, Spink & Co. 1915.

Compact and masterly. Contains a glorious collection of examples.

Rouse Ball, W. W. History of the Study of Mathematics at Cambridge. xvi + 264 pp. C.U.P. 1889.

3. ARITHMETIC

i. SHORT AND INTRODUCTORY BOOKS

Karpinski, L. C. The History of Arithmetic. 200 pp. Rand, McNally & Co. 1925.

An excellent book. Well illustrated. Has good bibliographies at the end of each chapter. Has a very long chapter on textbooks, but compresses the discussion of processes.

Smith, D. E. Number Stories of Long Ago. 150 pp. Ginn. 1919. 2*s.* 6*d.*

Expressly written for children. Shows how numbers reached their present form, and contains simple puzzles. Charming illustrations.

ii. FOR SPECIALISTS

De Morgan, A. Arithmetical Books from the Invention of Printing to the Present Time. London. 1847.

Contains 1,580 names of authors.

Steele, R. R. The Earliest Arithmetics in English. Early English Text Society. xviii + 184 pp. O.U.P. 1922. 15*s.*

Authoritative.

iii. TEXT BOOKS THAT MARK EPOCHS IN THE HISTORY OF ARITHMETIC

The Rhind Mathematical Papyrus, edited by Peet (Thomas Eric) in 1923.

Fibonacci (Leonardo) Pisano (1202). **Liber Abbaci,** ed. by Boncompagni. 1857.

The first European textbook on Arabic methods. Very full. Many examples.

Sacrobosco, 1490. **De arte numerandi liber.** The last flare of monastic arithmetic as based on Roman traditions.

Paccioli (Luca). 1494. **Suma de Arithmetica.**

Determined Arithmetic as a written art in Europe (Venice).

Recorde (Robert). 1543. **The groũd of artes.**

The first and the most lovable of arithmetics in the English language; pervaded by the notion that the boys themselves would read it.

Cocker (Edward). Arithmetic. 1765.
Superseded Recorde. Reduced Arithmetic to rules; written in a high-falutin style. Still exerts its suffocating influence.

4. PHYSICS AND CHEMISTRY

Cajori, F. History of Physics. 322 pp. Macmillan. 1919. 10*s.* 6*d.*
Excellent for teachers.

Hart, I. B. Makers of Science. 320 pp. O.U.P. 1923. 6*s.*
An excellent book for the top class in a central school. Reaches modern times and shows the inspiration behind modern research. Very good bibliography.

Haskins, C. H. Studies in the History of Medieval Science. xiv + 112 pp. Harvard Univ. Press. 1924.
A splendid but difficult book.

Holmyard, E. J. Chemistry to the Time of Dalton. 128 pp. O.U.P. 1925. 2*s.* 6*d.*
Very good, clear and interesting.

Libby, W. Introduction to the History of Science. x + 288 pp. Harrap. 1918. 5*s.*
Can be read with interest by the non-specialist. Physical and biological sides well balanced.

Turner, D. M. Makers of Science: Magnetism and Electricity. xv + 184 pp. O.U.P. 7*s.* 6*d.* 1927.
Lively, well illustrated and modern.

5. BIOLOGY AND MEDICINE

Singer, C. Greek Biology and Medicine. 128 pp. O.U.P. 1922. 2*s.* 6*d.*

Singer, C. Studies in the History and Method of Science. xiv + 304 pp. O.U.P. 1917 (out of print). Second series. xiv + 560 pp. 1921.

12. TEACHING METHODS: TIME CHARTS, MAPS, ETC.

A. BOOKS ON METHOD

Archer, R. L., Owen, L. V. D., Chapman, A. E. The Teaching of History in Elementary Schools. xi + 263 pp. A. & C. Black. 1916. 6*s.*
A practical and useful guide to beginners; Part I deals with general principles of method and Part II with the teaching of particular periods; especially useful in suggesting how European History can be combined with English.

Committee of Seven. The Study of History in Schools. ix + 267 pp. Macmillan. 1906.

A report drawn up by American educationalists. Although it deals mainly with secondary education and is more than twenty years old, its general principles and its suggestions for treating different periods are so valuable that it deserves to be remembered as a classic.

Findlay, J. J. History and its Place in Education. 182 pp. Univ. of London Press. 1923. 3*s*. 6*d*.

General essays discussing the aims of history teaching at each successive stage.

Firth, C. B. The Learning of History in Elementary Schools. viii + 224 pp. Kegan Paul. 1929. 6*s*.

A stimulating discussion of the theory and practice of learning history by children under fourteen. Gives practical suggestions for the encouragement of independent work.

Happold, F. C. The Approach to History. xvi + 102 pp. Christophers. 1928. 3*s*. 6*d*.

A most lively and stimulating sketch of methods of teaching history to children of 12–14 years. Although the school described is a secondary one, much of the material could be used in elementary school conditions, and the book as a whole is most suggestive to teachers.

Johnson, H. The Teaching of History in Elementary Schools. Teachers' Professional Library. xxix + 497 pp. 1915. 7*s*. 6*d*.

Useful for a general view of the subject; gives information as to the history syllabuses and aims of other countries.

Keatinge, M. W. Studies in the Teaching of History. viii + 232 pp. A. & C. Black. 1910. 7*s*. 6*d*.

A book dealing with the use of sources in history teaching in the middle forms of secondary schools. Teachers interested in this subject will find here suggestions which they can adapt to elementary school work.

Madeley, H. M. History as a School for Citizenship. 106 pp. O.U.P. 1920. 4*s*. 6*d*.

A charming, humorous and practical book, which, like Happold's, is fully illustrated from actual experience.

Memorandum on the Teaching of History: issued by the Incorporated Association of Assistant Masters in Secondary Schools. 75 pp. C.U.P. 1925. 2*s*. 6*d*.

An excellent guide to present-day methods; the study of it would be very useful to the teacher who wishes to maintain continuity of teaching between the elementary and secondary schools.

Report of a Conference on the Teaching of History in London Elementary Schools. 61 pp. L.C.C. 1911 (reprinted, 1923).

A valuable report, dealing with existing methods in England and in other countries, with numerous practical recommendations.

Report on the Teaching of History in London Elementary Schools. 22 pp. H.M.S.O. 1927. 2*d.*

An interesting and controversial report, many of whose constructive suggestions are of great value to teachers.

Robinson, J. H. The New History. vi + 266 pp. Macmillan. 1920. 8*s.* 6*d.*

A book of essays for students, especially valuable in stimulating thought as to the aims of history teaching.

Suggestions for Teachers, Handbook of. 112–140 pp. H.M.S.O. 1927. 2*s.*

By far the most useful guide to teachers, at once practical and progressive.

B. SOME AIDS TO HISTORY TEACHING

(*a*) EXERCISE BOOKS FOR CHILDREN

Bishop, M. C., Willard, R. C. and **Robinson, E. K. Practical Map Exercises.** Consists of 7 parts: general history, ancient history, medieval and modern European history, European history before 1714, after 1714, English history and American history. Clear and useful. Ginn. 2*s.* 6*d.* each.

Williams, W. T. and **McGrady, S. H. Practical Exercises in Junior History.** In 4 parts. A new series which contains some stimulating and thorough plans for individual work. Philip. 1929. 10*d.* each.

(*b*) MAPS

Muir, J. Ramsay. Historical Atlas: Medieval and Modern. Sixth edition. Philip. 15*s.* For the teacher's private use.

Historical wall maps are published by Johnston, W. and A. K. (British and European History: 7*s.* 6*d.* each) and by Philip (Wall Atlas of Modern History. Edited by J. Ramsay Muir and G. Philip. 7*s.* 6*d.* each or 47*s.* 6*d.* and 52*s.* 6*d.* the set of eight). For home-made maps (generally most valuable as regards clearness and adaptability to class needs) the teacher will find useful Philips' Mapbuilding Sheets on blackboard paper with red outlines, 3*s.*, 4*s.* 6*d.* and 6*s.* 6*d.* each, and Large Visual Contour Outline Maps on stout cartridge paper, 1*s.* 6*d.* each. All kinds of coloured mounting papers for map and diagram making can be obtained from Kettle's, 9, New Oxford Street, W.C.1.

(*c*) THEATRICALS

The Bankside Costume Book, by M. Stone, pub. by Wells Gardiner Darton & Co., is a very useful little guide to the making of dresses for historical pageants, &c. It gives practical help in cutting out, and is accurate, though of course not comprehensive. 5*s.*

(*d*) TIME CHARTS

There are two useful pamphlets explaining the use of Time Charts: **Time Charts,** by **H. Madeley** (Historical Association Leaflet: 1*s.* 1*d.* to non-members, 7*d.* to members) and **Historical Diagrams and Time Charts,** by **Dr. Robert Jones** (London Teachers' Association publication: 6*d.*). Nelson publishes a very useful series of time chart forms, on which the time line and general headings are printed in colour, while particulars are to be filled in by the children. The set complete with explanatory notes costs 1*s.* 6*d.*

13. SELECTED BIOGRAPHIES

These books have been placed in a separate section under the belief that through its human interest biography makes a stronger appeal to non-specialists than does any other form of history. The advantage to the children, also, of the teacher's reading from time to time a good biography on their period of study is far greater than can be measured by direct influence. The following list, though of course very incomplete, gives some of the best known biographies of some famous characters, as well as a few more popular sketches.

ALEXANDER THE GREAT. Wheeler, B. I. **Alexander the Great.** Putnam's. Heroes of Nations Series. 1900.

ALFRED. Lees, B. A. **Alfred the Great, the truth teller, maker of England.** Putnam's. Heroes of Nations Series. 1915.

—— Plummer, C. **The Life and Times of Alfred the Great.** O.U.P. 1902.

ANSELM. Church, R. W. **Saint Anselm.** Macmillan. 1888.

ARCH. **Arch, Joseph.** His Life by himself. Hutchinson. 1898.

AUGUSTUS. Firth, J. B. **Augustus Caesar and the Organization of the Empire of Rome.** Putnam's. Heroes of Nations Series. 1903.

BACH. Terry, C. S. **Bach. A biography.** O.U.P. 1928.

BAMFORD. Bamford, S. **Passages in the Life of a Radical.** 2 vols. Unwin. 1893.

BAXTER. **Baxter, Richard. Autobiography.** Dent. 1925.

—— Powicke, P. J. **A Life of the Reverend Richard Baxter.** Jonathan Cape. 1925.

BECKET. Hutton, W. H. **Thomas Becket, Archbishop of Canterbury.** C.U.P. 1926.

BEETHOVEN. Rolland, Romain. (Trans. Rothwell, F.) **Life of Beethoven.** Drane. 1907.

BERNARD. Morison, J. Cotter. **The Life and Times of S. Bernard.** Macmillan. 1868.

BISMARCK. Headlam, J. W. **Bismarck and the New German Empire.** Putnam's. Heroes of Nations Series. 1899.

—— Ludwig, E. **Bismarck. The story of a fighter.** Allen & Unwin. 1927.

—— Robertson, C. Grant. **Bismarck.** Constable. 1918.

BOLINGBROKE. Sichel, W. **Bolingbroke and his times.** 2 vols. Nisbet & Co. 1901–2.

BRIGHT. Trevelyan, G. M. **The Life of John Bright.** Constable. 1925 (2nd ed.).

BROUGHAM. Aspinall, A. **Lord Brougham and the Whig Party.** Manchester Univ. Press. 1927.

BRUCE, ROBERT. Maxwell, Sir Herbert. **Robert the Bruce.** Putnam's. Heroes of Nations Series. 1898.

BUNYAN. Hutton, W. H. **John Bunyan.** Hodder & Stoughton. The People's Library. 1928.

BURKE. Morley, J. **Burke : A political study.** Macmillan. 1879.

CABOT. Beazley, C. R. **John and Sebastian Cabot.** Unwin. 1898.

CAESAR. Fowler, W. Warde. **Julius Caesar and the Foundation of the Roman Imperial System.** Putnam's. Heroes of Nations Series. 1892.

CALVIN. Penning, L. (trans.). **Life and Times of Calvin.** Kegan Paul. 1912.

CAMPBELL-BANNERMAN. O'Connor, T. P. **Sir Henry Campbell-Bannerman.** Hodder & Stoughton. 1908.

CANNING. Temperley, H. W. **Life of Canning.** Finch. 1905.

CANUTE. Larson, M. **Canute the Great.** Putnam's. Heroes of Nations Series. 1912.

CAVOUR. Cesaresco, E. M. **Cavour.** Macmillan. 1898.

—— Thayer, W. R. **Life and Times of Cavour.** 2 vols. Constable. 1915.

CAXTON. Blades. **Life and Typography of William Caxton.** Trübner. 1882.

CECIL LORD BURGHLEY. Innes, A. D. *In* **Ten Tudor Statesmen.** Nash. 1906.

CHADWICK. Marston, M. **Sir Edwin Chadwick.** Leonard Parsons. Roadmakers' Series. 1925.

CHAMBERLAIN. Gulley, E. E. **Joseph Chamberlain and English Social Politics.** Columbia Univ. Press. 1926.

CHARLEMAGNE. Davis, H. W. C. **Charlemagne.** Putnam's. Heroes of Nations Series. 1900.

—— Einhard (trans. A. J. Grant). *In* **Early Lives of Charlemagne.** King's Classics. 1905.

—— Hodgkin, T. **Charles the Great.** Macmillan. Foreign Statesmen Series. 1897.

CHARLES II. Airy, O. **Charles II.** Longmans. 1904.

CHARLES V. Armstrong, E. **Charles V.** Macmillan. 1910.

CHARLES THE BOLD. Putnam, R. **Charles the Bold.** Putnam's. Heroes of Nations Series. 1908.

CHATHAM. Green, W. D. **William Pitt, Earl of Chatham.** Putnam's. Heroes of Nations Series. 1890.

CHAUCER. Coulton, G. G. **Chaucer and his England.** Methuen. 1908. 12*s.* 6*d.*

CHURCHILL, RANDOLPH. Churchill, Winston. **Randolph Churchill.** Macmillan. 1907.

CICERO. Strachan-Davidson, J. L. **Cicero and the Fall of the Roman Republic.** Putnam's. Heroes of Nations Series. 1894.

CID. Clarke, H. B. **The Cid Campeador.** Putnam's. Heroes of Nations Series. 1902.

CLIVE. Forrest, Sir G. **The Life of Lord Clive.** Cassell. 1918.

COBBETT. Carlyle, E. I. **William Cobbett. A study of his life as shown in his writings.** Constable. 1904.

—— Chesterton, G. K. **Cobbett.** Hodder & Stoughton. 1925. (Popular.)

—— Cole, G. D. H. **Cobbett.** Collins. 1925.

COBDEN. Morley, J. **The Life of Richard Cobden.** 2 vols. Chapman & Hall. 1881. Abridged edition published by Nelson, 1910.

COLET. Seebohm, F. **Oxford Reformers.** Longmans. 1887. Dent. Everyman's Library. 1914.

COLUMBA. Adamnan. **Life of St. Columba.** (Tr. by J. T. Fowler.) O.U.P. 1895.

COLUMBUS. Irving, W. **Life and Voyages of Christopher Columbus.** Harrap. 1909. (Orig. date 1828.)

COOK. Besant, Sir W. **Captain Cook.** Macmillan. 1890.

CRANMER. Pollard, A. F. **Thomas Cranmer and the English Reformation.** Putnam. 1904.

CROMWELL. Carlyle, T. **Oliver Cromwell's Letters and Speeches.** Dent. Everyman's Library. 3 vols. 1908.

CROMWELL. Firth, C. H. **Oliver Cromwell, and the Rule of the Puritans in England.** Putnam's. Heroes of Nations Series. 1900.

CROMWELL. Morley, J. (Viscount Morley of Blackburn). **Oliver Cromwell.** Macmillan. 1904.

—— Gardiner, S. R. **Cromwell's Place in History.** Longmans. 1897 (3rd Ed.).

DANTON. Madelin, L. **Danton.** Heinemann. 1921.

DISRAELI. Maurois, A. **Disraeli.** Lane. 1927. (Brilliant sketch.)

—— Monypenny, W. F. and Buckle, G. E. **The Life of Benjamin Disraeli, Earl of Beaconsfield.** 6 vols. Murray. 1910–20.

DOMINIC. Bede, Jarrett. **Life of S. Dominic.** Burns, Oates and Washbourne. 1924.

DRAKE. Benson, E. F. **Sir Francis Drake.** John Lane. 1927. (Dramatically told sketch.)

—— Corbett, Sir J. S. **Drake and the Tudor Navy.** 2 vols. Longmans. 1899 (2nd ed.). (The foundation of all later works.) **Sir Francis Drake.** Macmillan. 1890. (Short sketch.)

DUNSTAN. Robinson, J. Armitage. **The Times of Saint Dunstan.** O.U.P. 1923.

DURHAM. Reid, Stuart J. **Life and Letters of the first Earl of Durham.** 2 vols. Longmans. 1906.

EDWARD I. Jenks, E. **Edward Plantagenet, the English Justinian.** Putnam's. Heroes of Nations Series. 1902.

ELIOT. Forster, J. **Life of Sir John Eliot.** 2 vols. 1872. (2nd ed.).

ELIZABETH. Beesley, E. S. **Queen Elizabeth.** Macmillan. 1892.

—— Creighton, M. **The Age of Elizabeth.** Longmans. 1876.

—— Dark, S. **Queen Elizabeth.** Hodder & Stoughton. People's Library. 1926. (Popular.)

—— John, Gwen. **Queen Elizabeth.** The Roadmaker Series. Leonard Parsons. 1924. (Popular.)

—— Strachey, G. Lytton. **Elizabeth and Essex.** Chatto & Windus. 1928.

ELIZABETH FARNESE. Armstrong, E. **Elizabeth Farnese.** Longmans. 1892.

ERASMUS. Froude, J. A. **Life and Letters of Erasmus.** Longmans. 1894.

—— Huizinga, J. **Erasmus.** Scribners. 1924.

—— Smith, P. **Erasmus. A study of his Life, Ideals and Place in History.** Harper. 1923.

C. J. FOX. Hammond, J. L. **Charles James Fox. A political study.** xi + 370 pp. Methuen. 1903.

—— Trevelyan, G. O. **Early History of C. J. Fox.** Longmans. 1908 (new ed.). Nelson. 1911 (cheap ed.).

FRANCIS. Cuthbert, O. S. F. C. **Life of S. Francis of Assisi.** Longmans. 1921.

—— Sabatier, P. **Life of S. Francis of Assisi.** Hodder & Stoughton. 1894.

FREDERICK II. Reddaway, W. **Frederick the Great and the Rise of Prussia.** Putnam's. Heroes of Nations Series. 1904.

FREDERICK WILLIAM THE GREAT ELECTOR. Maurice, C. E. **Life of Frederick William, the Great Elector of Brandenburg.** Allen & Unwin. 1926.

GARIBALDI. Trevelyan, G. M. **Garibaldi and the Defence of the Roman Republic. Garibaldi and the Thousand. Garibaldi and the Union of Italy.** Nelson. 1920 (cheap ed.).

GLADSTONE. Morley, J. **The Life of Gladstone.** 3 vols. Macmillan. 1903. Abridged ed. published by Hodder & Stoughton. 1927.

—— Somervell, D. C. **Disraeli and Gladstone.** Jarrolds. 1925.

GORDON. Strachey, G. Lytton. **Eminent Victorians.** Chatto & Windus. 1918. Issued by Chatto & Windus in Phoenix Library. 1928.

GREGORY. Dudden, F. H. **Gregory the Great ; his place in History and Thought.** 2 vols. Longmans. 1905.

GREY. Trevelyan, G. M. **Lord Grey of the Reform Bill.** Longmans. 1920.

GUSTAVUS ADOLPHUS. Fletcher, C. R. L. **Gustavus Adolphus.** Putnam's. Heroes of Nations Series. 1892.

HADRIAN IV. Mann, H. K. **Nicholas Breakspear (Hadrian IV).** Kegan Paul. 1914.

HALIFAX. Foxcroft, H. C. **The Life and Letters of Sir George Saville, Bart., first Marquis of Halifax.** Longmans. 1898.

HANNIBAL. Morris, W. O'Connor. **Hannibal.** Putnam's. Heroes of Nations Series. 1899.

HARDIE, KEIR. Stewart, W. **J. Keir Hardie.** Cassell. 1921.

HASTINGS, WARREN. Lyall, A. **Warren Hastings.** Macmillan. 1889.

HAWKINS. Williamson, J. A. **Sir John Hawkins : the Time and the Man.** O.U.P. 1927.

HENRY II. Green, Mrs. J. R. **Henry II.** Macmillan. 1903.

—— Salzmann, L. F. **Henry II.** Constable. 1917.

HENRY V. Kingsford, C. L. **Henry V.** Putnam's. Heroes of Nations Series. 1923 (latest issue).

—— Mowat, R. B. **Henry V.** Constable. 1919.

HENRY VII. Gairdner, J. **Henry VII.** Macmillan. Twelve English Statesmen Series. 1902.

HENRY VII. Innes, A. D. *In* **Ten Tudor Statesmen.** Nash. 1906.

HENRY VIII. Pollard, A. F. **Henry VIII.** Longmans. 1905.

—— Innes, A. D. *In* **Ten Tudor Statesmen.** Nash. 1906.

PRINCE HENRY THE NAVIGATOR. Beazley, C. R. **Prince Henry the Navigator.** Putnam's. Heroes of Nations Series. 1904.

HILL, OCTAVIA. Ed. Maurice, C. E. **Life of Octavia Hill as told in her Letters.** Macmillan. 1913.

HOBBES. Stephen, L. **Hobbes.** Macmillan. 1904.

HUGH. Woolley, R. M. **S. Hugh of Lincoln.** Sheldon Press. 1927.

ISABELLA. Plunket, I. L. **Isabel of Castile.** Putnam's Sons. 1915.

JACKSON, STONEWALL. Henderson, G. F. R. **Stonewall Jackson.** 2 vols. Longmans. 1902.

JAMES II. Clarke, J. S. **The Life of King James the Second.** 2 vols. London. 1816.

JAMESON. Colvin, Ian Duncan. **The Life of Jameson.** 2 vols. Arnold. 1922.

JOAN OF ARC. Lang, Andrew. **The Maid of France.** Longmans. 1922.

JOHN. Norgate, Kate. **John Lackland.** Macmillan. 1902.

JOHN OF GAUNT. Smith, Sydney Armitage. **John of Gaunt.** Constable. 1904.

KITCHENER. Arthur, Sir George C. A. **Life of Lord Kitchener.** 3 vols. Macmillan. 1920.

LANFRANC. Macdonald, A. J. **Lanfranc. A Study of his Life, Work, and Writing.** O.U.P. 1926.

LANGTON, STEPHEN. Powicke, F. M. **Stephen Langton.** O.U.P. 1928.

LAUD. Hutton, W. H. **William Laud.** Methuen. 1913 (4th Ed.).

LEE, ROBERT E. Maurice, Sir Frederick B. **Robert E. Lee, the Soldier.** Constable. 1925.

LINCOLN. Charnwood, G. R. B. **Abraham Lincoln.** Hodder & Stoughton. 1916.

LOUIS IX. Perry, F. J. E. **Saint Louis, the most Christian King.** Putnam's. Heroes of Nations Series. 1901.

—— Joinville, Jean de. **S. Louis, King of France.** (1) translated by T. Hutton. London. 1868. Part of Bayard Series. (2) Everyman's Library. 1908.

LOUIS XIV. Hassall, A. **Louis XIV.** Putnam's. Heroes of Nations Series.

LOYOLA. Sedgewick, H. D. **Ignatius Loyola.** Macmillan. 1923.

LUTHER. Lindsay, T. **Luther and the German Reformation.** Clark. 1900.

—— Smith, P. **The Life and Letters of Martin Luther.** Houghton Mifflin Co. 1911.

MACHIAVELLI. Villari, (Pasquale) Nicolo. **Life and Times of Machiavelli.** 2 vols. Fisher Unwin. 1892.

MAGELLAN. Hildebrand, A. S. **Magellan. A general account of the life and times and remarkable adventures of Ferdinand Magellan.** Cape. 1925. (Lively sketch.)

MAHOMET. Margoliouth, D. S. **Mohammed and the Rise of Islam.** Putnam's. Heroes of Nations Series. 1905.

MANIN. Trevelyan, G. H. **Manin and the Venetian Revolution. 1848.** Longmans. 1923.

MANNING. Hutton, A. W. **Life of Cardinal Manning.** Methuen. 1892. 3*s*.

—— Strachey, G. Lytton. **Eminent Victorians.** Chatto & Windus. 1918. Issued by Chatto & Windus in Phoenix Library. 1928.

MARCUS AURELIUS. Renan, J. E. **Marcus Aurelius.** Walter Scott. 1892.

MARIE ANTOINETTE. Belloc, H. **Marie Antoinette.** Methuen. 1923.

MARLBOROUGH. Atkinson, C. T. **Marlborough.** Putnam. 1921.

—— Edwards, H. J. and E. A. **A Short Life of Marlborough.** Bell. 1926.

MARY I. Davey, R. **Mary Tudor.** Roxburghe Press. 1897. Stone, J. M. **Queen Mary I.** Sands & Co. 1901.

MEDICI, COSIMO DE'. Ewart, K. D. **Cosimo de' Medici.** Macmillan. Foreign Statesmen Series. 1899.

MEDICI, LORENZO DE'. Armstrong, E. **Lorenzo de' Medici.** Putnam's. Heroes of Nations Series.

—— Horsburg, E. L. S. **Lorenzo the Magnificent.** Methuen. 1908.

METTERNICH. Sandeford, G. O. C. Methuen. 1911.

MILTON. Pattison, Mark. **Milton.** English Men of Letters Series. 1879.

MIRABEAU. Willert, P. F. **Mirabeau.** Macmillan. Foreign Statesmen Series. 1896.

MONTFORT, SIMON DE. Prothero, Sir George Walter. **Simon de Montford.** London. 1877.

—— Bateman, S. **Simon de Montfort.** Cornish. 1925.

MORE. Hutton, W. H. **Life of More.** Methuen. 1895.

—— Roper, W. **The Life of Sir Thomas More, Knight.** The King's Classics. 1902. (The contemporary account by More's son-in-law.)

NAPOLEON. Fisher, H. A. L. **Napoleon.** Home Univ. Lib. 1912. (Brilliant introductory sketch.)

—— Ludwig, E. Translated. Allen & Unwin. 1927.

—— Rose, J. H. **Life of Napoleon I.** Bell. 1920. (Cheap ed. 10*s*. Best scholarly account.)

NAPOLEON III. Guedalla, P. **The Second Empire.** Constable. 1922.
NELSON. Mahan. **Life of Nelson.** S. Low & Co. 1899.
NEWMAN. Barry, W. **Cardinal Newman.** Hodder & Stoughton. People's Library. 1927. (Latest ed.) A sympathetic survey.
—— Strachey, G. Lytton. **Eminent Victorians.** Chatto & Windus. 1918. (Cheap ed.)
NIGHTINGALE, F. Cook, Sir E. **Life of Florence Nightingale.** Macmillan. 1925.
—— Strachey, G. Lytton. **Eminent Victorians.** Chatto & Windus. 1918. Issued by Chatto & Windus in Phoenix Library. 1928.
OLDKNOW. Unwin, G. **Samuel Oldknow and the Arkwrights.** Manch. Univ. Press. 1924.
OWEN, R. Cole, G. D. H. **Robert Owen.** Benn. 1925.
PAINE. Gould, F. S. **Thomas Paine, 1737-1809.** Leonard Parsons. Roadmakers Series. 1925.
PALMERSTON. Guedalla, P. **Palmerston.** Benn. 1926.
PEEL. Ramsay, A. A. W. **Sir Robert Peel.** Constable. 1928.
PEPYS. Tanner, J. H. **Mr. Pepys.** Bell. 1925.
PERICLES. Abbott, Evelyn. **Pericles and the Golden Age of Athens.** Putnam's. Heroes of Nations Series. 1891.
PETER THE GREAT. Schuyler, Eugene. **Peter the Great.** 2 vols. Sampson Low & Co. 1884.
PHILIP AUGUSTUS. Hutton, W. H. **Philip Augustus.** Macmillan. 1896.
PITT (YOUNGER). Rose, J. H. **A Short Life of William Pitt.** Bell. 1925.
—— Rosebery, Lord. **William Pitt.** Macmillan. Twelve English Statesmen. 1891.
PIUS II. Ady, C. M. **Pius II the Humanist Pope.** Methuen. 1913.
PLACE. Wallas, Graham. **Francis Place.** Allen & Unwin. 1918.
RALEIGH. Hume, M. A. S. **Raleigh.** T. Fisher Unwin. 1926.
—— Innes, A. D. *In* **Ten Tudor Statesmen.** Nash. 1906.
RHODES. McDonald, J. G. **Rhodes : A Life.** P. Allen & Co. 1927.
—— Williams, Basil. **Cecil Rhodes.** Constable. 1921.
RICHARD I. Norgate, K. **Richard the Lion Heart.** Macmillan. 1924.
RICHARD III. Gairdner, J. **History of the Life and Reign of Richard III.** C.U.P. 1898.
RICHELIEU. Federn, K. (trans.). **Richelieu.** Allen & Unwin. 1928.
—— Perkins, J. B. **Richelieu.** Putnam's. Heroes of Nations Series. 1900.

ROBERT OF NORMANDY. David, C. W. **Robert Curthose, Duke of Normandy.** O.U.P. 1920.
ROBESPIERRE. Belloc, J. H. P. **Robespierre.** Nisbet. 1927.
RODNEY. Hannay, D. **Rodney.** Macmillan. English Men of Action Series. 1891.
ROUSSEAU. Morley, John. **Rousseau.** 2 vols. Macmillan & Co. 1886.
RUPERT. Scott, Eva. **Rupert, Prince Palatine.** Constable. 1899.
SALADIN. Poole, S. L. **Saladin and the Fall or Jerusalem.** Putnam's. Heroes of Nations Series. 1906.
SALISBURY. Lady Gwendoline Cecil. **Life of Robert Marquis of Salisbury.** 2 vols. Hodder & Stoughton. 1921.
SAVONAROLA. Villari, P. **Savonarola and his Times.** Fisher Unwin. 1888.
SHAFTESBURY (THE FIRST LORD). Christie, W. D. **A Life of Anthony Ashley Cooper, First Earl of Shaftesbury.** London. 1871.
SHAFTESBURY (THE SEVENTH EARL). Hammond, J. and B. **Lord Shaftesbury.** Constable. 1923.
SHAKESPEARE. Lee, Sir Sidney. **A Life of William Shakespeare.** (4th Edition: revised version.) Murray. 1925.
SOMERSET. Pollard, A. F. **England under Protector Somerset. An essay.** Kegan Paul & Co. 1900.
—— Innes, A. D. *In* **Ten Tudor Statesmen.** Nash. 1906.
STRAFFORD. Traill, H. D. **Strafford.** Macmillan. English Men of Action. 1889.
THEODORIC. Hodgkin, T. **Theodoric the Goth.** Putnam's. Heroes of Nations Series. 1906.
VANE. Hearnshaw, F. J. C. **The Life of Sir Harry Vane.** Congregational Union of England and Wales. 1910.
VICTORIA. Strachey, G. Lytton. **Life of Queen Victoria.** Chatto & Windus. 1928. (Cheap ed.)
VOLTAIRE. Morley, J. **Voltaire.** Macmillan & Co. 1886.
WALPOLE, HORACE. Stuart, D. M. **Horace Walpole.** Macmillan. 1927.
WALPOLE, ROBERT. Morley, J. **Sir Robert Walpole.** Macmillan. Twelve English Statesmen Series. 1902.
WALSINGHAM. Innes, A. D. *In* **Ten Tudor Statesmen.** Nash. 1906.
WARWICK. Oman, Sir C. W. C. **Warwick the Kingmaker.** Macmillan. English Men of Action. 1889.
WELLINGTON. Fortescue, J. W. **Wellington.** Williams & Norgate. 1925.
WESLEY. Hutton, W. H. **John Wesley.** Macmillan. 1927.
WILBERFORCE. Coupland, R. **Wilberforce. A narrative.** O.U.P. 1924.
WILHELM II. Ludwig, E. **Wilhelm II.** Putnam's. 1926.

WILLIAM I. Stenton, F. M. **William the Conqueror.** Putnam's. Heroes of Nations Series. 1908.

WILLIAM III. Traill, H. D. **William III.** Macmillan. English Statesmen. 1902.

WILLIAM THE SILENT. Putnam, R. **William the Silent, the Founder of the Dutch Republic.** Putnam's. Heroes of Nations Series.

WOLSEY. Innes, A. D. *In* **Ten Tudor Statesmen.** Nash. 1906.

—— Creighton, M. **Wolsey.** Macmillan. Twelve English Statesmen Series.

—— Cavendish, George. **Life of Wolsey.** Edited with notes by Mary Tout. Macmillan. 1908.

WOLFE. Parkman, F. **Montcalm and Wolfe.** 6th edition, Macmillan. 1885.

—— Bradley, A. G. **Life of Wolfe.** Macmillan. English Men of Action. 1889.

WYCLIF. Workman, Herbert Brook. **John Wyclif. A study of the English Medieval Church.** O.U.P. 1926.

—— Poole, R. Lane. **Wycliffe and Movements of Reform.** Longmans. Epochs of Church History. 1889.

V

SOME SUGGESTED SOURCES FOR THE PREPARATION OF HISTORY STORIES BY THE TEACHER

THIS is a section for enthusiasts. The teacher who is preparing a story in a hurry will find in the class library section suggestions for books of 'ready made' stories, many of them excellent of their kind, which will supply his needs. But nobody will deny that there is a very different flavour about a story which the narrator has arranged for himself; and there are many teachers who possess the energy, skill, and understanding of children's powers which are needed for the making of such an arrangement, but do not possess the specialized knowledge which will enable them to find material for it. This section is intended for them; and it is hoped that the material suggested here will also be of use to students in training colleges who are learning under the guidance of their lecturers to prepare stories for themselves.

It is clearly much easier, as well as much better, to prepare stories for young children from a big book. Only a book on the grand scale will give the minute and vivid detail that makes the subject live in a child's mind. The stories given here are taken whenever possible from a translated contemporary source; where this is impossible or unsuitable, they are generally taken from the great secondary authorities who tell their stories in a leisurely and graphic style. In either case, the matter suggested here gives only the raw material of the child's story; it is the teacher's task to decide what parts of it should be read or told. Hardly one of the references, particularly in the later sections, is suited for telling as it stands. But the story prepared from it would have a glow and reality which the best second-hand story in the world could never possess: the teacher would tell better all his life the story which he has once thoroughly prepared from a good source. In some cases the contributors have sketched out the broad lines of a possible arrangement. The main consideration throughout has been to find material that lent itself to dramatic and vivid treatment, and as the stories will generally be told to young children an occasional legendary or traditional story has not been excluded, even though the more scientific history of a later stage must abandon it.

It should be carefully noted that this list is not a syllabus; it is simply a collection of famous historical episodes suited for telling to young children, and chosen for their romantic value and compactness as well as for their historical significance.

I. STORIES OF GREECE AND ROME

[This section has been edited by S. Ridout, M.A., Lecturer in History at Goldsmiths' College.]

Recommended Translations to which reference is made in the list of stories. Where an alternative is given, the reference applies to the first work.

Lang, A., Leaf W. and **Myers, E., The Iliad** (translated). Macmillan. 4*s*. 6*d*.

Butcher, S. H. and **Lang, A., The Odyssey** (translated). Macmillan. 4*s*. 6*d*. Or O.U.P.

Macaulay, G. C. Herodotus: Histories (translated). Macmillan. 1904. 15*s*. Or Dent. Everyman's Library. 2 vols. 2*s*. each.

Jowett, B. Thucydides (translated). 2 vols. O.U.P. 18*s*.

Stewart, A. and **Long, G. Plutarch's Lives** (translated). Bell. 4 vols. 2*s*. each. Or Dent. Everyman's Library. 3 vols. 2*s*. each.

Shuckburgh, E. S. The Histories of Polybius (translated). Macmillan. 24*s*.

Foster, B. O. Livy (translated). Heinemann. Or by W. M. Roberts. Dent. Everyman's Library. 6 vols. 2*s*. each.

Holmes, Rice. Caesar's Gallic War (translated). Macmillan. 5*s*. 6*d*. Or by E. P. Long. O.U.P. 5*s*.

Ramsay, G. G. Tacitus. Annals (translated). Murray. 2 vols. 18*s*. each. Or in Dent. Everyman's Library. 2*s*.

Fyfe, W. F. Tacitus. Histories (translated). O.U.P. 2 vols. 5*s*. each, or 8*s*. 6*d*. together. Or by Ramsay, G.C. Murray. 18*s*.

Fyfe, W. H. Tacitus. Agricola and Germania (translated). O.U.P. 5*s*.

1. STORIES FROM HOMER

i. Iliad

The quarrel. Bk. 1, p. 7.
The duel of Paris and Menelaus. Bk. 3, p. 59.
The story of Diomed. Bk. 5, p. 52; also Bks. 6 and 10 (*passim*).
Hector and Andromache. Bk. 6, p. 123.
Hector and Ajax. Bk. 7, p. 134 *seq*.
The battle of the ships. Bk. 8.
The embassy to Achilles. Bk. 9, p. 166.
Death of Patroclus. Bk. 16.
The grief of Achilles. Bk. 18, p. 366 *seq*.
The fight between Hector and Achilles. Bk. 22, p. 434 *seq*.
The funeral games. Bk. 23.
The ransom of Hector's body by Priam. Bk. 24, p. 492.

ii. Odyssey

Ulysses and his raft. Bk. 5, p. 83.
Nausicaa. Bk. 6, p. 92.
The minstrel Demodocus. Bk. 8, p. 130.
The Lotus-eaters. Bk. 9, p. 135.
The Cyclops Polyphemus. *ib.*, p. 137.
Aeolus and the winds. Bk. 10, p. 153.
Circe. *ib.*, p. 157.
The trial of the bow. Bk. 21, p. 345.
Ulysses and the ghosts. Bk. 11, p. 172.
The Sirens. Bk. 12, p. 193.
Scylla and Charybdis. *ib.*, p. 193.
Ulysses and his dog. Bk. 17, p. 284.
The slaying of the suitors. Bk. 22, p. 359.

N.B.—As an alternative, stories from the Odyssey and Iliad can be read in A. J. Church (Seeley & Co., London, 1902).

2. STORIES FROM HERODOTUS

Vol. I

The story of Helen, pp. 2, 3.
How the Lydian kings made war, pp. 8 and 9.
The story of King Croesus, pp. 11–16.
Croesus and the oracle, pp. 21–24.
How Pisistratus became ruler of Athens, pp. 26–30.

The fall of Croesus, pp. 36–45.
How Cyrus became king of the Persians, pp. 54–67.
The taking of Babylon, pp. 93–4.
The death of Cyrus, pp. 99–108.
The story of Cheops, pp. 173–5.
The building of the Pyramids, p. 174.
How Darius conquered Babylon, pp. 281–5.
Darius and the Scythians, pp. 324–30 and 340–5.

Vol. II

The message of Histiaeus, pp. 12–15.
The revolt of Ionia, pp. 49–51, 55–7.
How Miltiades became king of the Chersonese, pp. 74–5.
The first expedition to conquer Athens, pp. 100–5.
The battle of Marathon, pp. 104–10.
Miltiades and the Naval War, pp. 116–9.
The dreams of Xerxes, pp. 134–6.
How Xerxes surveyed his army, pp. 148–9.
The crossing of the Hellespont, pp. 152–3.
The wooden walls of Athens, pp. 180–2.
Leonidas at Thermopylae, pp. 213 *seq.*
The battle of Salamis, pp. 259–69.
The battle of Plataea, pp. 320–30.
How the Greeks won Mycale, pp. 314–28.

3. STORIES FROM THUCYDIDES

Corcyra and Corinth. Bk. 1, pp. 17–39.
Athens and Sparta. *ib.*, pp. 45–61.
Cylon and the curse. *ib.*, pp. 83–5.
Pausanias. *ib.*, pp. 86–91.
The speech of Pericles. *ib.*, pp. 94–101.
The Thebans surprise Plataea. Bk. 2, pp. 102–7.
The Funeral Speech of Pericles. *ib.*, pp. 125–35.
The plague at Athens. *ib.*, pp. 135–40.
Siege of Plataea. *ib.*, pp. 157–60. Bk. 3, pp. 196–9, 220–33.
Mytilene. *ib.*, pp. 185–201, and 205–18.
Pylos. Bk. 4, pp. 3–31.
Brasidas in Thrace. *ib.*, pp. 52–67.
Battle of Delium. *ib.*, pp. 57–76, 92. Bk. 5, pp. 102–11.
Mantinea. *ib.*, pp. 152–60.
Sicilian expedition and mutilation of the Hermae. Bk. 6, pp. 178–204.
Athenians at Syracuse. *ib.*, pp. 228–60.
Sea fights in the great harbour. Bk. 7, pp. 287–93, 310–20.
Alcibiades at Athens. *ib.*, pp. 365 *seq.*

4. STORIES FROM PLUTARCH

i. *Stories*

Theseus and Ariadne. Vol. 1, pp. 12–15.
Theseus and the union of Attica, pp. 17–19.
Romulus and Remus, pp. 32–7.
The foundation of Rome, pp. 37–43.
The story of Tarpeia, pp. 46–7.
How Lycurgus trained the Spartans, pp. 68–80.
Numa, King of Rome, pp. 103–9.
Solon and Croesus, pp. 140–56.
The story of Horatius, pp. 174–5.
How the sacred geese saved Rome, p. 235.
How Pisistratus governed Athens, p. 257–70.
Fabius and Hannibal, pp. 290–311.
Coriolanus and Rome, p. 387.
Battle of Leuctra. Vol. 2, pp. 15–21.
Aristides the Just and Themistocles, pp. 68–77.
A Pyrrhic Victory, pp. 193–209.
How Pompey destroyed the Pirates. Vol. 3, pp. 221–5.
How Caesar crossed the Rubicon, pp. 416–23.
The death of Caesar, pp. 441–64.
Cleomenes and Macedonia. Vol. 4, pp. 37–42.
The story of Antony, pp. 264–351.
Brutus, pp. 414–53.
Artaxerxes, pp. 475–84.

ii. *Biographies.* (*a*) *Greek*

Vol. 1. Theseus, p. 1. Lycurgus, p. 67. Solon, p. 130. Themistocles, p. 185. Pericles, p. 252. Alcibiades, p. 318. Timoleon, p. 395.
Vol. 2. Pelopidas, p. 1. Aristides, p. 67. Philopoemen, p. 134. Pyrrhus, p. 180. Lysander, p. 285. Cimon, p. 391.
Vol. 3. Nicias, p. 1. Agesilaus, p. 152. Alexander, p. 300.
Vol. 4. Agis, p. 1. Cleomenes, p. 19. Demosthenes, p. 119. Demetrius, p. 215. Dion, p. 352. Artaxerxes, p. 458. Aratus, p. 485.

(*b*) *Roman*

Vol. 1. Romulus, p. 30. Numa, p. 99. Fabius Maximus. Coriolanus, p. 357.
Vol. 2. Marius, p. 221. Sulla, p. 317. Lucullus, p. 414.
Vol. 3. Crassus, p. 36. Pompey, p. 195. Julius Caesar, p. 379. Cato, p. 500.

Vol. 4. Tiberius Gracchus, p. 53. Caius Gracchus, p. 90. Cicero, p. 146. Antonius, p. 263. Brutus, p. 398. Galba, p. 530. Otho, p. 556.

5. STORIES FROM POLYBIUS

Book I. How the Romans built ships, pp. 21–6.
Story of Regulus, pp. 35–40.
The mercenaries of Sicily, pp. 72–97.
Book II. Queen Teuta, pp. 102–10.
Achaeans and Aetolians, pp. 134–62.
Book III. Hannibal's oath, pp. 175–81.
His preparations and march, pp. 194–216.
Battles of Ticinus and Trebia, pp. 224, 227–34.
Battle of Trasimene, pp. 240–4.
Fabius Cunctator and Hannibal, pp. 246–52.
Fabius and Minucius, pp. 258–62.
Battle of Cannae, pp. 266–73.
Book IV. The story of Aratus, pp. 283–312, 332–57.
Book V. Battle of Raphia, pp. 432–6.
Book VIII. Hannibal at Tarentum, pp. 550–60.
Book XI. Siege of Capua. Fragment.
Scipio and the mutiny. *ibid*, pp. 70–4.
Book XIX. Syphax and Masannasa, pp. 124–33.
Battle of Zama, pp. 140–50.
The Phalanx at Cynoscephale, pp. 220–30.

6. STORIES FROM LIVY

Book I. Hercules and Cacus, p. 27 *seq.*
The Sabine women, pp. 33–9, 47–9.
Horatii and Curiatii, pp. 23–6, 76–95.
Tullia and Servius Tullius, pp. 46–8, 159–71.
Brutus and the Tarquins, pp. 59–60, 205–9.
Book II. Horatius and the Bridge, pp. 8–11, 245–54.
Mucius the left-hander, pp. 12–13, 255–61.
The story of Cloelia, pp. 13, 261–3.
The Sacred Mount, pp. 23 *seq.* and 289 *seq.*
Coriolanus, pp. 34–40, 331–51.
Book III. Cincinnatus, pp. 26–9, 89–101.
Virginia, pp. 43–44, 143–71.
Book IV. Spurius Maelius, pp. 13–16, 299–311.
Book V. Rome and Veii, pp. 15–21, 53–77.
The Gauls capture Rome, pp. 35–43, 121–47.
The geese in the Capitol, pp. 47–8, 157–65.
Book VI. Marcus Manlius, pp. 15–20, 245–269.
Book VII. Titus Manlius, pp. 385–9.

Book VIII. Manlius and his son, pp. 385–9.
Book IX. Caudinae Fauces, pp. 1–7, 163–89.
Story of Pyrrhus, Bks. XII, XIII, XIV (*passim*).
Book XVIII. Regulus in Africa.

7. SUPPLEMENT ON ROMAN BRITAIN

Caesar's First Expedition, 55 B.C. Gallic War, Bk. 4, pp. 20–36.
ib. Second Expedition, 54 B.C. Bk. 5, pp. 8–23.
The story of Caractacus. Tac. Ann. XII, pp. 31–40.
The story of Boudicca. Tac. Ann. XIV, pp. 29–39.

N.B.—The above and many other extracts can be read in **England before the Norman Conquest,** by **R. W. Chambers** (with a foreword by Dr. Cary). Longmans, Green & Co., 1926. 10*s.* 6*d.* 314 pages.

II. STORIES FROM MEDIEVAL HISTORY

A. A.D. 410–1066

I. ENGLISH STORIES

1. Stories of the Barbarian Settlement and Conversion in England

The Story of S. Patrick. Bury, J. B. The Life of S. Patrick. (Macmillan. 1905). His youth, pp. 16–32: his mission, p. 42: comes to Ireland, pp. 80–92: legends, pp. 104–13: his death, pp. 206–11.

The Story of the coming of the Saxons. There is no one good source. The romantic legendary accounts (including stories of Hengist, Vortigern and Arthur) are given in **Nennius' Chronicle** and **Geoffrey of Monmouth's Historia Britonum.** Evidence of the Saxon ravages is given in **Gildas,** pp. 307–13. All these are contained in **Giles, J. A., Old English Chronicles.** (Bell. 1910.) Their accuracy is discussed and the true story sifted out in **Oman, Sir Charles. England before the Norman Conquest.** (Methuen. 1910.) Chapter XI. The stories of Arthur as told at a later date will be found in **Malory's Morte d'Arthur** (Dent. Everyman's Library. Nos. 45, 46).

Story of S. Columba. Adamnan. Life of S. Columba (trans. by J. T. Fowler. O.U.P. 1895). His birth and manner of life (pp. 2–4); a vision of his boyhood (p. 111); the story of the crane, an example of his prophecies (p. 48); the miracle of the apples (p. 57); the cornfield (p. 58); the unclosing of the church (p. 87); the vision of the swift angel (p. 122); death (pp. 129–40).

How Gregory I came to desire the conversion of England. Bede. Ecclesiastical History. (Everyman's Library. Dent.) Book II, chap. I (pp. 59–65).

A story which has been rather over-done: puns are out of fashion.

How S. Augustine converted Kent. Bede. Ecclesiastical History (as above). Book I, chaps. XXIII–XXVII (pp. 32–7), and Book II, chaps. II and III (pp. 65–9).

How Paulinus converted Northumbria. Bede. Ecclesiastical History (as above). Book II, chaps. XII (pp. 87–90); IX (pp. 79–81); XIII, XIV (pp. 90–4); XVI (pp. 95–6).

A most beautiful story, too often omitted.

The Story of Aidan and Oswald. Bede. Ecclesiastical History (as above). Book III, chaps. I, II (pp. 103–6); V, VI (pp. 110–12); IX (p. 117).

Useful as bringing in Celtic monasticism.

The Story of the Council at Whitby and of Archbishop Theodore. Bede. Ecclesiastical History (as above). Book III, chap. XXV (pp. 146–52). Book IV, chap. II (p. 164).

Shows the choice between Roman and Celtic church.

Stories of Wilfrid. Eddius Stephanus. The Life of Bishop Wilfrid (trans. by B. Colgrave. C.U.P. 1927).

Story of the Abbess Hilda and of Caedmon. Bede. Ecclesiastical History (as above). Book III, chaps. XXIII, XXIV (pp. 201–8).

Stories of S. Cuthbert. Bede. The Life and Miracles of St. Cuthbert. (Everyman's Library (bound up with the Ecclesiastical History). Dent. 1910.)

These stories are included for their interest and beauty, but they do not play as great a part in English History as the earlier stories.

2. Stories from the Sagas

I. Stories of Grettir the Strong. (Everyman's Library. Dent.)

Adventures of Onund Tree-foot. Wooden-leg. Chaps. I–XI, pp. 1–19.

Battle of the Stranded Whale. Chap. XII, pp. 21–4.

Childhood of Grettir. Chaps. XIV–XV, pp. 26–33.

Journey to the Althing. Grettir is Outlawed. Chap. XVI, pp. 33–6.

His Adventures in Exile.

(1) Storm and Shipwreck. Chap. XVII, pp. 37–41.

(2) Fight with a Treasure Ghost. Chap. XVIII, pp. 42–5.

(3) A Fight with Berserks. Chaps. XIX–XX, pp. 46–57.
(4) Grettir's Adventure with a Bear. Chap. XXI, pp. 57–61.

Grettir returns to Iceland. A Wrestling Match. Chap. XXVIII, pp. 75–8.

A Horse Fight. Chap. XXIX, p. 78.

Grettir's Adventure with Glam's Ghost. Chaps. XXXII–XXXV, pp. 86–100.

Grettir in Norway.
(1) A Swimming Feat. Chap. XXXVIII, pp. 104–7.
(2) Adventure with a Berserk. Chap. XL, pp. 110–12.

Grettir Outlawed the Second Time. Chap. XLVI, pp. 121–2.
(1) Adventure with Gisli. Chap. LIX, pp. 155–60.
(2) Another Adventure with an Ogress and a Ghost, and a Giant under a Waterfall. Chaps. LXIV–LXVII, pp. 170–77.
(3) Witchcraft Practised against Grettir, bringing about his Death. Chaps. LXXVIII–LXXXII, pp. 199–214.

II. **ASGARD AND THE NORSE HEROES.** (Everyman's Library. Dent.)

Part I

Settlement of Iceland, pp. 1–9 (*v.* Landnámabók in Origines Islendicae).

Tales of the Norse Gods, Odin, Frigga, Thor, Balder, Tyr, Loki, etc., pp. 10–128 (*v.* Snorra Edda (= Younger or Prose Edda).)

The Adventures of King Gylfi in Search of Knowledge. The Enchanted Palace of High, Even High and Third, pp. 15–19.

The Creation of the World and of Man, pp. 19–26.

Odin Seeks Knowledge—giving his right eye for it, pp. 27–36.

Frey and Gerd, pp. 37–44.

Freyja and the Necklace of the Dwarfs, pp. 45–52.

Bragi the Poet and the Spirit of Youth, pp. 53–8.

Thiassi the Storm Giant, pp. 59–68.

The Wedding of Skadi, Daughter of Thiassi, pp. 69–72.

Adventures of Thor, pp. 73–100.

Balder's Death. CXII, pp. 101–9.

Lament for Balder. CXIII, pp. 110–15.

Loki and his Children. CXIV–XV, pp. 116–27.

The Twilight of the Gods. CXVI, pp. 128–33.

Part II

Sigurd the Volsung. Chaps. I–XII, pp. 137–212.

Weland the Smith, pp. 213–28.

Ragnar Lodbrog. Chaps. I–V, pp. 229–62.

III. Beowulf. *In* Anglo-Saxon Poetry: Selected and edited by Professor R. K. Gordon. (Everyman's Library. Dent.)

Part I. 1st Adventure—The Fight with Grendel, p. 4.
The Building of Heorot, p. 5.
The Coming of Grendel, pp. 5–7.
Beowulf arrives from Sweden, p. 8.
Challenged by the Coastguard—Received by Hrothgar. Unferth's Taunt and Beowulf's Reply, pp. 8–17.
The Fight with Grendel, pp. 17–21.
The Rejoicing after the Victory—Minstrel Tales, &c., pp. 21–30.

Part II. 2nd Adventure. The Fight with Grendel's Mother, pp. 30–8. Beowulf is rewarded, pp. 38–43.

Part III. 3rd Adventure. Beowulf and the Dragon, pp. 43–70.
Beowulf's Home Coming, pp. 43–45.
Beowulf's Account, pp. 45–50.
The Dragon's Hoard, pp. 50–51.
The Hoard is Raided and the Dragon's Revenge, pp. 51–52.
Beowulf's Last Fight, pp. 52–70. (Fight, Death, Funeral.)

3. Stories of the Age of the Danish Invasions

The Story of Alfred's childhood. Asser's Life of Alfred (King's Classics edition). His visit to Rome, pp. 6, 7; his early learning, pp. 17–20.

The Story of Alfred at Athelney. Asser's Life of Alfred (King's Classics). Alfred at Athelney, p. 37: the burning of the cakes (a later interpolation), p. 38; the Danes and their Raven banner, p. 41; Alfred comes out of hiding and defeats the Danes, pp. 41–3.

The Story of Alfred's wisdom and government. Asser's Life of Alfred (King's Classics). His virtues, p. 54; his learning, pp. 56 and onwards, 69–72; his government and inventions, pp. 82–91.

The Story of the battle of Brunanburh. Anglo-Saxon Poetry. (Everyman's Library. Dent.) pp. 359–60. See Tennyson's versified translation of the chronicle account.

The Story of S. Dunstan. Can be found in J. Armitage Robinson's The Times of Saint Dunstan (O.U.P. 1923). It is very well retold in N. Niemeyer, Stories from History: Patrick to Dunstan. (Dent.)

The Battle of Maldon. Anglo-Saxon Poetry. (Everyman's Library. Dent.) pp. 361–7. Also in England before the Norman Conquest. (Intermediate Source Book. Longman. 1926.)

The Story of S. Brice's Day. Du Chaillu, P. B. The Viking Age. (Murray. 1889.) Vol. II, pp. 481–3.

The Story of Edmund Ironside's fight with Cnut. Freeman, E. A. Norman Conquest. (O.U.P. 3rd edition.) Vol. I, pp. 380–400.

This is an old book, out of date in places, and should not be used for serious study: but its picturesque detail makes it a treasure house for the story-teller.

The Story of Cnut. Du Chaillu, P. B. The Viking Age. (Murray. 1889.) Vol. II, chapter XXXI.

4. Stories of the Time of Edward the Confessor and the Norman Conquest

The Story of Earl Godwin. Ramsay, Sir J. H. The Foundations of England (Sonnenschein. 1898). Vol. I. His greatness, pp. 439–42; the quarrel and outlawry, pp. 452–5; the return and death of Godwin, pp. 462–9.

The Story of Harold Hardrada and the battle of Stamford Bridge. Freeman, E. A. Norman Conquest. (O.U.P.) His adventurous youth. Vol. II (3rd edition), pp. 75–80. His invasion of England. Vol. III, pp. 339–74; *or* Du Chaillu, P. B. The Viking Age. (Murray. 1889.) Vol. II, chapter XXXII.

The Story of Hastings. The most picturesque account is found in Freeman's Norman Conquest, chapter XV. But Freeman's account of the English tactics has been much revised by later historians. The up-to-date facts are given briefly in Haskins, C. H. The Normans in European History (Constable), pp. 76–80.

The Story of William's coronation. Freeman, E. A. Norman Conquest. (O.U.P. 3rd ed.) Vol. III, pp. 553–62.

II. EUROPEAN STORIES

1. Stories of the Barbarian Invasions, Settlements and Conversion

The Story of Alaric and the Sack of Rome, 410. Hodgkin, T. Italy and her Invaders. (O.U.P. 1892.) Vol. I. His birth and election, pp. 651–4; he enters Italy, p. 709; the Gothic council and the battle of Pollentia, pp. 717–23; the first siege, pp. 792–9; the southward march and death of Alaric, pp. 806–9.

Important as showing that the barbarian invasions affect the whole Roman Empire, not only Britain.

The Story of Attila and the Huns. Hodgkin, T. Italy and her Invaders. (O.U.P. 1892.) Vol. II, Attila's appearance and character, pp. 41–2; he invades Gaul, p. 106; is defeated at Troyes, pp. 124–36; he enters Italy, pp. 146–7; the embassy of Pope Leo I, pp. 155–61.

The Story of the Conversion of the Franks. Gregory of Tours (trans.). History of the Franks. (O.U.P. 1927.)

Vol. II. Accession of Clovis, his wars and character, pp. 65–6; story of his conversion, pp. 66–70.

A very good tale: brings out the character of the barbarians and the point of view of the Church: told by a Churchman.

The Story of S. Benedict. Dudden, F. H. Gregory the Great. (Longmans. 1905.) His life. Vol. II, pp. 162–9. His rule. Vol. I, pp. 109–15.

[The rule has been translated by Gasquet in the King's Classics Series.]

The Story of Mahomet. Gibbon, E. The Decline and Fall of the Roman Empire. (Dent. Everyman's Library.) Vol. V, Chap. 50, especially pp. 230–72.

2. Stories of the Empire of Charles the Great

The Story of a Frankish peasant in Charlemagne's time. Power, E. Medieval People (Methuen. 1925), ch. I.

The Story of Charles the Great and how he became Emperor. Eginhard (trans.). Life of Charlemagne. (Chatto & Windus. 1922.) His appearance and character, pp. 37–43. Bryce, Viscount. The Holy Roman Empire. (Macmillan. 1913.) His coronation, pp. 53–64. Bryce gives three contemporary accounts of the coronation and an invaluable discussion of its significance.

3. Stories of the Viking Invasions in Europe and the Origins of the French Monarchy

The Story of the Great Siege of Paris by the Vikings. Keary, C. F. The Vikings in Western Christendom. (Fisher Unwin. 1891.) pp. 420–33.

Useful as showing the widespread nature of the Viking raids and introducing the city of Paris.

The Story of Hugh Capet and how he became King of France. Not a very good story, but a useful milestone in French history: shows how the dynasty of Charles the Great with its imperial traditions gives place to a new monarchy with a national future. Funck-Brentano, Fr. The Middle Ages. (Heinemann. 1922.) pp. 37–47.

B. A.D. 1066–1272

I. ENGLISH STORIES

1. Stories of the Age of the Norman Kings

Legends of Hereward the Wake. Kingsley, C.: Hereward the Wake. N.B.—A discussion as to the truth of these legends is given in Freeman's Norman Conquest, vol. III, p. 804.

How William I had to fight for his crown. Ramsay, Sir J. H., The Foundation of England. (Sonnenschein. 1898.) Vol. II, pp. 155–62. For William's appearance and character, see p. 223.

The Story of the Rising of the Earls. Ramsay, Sir J. H. The Foundations of England. (Sonnenschein. 1898). Vol. II, pp. 102–7.

The Story of Domesday Book. Ballard, A. The Domesday Inquest. (Antiquary's Books : Methuen. 1906.) What the chronicle tells us (quoted), p. 7; purpose of the inquest, pp. 8–11; how it was compiled and what questions were asked, pp. 11–17.

How Anselm became Archbishop of Canterbury. Church, R. W. Saint Anselm (Macmillan. 1890), pp. 206–26.

How Anselm quarrelled with William II. Church, R. W. Saint Anselm (Macmillan. 1890), pp. 230–66.

How Anselm quarrelled with Henry I. Church, R. W. Saint Anselm (Macmillan. 1890). The quarrel, pp. 293–321; the reconciliation, pp. 333–5. [Much of this is, of course, too difficult for children: but the account will give the teacher enough grasp of the real issues to simplify them for children, and gives many personal details and incidents of the kind that children like.]

The Story of Matilda. Ramsay, Sir J. H. The Foundations of England (Sonnenschein. 1898). Vol. II. The vow taken to her, pp. 307, 314; Stephen made king in her place, p. 348; his bad government, pp. 374–5; his defeat at Lincoln, pp. 397–400; Matilda's attempt to rule, pp. 401–31.

2. Stories of Henry II

The Death of Thomas Becket. Grim, E. A translation given in S. Thomas of Canterbury (English History by contemporary writers: Nutt: 1899), pp. 234–45. Quoted in Keatinge and Frazer's Documents of British History. (Black. 1913.)

The Rebellion of Henry II's sons and his death. Stubbs, W. Historical Introductions to the Rolls Series, ed. Hassall, A. (Longmans. 1902), pp. 173–81. [N.B.—A most valuable description of Henry's person and character is included in the same volume, pp. 104–8.]

3. Stories of Richard I

For the story of Richard's Crusade, see the Crusades section below.

The Story of Richard's Return Home. Norgate, K. Richard the Lion Heart (Macmillan. 1924). Book III, chap. I.

4. Stories of King John

A story about the electing of an abbot. Chronicle of Jocelin of Brakelond (King's Classics). Chap. III.

The story of John and Arthur. Norgate, K. John Lackland (Macmillan. 1902). The rivalry, pp. 56–9; his capture, pp. 85–6; his death, pp. 90–2.

How John lost Normandy. Norgate, K. John Lackland (Macmillan. 1902), pp. 93–102.

The Story of Runnymede. McKechnie, W. S. Magna Carta, 1914, part I, pp. 31–41. *Or* Norgate, K. John Lackland (Macmillan. 1902), pp. 232–7. See 'History,' Vol. XIII, No. 51, Oct. 1928, for an exact up-to-date statement.

5. Stories of Henry III

Story of how the Provisions of Oxford were signed. Ramsay, Sir J. H. The Dawn of the Constitution (Sonnenschein. 1908), pp. 166–75. A great event: but not an exciting story. The details of the terms should, of course, be omitted.

The Story of the Battle of Lewes. Ramsay, Sir J. H. The Dawn of the Constitution (Sonnenschein. 1908), pp. 219–26. See also for extracts from contemporary writers Simon de Montford and his Cause, ed. W. H. Hutton (Nutt. 1907).

The Story of Simon de Montfort's death. Ramsay, Sir J. H. The Dawn of the Constitution (Sonnenschein. 1908), pp. 239–47. See also contemporary extracts as above.

II. EUROPEAN STORIES

1. Stories of the Wars of Empire and Papacy

The Story of Hildebrand. Gregorovius, F. History of the City of Rome in the Middle Ages. Bell. 1896. Vol. IV. Part I. His accession, pp. 167–73; he forbids lay investiture, pp. 187–9; Henry IV defies him at the synod of Worms, pp. 195–7; Hildebrand excommunicates Henry, pp. 198–203; Henry's dilemma and the submission at Canossa, pp. 204–9; the second excommunication of Henry, pp. 220–2; Henry's advance on Rome, pp. 223–5; his victory, p. 239; the sack of Rome and death of Hildebrand, pp. 242–8 and 254–6.

This is probably the best single account in English of this great drama: but it describes Hildebrand as of a too consistently cold and ambitious nature.

The Story of Frederick Barbarossa. *Ibid.* Vol. IV. Part II. His accession, p. 518; his meeting with the pope and coronation, pp. 530–43; development of conflict between

Frederick and the Italian cities and the Papacy, pp. 553–62, 563–71; the defeat of Frederick, pp. 597–602.

The Story of Innocent III. *Ibid.* Vol. V. Part I. His accession, pp. 5–8; the story of his relations with the empire, pp. 64–101. There is also a good sketch of Innocent III in D. C. Somervell's Studies in Statesmanship.

This should, of course, be connected with the English story of Innocent's relations with John.

The Story of Frederick II. *Ibid.* Vol. V. Part I. His childhood, p. 50; his accession, pp. 96–100; the first conflict with the papacy, pp. 142–56; the fiercest quarrel, pp. 182–204; the final stages and death of Frederick, pp. 253–66.

2. Stories of French History from Hugh Capet—Louis IX

The Story of Fulk of Anjou. Cambridge Medieval History. C.U.P. 1922. Vol. III, pp. 125–7.

A good story to illustrate the violence of the great feudal nobles and the influence of the Church upon them.

The Story of Philip II and the siege of Château Gaillard. Ramsay, Sir J. H. The Angevin Empire (Sonnenschein. 1908), pp. 398–403. An example of the strength of the French Monarchy.

Stories of S. Louis, illustrating his virtues and character. Joinville (trans.). Chronicle of the Crusade of St. Lewis. (Dent. Everyman's Library), pp. 139–48.

Stories of S. Louis, illustrating his government. Joinville (trans.). Chronicle of the Crusade of St. Lewis. (Dent. Everyman's Library), pp. 148–52, 300–1, 308–9, 311–6.

3. Stories of the Crusades

The Story of the First Crusade. The Legendary Story. William, Archbishop of Tyre (trans. by William Caxton). Godeffroy of Boloyne, or The Siege and Conqueste of Jerusalem. Kegan Paul. 1893. Peter the Hermit and his vision, pp. 36–40; the Council of Clermont and the gathering of the crusaders, pp. 42–7; the taking of Antioch, pp. 179–84; the finding of the Holy Lance, p. 200; the Battle of Antioch, pp. 204–14; Jerusalem besieged, p. 255, and taken, pp. 271–5; Godfrey chosen king, p. 281; but refuses to wear a crown, p. 290; his death, p. 311.

This story has great romantic qualities, but it must be regarded as 'intermediate between legend and history'. The true story of the crusade together with comments on William of Tyre's story will be found in H. von Sybel. The History and Literature of the Crusades. Routledge. Part I, chap. II. Part II, chap. II.

The Story of the Third Crusade. A good short account is given by T. A. Archer. Crusades (Fisher Unwin. Stories of the Nation.) A much fuller account is given in Norgate, K. Richard the Lion Heart (Macmillan. 1924), Book II. A collection of sources from which a splendid story could be made is published by T. A. Archer, under the title of The Crusade of Richard I (Nutt. 1900).

A Story of the Fourth Crusade and the Fall of Constantinople to the Crusaders. Villehardouin (trans.). Chronicle of the Fourth Crusade and the Conquest of Constantinople. (Dent. Everyman's Library.) The preaching of the crusade, pp. 1–2 ; the deflecting of the crusade to Constantinople, pp. 22–4 ; the capture of Constantinople, pp. 32–44 ; the quarrel between Alexius and the crusaders, pp. 52–3 ; the second capture of the city, pp. 53–66 ; Baldwin made emperor, pp. 67–8. The full story of the crusade by a secondary authority will be found in E. Pears. The Fall of Constantinople : being the story of the Fourth Crusade. (Longmans.)

The Story of S. Louis' First Crusade. Joinville (trans.). Chronicle of the Crusade of St. Lewis. (Dent. Everyman's Library.) The starting and journey of the crusaders, pp. 162–76. The King and (later) Joinville taken by the Saracens, pp. 211–20. Their great danger and release, pp. 227–32. The crusaders and their plans, pp. 236–45. Many incidents of the fighting will be found in the succeeding pages. The return of the crusaders, pp. 289–300.

The Story of S. Louis' Second Crusade and Death. Joinville (trans.). Chronicle of the Crusades of St. Lewis. (Dent. Everyman's Library), pp. 319–24.

4. Stories of Monks and Scholars

The Story of S. Bernard. Morison, J. C. Life and Times of S. Bernard. (Macmillan. 1901.) His parentage and early life, pp. 1–8 ; he enters Citeaux, pp. 9–18 ; he founds Clairvaux, pp. 23–30 ; examples of his preaching and miracles, pp. 62–6, 406–7 ; his death, p. 436.

The Story of Abelard's Early Life. Morison, J. C. Life and Times of S. Bernard. (Macmillan. 1901), pp. 258–73. [Needs expurgation—the point to bring out is the adventures of Abelard as a scholar and lecturer, which prepares the way for the rise of universities.]

The Story of Bernard and Abelard. Morison, J. C. Life and Times of S. Bernard (Macmillan. 1901), pp. 308–22.

5. Stories of the Friars

Stories of the Life of St. Francis.

Reference No. I is to the two contemporary lives of St. Francis by Thomas of Celano (Methuen. 1908). Reference No. II is to the modern life by P. Sabatier (Hodder and Stoughton. 1899).

His Youth. II. Chap. I, pp. 1–8.
His Conversion. I. First Life. Chap. II, pp. 5–9. II. Chap. II, pp. 15–27.
The Restoration of San Damiano and breach with his father. I. First life, Chaps. IV–VII, pp. 10–19. II. Chap. IV, pp. 54–64.
He begins to preach. I. First Life, Chaps. VIII, IX, X. II. pp. 64–87.
He is received at Rome by Innocent III. I. First Life, Chap. XIII, pp. 31–3. Second Life, Chap. XI, pp. 160–2. II. Chap. VI, pp. 92–101.
The Early Friars and the Portiuncula. I. Second Life, Chap. XII, pp. 162–4. II. Chap. VIII, pp. 120–42.
The Story of St. Clare. I. First Life, Chap. VIII, pp. 19–20. Second Life, Chap. CLV, pp. 332–3. II. Chap. IX, pp. 147–67.
The Canticle of the Sun. II. Chap. XVIII, pp. 303–7.
The Will of St. Francis. II. Chap. XX, pp. 337–9.
The Death of St. Francis. I. First Life, Chap. VIII, pp. 108–111. Second Life, Chap. CLXIII, pp. 342, 345. II. Chap. XX.
Appearance and Character. I. First Life, Chap. XXIX, p. 81. II. Chap. X, p. 182. Chap. XI, p. 195. His cheerfulness. I. Second Life, Chaps. XC, XCI, pp. 264–5. II. Chap. XI, p. 196. His Humility. I. Second Life, Chap. CII, p. 273. II. Chap. XIV, pp. 239, 249. His love of animals. I. First Life, Chap. XXIX, pp. 78, 79. Second Life, pp. 299–303. II. Chap. X, pp. 177–80.

Legends of the Franciscans.

Fioretti. (Dent: Everyman's Library. 1912.)

Bernard of Quintavalle, the first companion. Chap. II, pp. 2–4.
Lent on Lake Trasimene. Chap. VII, p. 14.
Perfect Joy to St. Francis and Leo. Chap. VIII, pp. 15, 16.
Praise of Poverty to Brother Masseo. Chap. XIII, pp. 22–5.
St. Clare eats with Francis. Chap. XV, pp. 26–7.
St. Francis preaches to the birds. Chap. XVI, pp. 28–30.
The Vision of the boy Friar. Chap. XVII, p. 31.
The Chapter of the Mats. Chap. XVIII, pp. 32–5.
The Conversion of the wolf at Gubbio. Chap. XXI, pp. 38–41.

St. Francis converts the Soldan of Babylon. Chap. XXIV, pp. 42–4.
St. Francis heals a leper. Chap. XXV, pp. 44–6.
St. Clare blesses the bread. Chap. XXXIII, p. 62.
St. Louis, king of France, visits Brother Giles. Chap. XXXIV, pp. 63–4.
The Fair Vision of Friar Leo. Chap. XXXVI, p. 65.
St. Anthony preaches to the fishes. Chap. XL, pp. 70–2.
Stories of Friar Juniper. Chap. IV, p. 140; V, pp. 140–2; IX, p. 144; X, pp. 144–5. These are perhaps the most popular of all the Franciscan stories to children.
The Story of Brother Giles. Chap. V, pp. 151–2.

Stories of the coming of the Friars to England can be prepared from Thomas of Eccleston (trans. by E. Gurney Salter. Dent. 1926), The Coming of the Friars.

C. A.D. 1272–1492

I. ENGLISH STORIES

1. Stories of Edward I and II

The Government of Edward I. Stubbs, W. The Constitutional History of England (O.U.P. 1880). Vol. II, pp. 138–56. The subject of Parliament under Edward I is very controversial. This reference is not suggested as an authoritative account, but because it contains some lively incidents suited to children.

The Story of Edward I and Wales. Edwards, O. M. Wales. (Fisher Unwin. Stories of Nations Series. 1925.) Chapters X, XI.

The Story of Wallace. Scott, Sir W. Tales of a Grandfather. (Black. 1925.) Chapter VII. *Or* Lang, A. History of Scotland. (Blackwood. 1900.) Vol. I, pp. 181–196.

The Story of Edward I and Bruce. Scott, Sir W. Tales of a Grandfather. (Black. 1925.) Chapters VIII and IX. *Or* Lang, A. History of Scotland. (Blackwood. 1900.) Pp. 200–11.

The Story of Gaveston. Ramsay, Sir J. H. The Genesis of Lancaster. (O.U.P. 1913.) Vol. I. Appearance and character, pp. 2–3; favouritism, pp. 5–8; his banishment by the nobles, p. 14; his return, p. 25; his end, pp. 43–6. Not a very valuable story, but might be included to explain the failure of Edward II.

The Story of Bannockburn. Ramsay, Sir J. H. The Genesis of Lancaster. (O.U.P. 1913.) Vol. I, pp. 61–73. *Or* Lang, A. History of Scotland. (Blackwood. 1900.) Pp. 211–41.

2. Stories of Edward III

The Story of Madame Eglentyne, Chaucer's Prioress in real life. Power, E. Medieval People (Methuen. 1925), Chap. III.

Stories of the Canterbury Pilgrims. Chaucer's Canterbury Tales (e.g. in Dent. Everyman's Library, No. 307).

For stories of the Hundred Years' War, see below under French History.

3. Stories of Richard II

The Story of the Peasants' Revolt. Oman, Sir C. Story of the Great Revolt. (O.U.P. 1906.) Pp. 32–80, for the adventures of Wat Tyler. For a contemporary account, see Froissart [Everyman's Library (abridged ed.)], pp. 207–24. Oman gives chapters on the rebellion in various particular districts which are useful for local history teaching.

The Banishment of Bolingbroke. Ramsay, Sir J. H. The Genesis of Lancaster. (O.U.P. 1913.) Vol. II, pp. 337–45. For contemporary detail, see Froissart [Everyman's Library (abridged ed.)], pp. 590–5.

This story forms the simplest and most dramatic way of explaining to children the arbitrary government of Richard II, and also introduces the figure of the future Henry IV.

The Deposition of Richard II. Ramsay, Sir J. H. The Genesis of Lancaster. (O.U.P. 1913.) Vol. II. Bolingbroke's expedition and the fall of Richard, pp. 350–60; Richard's abdication and death, pp. 360–70. For a contemporary account, see Froissart [Everyman's Library (abridged ed.)], pp. 609–15. See also Shakespeare's *Richard II.*

4. Stories of the Early Lancastrian Kings

The Story of Owen Glendower. Edwards, O. M. Wales. (Fisher Unwin. Stories of Nations Series. 1925.) Chapter XVI.

The Story of the Battle of Shrewsbury. Ramsay, Sir J. H. Lancaster and York. (O.U.P. 1892.) Vol. I, pp. 57–65.

The Story of Dick Whittington. Bourne, H. R. F. English Merchants, Vol. I, chap. III; *or* Bourne, H. R. F. Famous London Merchants, chap. I.

The Story of Thomas Betson, a merchant of the staple in the fifteenth century. Power, E. Medieval People (Methuen. 1925), chap. V.

For stories of the Hundred Years' War, see below under French history.

5. Stories of the Wars of the Roses

The Story of the Pastons and the Manor of Gresham. The Paston Letters. *Ed.* Gairdner, J. (Constable. 1901). Introduction, pp. xlviii–lii, and Letters 77 and 78.

One of the many stories that could be drawn from the Paston Letters to illustrate the lawlessness of the period. [For others, see Gairdner's Introduction, e.g. pp. ccxxxv–cclxv.]

The Death of the Duke of Suffolk. The Paston Letters. *Ed.* Gairdner, J. (Constable. 1901). Introduction, pp. lxvi–lxxix, and Letters 93 and 94.

Included as an illustration of the troubled politics of the period and for the dramatic value of Letter 93.

The Story of Jack Cade's Rebellion. The Paston Letters. *Ed.* Gairdner, J. (Constable. 1901). Introduction, pp. lxxix–lxxxviii; and A Short English Chronicle, *ed.* Gairdner (Camden Society. 1880), pp. 66–8.

The Story of the Indictment of Tuddenham and Heydon. The Paston Letters. *Ed.* Gairdner, J. (Constable. 1901). Introduction, pp. cii–cvi, and Letters 134, 135, 144, 145, 147, 148, 152, 155, 158.

A very good instance of the partiality of justice in this period.

The Lawlessness of Charles Nowell. The Paston Letters. *Ed.* Gairdner, J. (Constable. 1901). Introduction, pp. cxxviii–cxxx, and Letters 174–6, 179, 188, 201.

A very spirited account.

The Battle of Towton, 1461. Ramsay, Sir J. H. Lancaster and York. (O.U.P. 1892.) Vol. II, pp. 271–8.

The Siege of Caister, 1469. The Paston Letters. *Ed.* Gairdner, J. (Constable. 1901). Introduction, pp. cclxxxv–cclxxxix, and Letters 616, 618–22, 626–31.

A good example of the effects of the Wars of the Roses on public order.

The Story of Caxton. Blades, W. The Biography of William Caxton. (Trübner. 1882.) The story of his apprenticeship and why he learned printing, Chapters II and III. His work in England, Chapter VIII.

The Story of Edward V. Ramsay, Sir J. H. Lancaster and York. (O.U.P. 1892.) Vol. II, pp. 473–500.

The Battle of Bosworth, 1485. Ramsay, Sir J. H. Lancaster and York. (O.U.P. 1892.) Vol. II, pp. 546–54.

II. EUROPEAN STORIES

1. Stories of Eastern and Western Empires and Papacy in the Later Middle Ages

The Story of Boniface VIII and the affaire d'Anagni. Gregorovius, F. History of the City of Rome in the Middle

Ages. (Bell. 1897.) Vol. V, Part II. The jubilee festival in Rome, pp. 557–65; the quarrel with Philip of France, pp. 572–6; the affaire d'Anagni, pp. 578, 588–97.

A version of the story by an original authority can be found in Villani's Chronicle, trans. by R. E. Selfe (Constable. 1906), Book VIII, Chapters 36, 62, 63, 64.

The Legend of William Tell. Hug, L. and Stead, R. Switzerland. (Fisher Unwin. Stories of the Nations. 1920.) Chapter X gives a summary.

The story of Arnulf von Winkelried and the battles of Sempach and Naefels. Hug, L. (as above), Chapter XV.

The Story of Hus and the Emperor Sigismund at the Council of Constance. Creighton, M. History of the Papacy during the period of the Reformation. (Longmans. 1882.) Vol. I. [The early life of Hus and the development of his quarrel with the Church are described in Chap. IV.] The trial and death, Chap. V.

The Fall of Constantinople in 1453. Pears, E. The Destruction of the Greek Empire and the Story of the Capture of Constantinople by the Turks. (Longmans. 1903). Chapter XVI.

2. Stories of French History after 1270 and the Hundred Years' War with England

The Story of Creçy. Ramsay, Sir J. H. The Genesis of Lancaster (O.U.P. 1913), Vol. I. The march through Normandy, pp. 321–29; the battle, pp. 329–35 (with plan). Also for contemporary detail see Froissart [Everyman's Library (abridged ed.)], pp. 41–9; and a source book called 'Edward III and his Wars,' ed. Ashley, W. J. (Nutt. 1887.)

The Siege of Calais. Ramsay, Sir J. H. The Genesis of Lancaster (O.U.P. 1913). Vol. I, pp. 345–501. Also see Froissart [Everyman's Library (abridged ed.)], pp. 50–53, and Ashley (as above).

The Story of Poictiers. Ramsay, Sir J. H. The Genesis of Lancaster (O.U.P. 1913). Vol. I, pp. 402–17 (with plan), and Froissart [Everyman's Library (abridged ed.)], pp. 55–67. See also Ashley (as above).

The Story of Etienne Marcel. Funck-Brentano, Fr. The Middle Ages (Heinemann. 1922), pp. 461–470.

Interesting as showing the children the effects of the Hundred Years' War on France, and the failure of French attempts at democratic government.

The Sack of Limoges. Ramsay, Sir J. H. The Genesis of Lancaster (O.U.P. 1913). Vol. II, pp. 8–10, and Froissart [Everyman's Library (abridged ed.)], pp. 132–3. See also Ashley (as above).

The Adventures of Le Bastot de Mauleon, the Gascon squire. Froissart [Everyman's Library (abridged ed.)], pp. 311–13.

A good illustration of the free companies and their effect on public order in France.

The Story of Agincourt. Ramsay, Sir J. H. Lancaster and York (O.U.P. 1892), Vol. I, pp. 201–24. Contemporary accounts are quoted in Keatinge and Frazer's Documents of British History. (Black. 1913.)

Stories of Joan of Arc. These are well told in A. Lang, The Maid of France. (Longmans. 1922.) The main points are : the call of Joan ; the fighting at Orléans ; the coronation at Rheims ; her capture, trial and death.

The Story of Louis XI and Charles the Bold. Comines, P. de. History (trans. by T. Danett. Nutt. 1897). The Battle of Montl'hery. Vol. I, Book I, Chaps. II, III, IV. The interview at Péronne, Book II, Chaps. V–X. The last wars and death of Charles, Book V (especially Chaps. VIII and IX). The death of Louis, Book VI, Chaps. XI–XIII.

3. Stories of Travel and Exploration in the Later Middle Ages

The Story of Marco Polo. The Travels of Marco Polo, the Venetian. (Dent. 1926.) Introduction.

Book I, Bagdad, Chap. VII, pp. 42–3. Persia and the Fire Worshippers, Chap. XI, pp. 50, 51. The Desert of Lop (Gobi), Chap. XXXVI, pp. 99–101. Kubla Khan, Chap. LVII, pp. 145–51.

Book II, Kubla Khan's admirable deeds, Chaps. I, II, pp. 152–60.

Book III, India and the Islands, Chap. I, pp. 321–3 ; Japan, land of gold and pearls, Chap. II, pp. 323–7 ; the Province of Malabar, Chap. XX, pp. 351–3.

The story is excellently retold by E. Power in Medieval People.

4. Stories of the Italian Renaissance

The Story of Dante. Boccaccio. Life of Dante (trans. by P. H. Wicksteed. King's Classics. De La More Press. 1904). His birth, youth and love for Beatrice, pp. 7–21 ; his appearance and character, pp. 53–59 ; his exile and death, pp. 29–42.

The Story of Giotto. Vasari's Lives of Italian Painters. (Dent: Everyman's Library. 1927.) Vol. I, pp. 65–85.

The Story of Donatello. Vasari (as above). Vol. I, pp. 222–3, 301–14.

The Story of Fra Angelico. Vasari (as above). Vol. I, pp. 336–43.

The Story of Luca della Robbia. Vasari (as above). Vol. I, pp. 224–9.

The Story of Botticelli. Vasari (as above). Vol. II, pp. 84–90.

The Story of Pinturicchio. Vasari (as above). Vol. II, pp. 114–16.

The Story of Lorenzo de' Medici. Vasari (as above). Vol. II, p. 208. Vol. IV, pp. 111–12. The Garden for School of Painting. Young, F. The Medici. The Great Tournament, pp. 222–4 ; the Pazzi Conspiracy, pp. 229–42.

The Story of Leonardo da Vinci. Vasari (as above). Vol. II, pp. 156–67.

The Story of Michael Angelo. Symonds, J. A. The Life of Michelangelo Buonarroti. (Nimmo. 1893.) His youth and training, and how he lived in the house of Lorenzo, Vol. I, Chap. I. His appearance, pp. 83–5. Of the many examples that could be given of his work, children might perhaps be most interested in the story of the David, pp. 89–105. See also Vasari (as above), Vol. IV, pp. 108–116, 134–5, 175–9.

The Story of Raphael. Vasari (as above). Vol. II, pp. 221–6, 231, 240, 246–8.

The Story of Andrea del Sarto. Vasari (as above). Vol. II, pp. 303–23.

The Story of Titian. Vasari (as above). Vol. IV, pp. 199–214.

The Story of Tintoretto. Vasari (as above). Vol. IV, pp. 23–6.

The Story of Savonarola. Villari, P. Life and Times of Savonarola. (Fisher Unwin. 1923.) His boyhood, p. 3 ; he becomes a monk, pp. 14–21 ; his preaching and independence of Lorenzo, pp. 124–31 ; he opposes the Medici and becomes the chief force in Florence, e.g. pp. 368–370 ; the people turn against him : ordeal by fire, Chap. VII ; his arrest, Chap. VIII ; his death, Chap. XI.

III. STORIES OF MODERN HISTORY

These stories are arranged roughly in chronological order, but the order is slightly changed at times where it is thought to be more convenient to the teacher.

A. The Sixteenth Century

The Story of the Marriage of Ferdinand and Isabella, 1469. Prescott, W. M. History of the Reign of Ferdinand and Isabella (ed. J. F. Kirk. Bell. 1902). The marriage proposed, Vol. I, pp. 180–3. The betrothal, arrival of Ferdinand and marriage, pp. 193–200.

The Story of the Conquest of Granada from the Moors, 1491–2. Irving, Washington. The Conquest of Granada (Dent. Everyman's Library), pp. 288–31 (Chaps. 86–100).

The Story of Columbus' Voyage in 1492. Irving, Washington. Life and Voyages of Christopher Columbus (Harrap, 1909), pp. 84–160. N.B.—Columbus' offer to sail under the patronage of Henry VII is told in Hakluyt's Voyages (Dent. Illustrated ed., 1927), Vol. V, pp. 80–2.

The Story of Cabot, 1497. Hakluyt's Voyages (Dent. Illustrated ed., 1927). Portrait. Vol. I, p. 232. Voyage to North America, Vol. V, pp. 85–92.

The Conquest of Mexico. An abridged edition of W. H. Prescott's history, from which a story may easily be prepared, is published by W. H. D. Rouse in Blackie's English School Texts. 1906.

The Conquest of Peru. An abridged edition of W. H. Prescott's history is published by W. H. Rouse in Blackie's English School Texts. 1906.

The Story of Thomas Paycocke, an Essex clothier, in the days of Henry VII. Power, E. Medieval People. (Methuen, 1925.) Chap. 6.

The Story of Erasmus. Froude, J. A. Life and Letters of Erasmus (Longmans, 1895). The story of his youth, lecture I. A visit to England, lecture III. This is useful as illustrating in a way children can grasp the intellectual life of the time, the coming of the Renaissance to England, and the causes of the Reformation. The book contains generous extracts from Erasmus' own letters: the rest of the text is, like all Froude's work, vivid, spirited and anti-catholic. The book lends itself to the making of further stories on Erasmus' adventures.

Colet and the founding of S. Paul's School. Froude, J. A. Life and Letters of Erasmus (Longmans, 1895). There is a translated letter from Erasmus describing Colet and his school, pp. 105–7. An excellent full account is given in F. Seebohm. The Oxford Reformers. (Longmans. 1887.) Chap. VI.

The Story of Luther and the Sale of Indulgences. Seebohm, F. The Era of the Protestant Revolution (Longmans, 1915), pp. 94–100. His excommunication and the burning of the Bull, pp. 100–9. (Exciting, rather popular, very Protestant.)

The Story of Luther at the Diet of Worms. Seebohm, F. The Era of the Protestant Revolution (Longmans, 1915), pp. 109–30.

The Story of Wolsey. Cavendish, G. The Life of Cardinal Wolsey (Macmillan. Edited with notes by M. Tout. 1908). The story of Wolsey briefly and vividly told by his gentleman-usher.

The Story of Sir Thomas More. Roper, W. The Mirrour of Vertue in Worldly Greatnes, or the life of Sir Thomas More, Knight. (Moring: King's Classics. 1908.) The whole book is material for story-telling, e.g., see pp. 18–22, More as Speaker and in the King's favour; his fall and death, pp. 64–102.

The Story of the Pilgrimage of Grace. Fisher, H. A. L. Political History of England (Longmans. 1906). Vol. V, Chap. XV.

The Story of the Last Abbot of Glastonbury. Gasquet. Henry VIII and the English Monasteries (Bell), pp. 372–8.

The Story of the Abdication of Charles V, 1556. Robertson, W. and Prescott, W. H. History of the Reign of the Emperor Charles V (ed. W. H. Munro. Lippincott). Charles' resolution, his speech and Philip's acceptance, Vol. IV, pp. 98–110. His life after abdication, pp. 272–312.

The Story of Lady Jane Grey.

1. Her youth. See the letter of Roger Ascham, 1550, often quoted: e.g. in the Memoir prefacing Ascham's 'Schoolmaster' (Bell), p. 24.
2. The plot to make her queen. Pollard, A. F. Political History of England. (Longmans. 1910.) Vol. VI, Chap. V.
3. Wyatt's Rebellion and the execution of Lady Jane Grey. Pollard, A. F. (as above), pp. 107–11. There is a beautifully told contemporary account published by the Camden Society, 1850, entitled 'The Chronicle of Queen Jane and of Two Years of Queen Mary, and especially of the Rebellion of Sir Thomas Wyat'.

The Story of the Death of Cranmer. Pollard, A. F. 'Thomas Cranmer' (Putnam, 1904), Chap. XIII.

The Story of Sir Thomas Smythe the Customer. Retold in Bourne, H. R. F. Famous London Merchants, Chap. V.

The Story of the Flight of Queen Mary of Scots to England. Lang, A. A History of Scotland (Blackwood, 1902), Vol. II, Chap. VIII. (N.B.—The Adventures of Mary in Scotland are well told in earlier chapters.)

The Story of the Massacre of S. Bartholomew's Day. Baird, H. M. History of the Rise of the Huguenots (Hodder and Stoughton, 1880), Vol. II, Chap. XVIII. This story is sometimes useful in illustrating religious unrest abroad and introducing Henry of Navarre. The account given here is detailed: it requires considerable pruning and expurgation. Another vivid account is given in E. Sichel.

The Later Years of Catherine de' Medici (Constable, 1908), Chaps. VIII and IX. The subject might be followed up later by the story of Henry's abjuration and coronation as King of France (H. M. Baird. The Huguenots and Henry of Navarre. Kegan Paul, 1886. Vol. II, pp. 353–72), and his attempt to bring religious peace by the Edict of Nantes (*ibid*, pp. 414–20)—a theme that can be picked up again in telling the story of Louis XIV.

The Story of Hawkins. Hawkins' three voyages in 1562, 1564, 1567, told in Hakluyt (Dent. Illustrated ed., 1927), Vol. VII, pp. 5–62. Portrait: frontispiece. The third voyage is also well told by Sir J. S. Corbett. Drake and the Tudor Navy (Longmans, 1899), Vol. I, Chap. III.

The Story of the Siege of Leyden, 1574. Motley, J. T. The Rise of the Dutch Republic (Murray, 1904), Vol. II, Part IV, Chap. II. This glorious and romantic story can be used as an illustration of the revolt of the Netherlands against Spain and should be connected with the English story of the Armada.

The Story of Drake's Voyage to Nombre de Dios, 1572. Hakluyt's Voyages (Dent. Illustrated ed., 1927), Vol. VII, pp. 62–4. For a fuller secondary account, see Sir J. S. Corbett, 'Drake and the Tudor Navy' (Longmans, 1899), Vol. I, pp. 155–90, or (more popular) E. F. Benson, Sir Francis Drake (Lane), Chaps. IV and V.

The Story of Frobisher, 1576–7. Hakluyt's Voyages (Dent. Illustrated ed., 1927), Vol. V, pp. 131–64. Illustrations, pp. 145 and 154, and portrait, Vol. IV, frontispiece.

The Story of Drake's Voyage round the World. Hakluyt's Voyages (Dent. Illustrated ed., 1927).

1. Voyage round the Globe by Sir Francis Drake, 1577, pp. 48–74. Portrait, Vol. VIII. Frontispiece.
2. Voyage of M. John Winter by Strait of Magellan with Sir Francis Drake, 1577, pp. 87–99.

Illustrations. 1. Magellan, p. 90. 2. Straits of Magellan, p. 83.

See also 'The World Encompassed' in Blackie's English Texts; and for excellent secondary accounts, Sir J. S. Corbett, 'Drake and the Tudor Navy' (Longmans, 1899), Vol. I, Chaps. 8, 9, 10; or (more popular) E. F. Benson, 'Sir Francis Drake' (Lane, 1927), Chaps. 6–10.

How Drake was Knighted. Corbett, Sir J. S. Drake and the Tudor Navy (Longmans, 1899), Vol. I, pp. 310–20.

The Story of Sir Humphrey Gilbert, 1583. Hakluyt's Voyages (Dent. Illustrated ed., 1927). Voyage of Sir Humphrey Gilbert to Newfoundland, 1583, pp. 1–38. Illustration. Manner of making boats, p. 126.

The Story of Davis. Hakluyt's Voyages (as above), Vol. V, pp. 281–336.

The Story of Voyages to Virginia, 1584–90. Hakluyt's Voyages (as above), Vol. VI, pp. 121–227.

The Death of Mary Queen of Scots. Scott, Mrs. Maxwell. The Tragedy of Fotheringay (Sands, 1906). The whole book tells of the trial and sentence. The final tragedy is described, pp. 155–211.

How Drake Singed the King of Spain's beard. Corbett, Sir J. S. Drake and the Tudor Navy (Longmans, 1899), Vol. II, Chap. III. Hakluyt's Voyages (Dent. Illustrated ed., 1927), Vol. IV, pp. 281–5.

The Story of the Armada. Corbett, Sir J. S. Drake and the Tudor Navy (Longmans, 1899), Vol. II, Chaps. V, VI, VII, VIII. A fine and very full account. Hakluyt's Voyages (Dent. Illustrated ed., 1927), Vol. II, pp. 369–402. Illustrations, pp. 368, 371, 384. A spirited account of a more popular type given by E. F. Benson. Sir Francis Drake (Lane), Chaps. 13, 14.

The Story of Sir Richard Grenville and the Revenge, 1591. Hakluyt's Voyages (Dent. Illustrated ed., 1927), Vol. V, pp. 1–14. See also Froude's Short Stories. First Series. England's Forgotten Worthies.

Drake's Last Voyage. Corbett, Sir J. S. Drake and the Tudor Navy (Longmans, 1899), Vol. II, Chap. XI. Hakluyt's Voyages (Dent. Illustrated ed., 1927), Vol. VII, pp. 183–99. For a more popular but dramatically told account, see E. F. Benson, 'Sir Francis Drake' (Lane), Chap. XVII.

The Voyages of Sir Walter Raleigh. Hakluyt's Voyages (Dent. Illustrated ed., 1927). The voyage to Trinidad, 1595. Vol. VII, pp. 287–350. Portrait, Vol. VI, Frontispiece. The Voyage to Guiana. Vol. VIII, pp. 1–13.

B. The Seventeenth Century

The Story of the Gunpowder Plot. Gardiner, S. R. History of England, 1603–42 (Longmans, 1883), Vol. I, Chap. VI. Gives the narrative in full detail: a most exciting story can be constructed by simplifying and selecting.

The Story of Arabella Stuart. Gardiner, S. R. History of England, 1603–42 (Longmans, 1883), Vol. II, pp. 113–9. A romantic but sad story.

The Last Voyage of Raleigh. Gardiner, S. R. History of England, 1603–42 (Longmans, 1883), Vol. III, Chap. 25.

The Death of Raleigh. Gardiner, S. R. History of England, 1603–42 (Longmans, 1883), Vol. III, pp. 140–53.

The Story of the Mayflower. Gardiner, S. R. History of England, 1603–42 (Longmans, 1883), Vol. IV, Chap. 36, particularly pp. 157–68.

The Protest of the Commons in 1621. Gardiner, S. R. History of England, 1603–42 (Longmans, 1883), Vol. IV, Chap. 39. The earlier part of the chapter describes the speeches on foreign policy and money matters which led up to the great quarrel on freedom of speech. The quarrel itself is described, pp. 249–53, the King's letter forbidding freedom of speech, the Commons' petition and his reply: pp. 258–65, the king's second letter and the crisis.

The Story of the Petition of Right. Gardiner, S. R. History of England, 1603–42 (Longmans, 1884), Vol. VI, Chap. LXIII, pp. 297–310. Describes the stirring debate held after Charles had virtually refused the petition, the remonstrance of the Commons, and Charles' final surrender.

The Passing of the Three Resolutions. Gardiner, S. R. History of England, 1603–42 (Longmans, 1884), Vol. VII, pp. 67–76. This is the dramatic tale of the final breach between Charles and his Third Parliament, when the House refused to adjourn until it had passed resolutions on taxation and religion.

The Assassination of Buckingham. Gardiner, S. R. History of England, 1603–42 (Longmans, 1884), Vol. VI, pp. 347–60.

The Story of Richelieu. A good brief sketch of his life and work given in D. C. Somervell's Studies in Statesmanship (Bell, 1923), Chap. V.

The Story of Wallenstein in the Thirty Years War. Gardiner, S. R. The Thirty Years War (Longmans, 1874). His early life and rise to fame, pp. 86–91; the Siege of Stralsund, pp. 104–8; his dismissal, pp. 122–7; his reinstatement, pp. 150–3; the battle of Lutzen, pp. 158–61; final efforts and assassination, pp. 167–78.

The Making of a Puritan. Memoirs of the Life of Colonel Hutchinson by his widow Lucy (Nimmo, 1885), Vol. I. His birth, p. 57; education, pp. 66–74; the story of his marriage, pp. 81–92; appearance and character, pp. 32–50; why he was called a Puritan, pp. 140–1, 169–72. There is not much incident in this, but it gives an excellent picture of Puritan ideals.

The Trial and Death of Strafford. Gardiner, S. R. History of England, 1603–42 (Longmans, 1884), Vol. IX, Chap. XCVII, describes the attempt to impeach Strafford, which failed. Chapter XCVIII describes the successful attack on him by bill of attainder. The King's assent to the bill and the death of Strafford are described, pp. 361–71.

The Attempted Arrest of the Five Members. Gardiner, S. R. History of England, 1603–42 (Longmans, 1884), Vol. X, pp. 129–41.

The Battle of Edgehill, 1642. Gardiner, S. R. History of the Great Civil War (Longmans, 1910), Vol. I, pp. 40–51. A valuable story because it brings out the peculiar qualities of each side in the civil war, especially as regards Rupert and Cromwell. A good contemporary account is given in Ludlow's Memoirs (ed. Firth, O.U.P., 1894), pp. 41–6.

The First Battle of Newbury, 1643. Gardiner, S. R. (as above), Vol. I, pp. 209, 219. Tells of the death of Falkland.

The Siege of Wardour Castle, 1643-4. Ludlow's Memoirs (ed. Firth. O.U.P., 1894), pp. 59–78. This story is not of great importance in itself, but it illustrates in a vivid way the small local fighting of the Civil War.

The Battle of Marston Moor, 1644. Gardiner, S. R. (as above), Vol. I, pp. 366–7, 370–82. An important turning point in the war, and a further illustration of the characters of Rupert and Cromwell.

The Story of Montrose. Gardiner, S. R. (as above), Vol. II. He begins his adventure, pp. 132–5; the campaign of Tippiemuir and Aberdeen, pp. 139–49; Inverlochy and the invitation to Charles, pp. 153–5; the victory of Kilsyth, pp. 291–300; his defeat at Philiphaugh, pp. 347–56. Or the story can be told from Sir Walter Scott's Tales of a Grandfather (Black, 1925), Chapters XLII, XLIII and (for his death) pp. 516–19.

The Story of Naseby, 1645. Gardiner, S. R. (as above). Vol. II, pp. 239–53.

How the Army abducted the King, 1647. *Ibid.* Vol. III, pp. 266–74. Useful as showing the split between Army and Parliament.

The Battle of Preston, 1648. *Ibid.* Vol. IV, pp. 183–93.

The Trial and Death of Charles, 1649. *Ibid.*, Vol. IV, pp. 296–330.

The Story of the Dissolution of the Rump. Carlyle, T. Cromwell's Letters and Speeches. (Everyman's Library. Dent.) Vol. II, pp. 306–11.

The Story of Cromwell as Protector. Carlyle, T. Cromwell's Letters (as above). The abdication of the Little Parliament and the establishment of the Protectorate, Vol. II, pp. 344–9. The Major-Generalships, Vol. III, pp. 93–4. Cromwell refuses the title of king, Vol. III, pp. 274–8. Dissolves the Second Protectorate Parliament, Vol. III, pp. 337–48.

The Story of the Restoration. Pepys' Diary (Dent: Everyman's Library). Desire for the Restoration. Vol. I, pp. 32–3. The Restoration, pp. 51–69.

The Story of Plague and Great Fire. The Plague. John Evelyn's Diary (Dent: Everyman's Library), Vol. I, pp. 403–6. Pepys' Diary (Dent: Everyman's Library), Vol. I, pp. 582, 622. The Fire. Evelyn's Diary (as above), Vol. II, pp. 11–17.

The Story of Louis XIV and the Revocation of the Edict of Nantes. Hassall, A. Louis XIV (Putnam's), pp. 242–52. For an interesting description of Louis XIV see pp. 82–90.

The Story of Monmouth. Macaulay, Lord. The History of England (ed. C. H. Firth. Macmillan, 1914), Vol. II, pp. 561–624 (part of Chap. V).

The Trial of the Seven Bishops. Macaulay, Lord. The History of England (as above), Vol. II, pp. 990–1039 (part of Chap. VIII).

How William III Landed in England. Macaulay, Lord. The History of England (as above), Vol. III, pp. 1116–40 (part of Chap. IX).

The Flight of James II. Macaulay, Lord. The History of England (as above), Vol. III, pp. 1197–1242 (parts of Chaps. IX and X).

The Story of Blenheim. Atkinson, C. T. Marlborough and the Rise of the British Army (Putnam's, 1921), Chaps. IX, X. Other battle stories of the War of the Spanish Succession can be found in the same volume.

C. The Eighteenth Century

The Rebellion of 1715. Full accounts of each episode are given in C. S. Terry's 'The Jacobites and the Union' (C.U.P., 1922), in which the editor combines several contemporary narratives into one story. Chap. 2, Sheriffmuir; Chap. 3, Preston; Chap. 4, Glenshiel.

The Rebellion of 1745: the Entry to Edinburgh, and the Battle of Prestonpans. Terry, C. S. 'The Forty-five' (C.U.P., 1922), pp. 45–58. Several contemporary narratives are combined into one story by the Editor.

The Rebellion of 1745: the March to Derby and the Retreat. Terry, C. S. 'The Forty-five', Chap. 4.

The Rebellion of 1745. Culloden. Terry, C. S. 'The Forty-five', Chap. 6.

The Rebellion of 1745. Flora Macdonald and the Escape of Prince Charlie. Terry, C. S. 'The Forty-five', Chap. 7 (very exciting and romantic).

Wesley's Boyhood. Tyerman, L. The Life and Times of John Wesley (Hodder & Stoughton, 1871), pp. 15–21.

The Story of John Wesley's Preaching. Wesley's Journal (Everyman's Library), Vol. I, pp. 438–43. An account of

Wesley's preaching at Wednesbury, of the attack of the mob upon him, and of his victory. An exciting episode which illustrates the general character of Wesley's work.

The Story of Mozart. Parry, C. H. H. Studies of Great Composers (Routledge, 1887), Chap. V. A child prodigy and his career: full of entertaining detail, and illustrates social life as well as introducing the children to the name of a great musician.

The Story of Clive's Boyhood and Arrival in India. Forrest, Sir G. The Life of Lord Clive (Cassell, 1918), Chap. I.

The Story of Plassey. Forrest, Sir G. The Life of Lord Clive (Cassell, 1918), pp. 450–60.

The Battle of Quiberon Bay. Corbett, Sir J. England in the Seven Years' War (Longmans, 1907), Vol. II, pp. 52–70.

The Capture of Quebec. Corbett, Sir J. England in the Seven Years' War (Longmans, 1907), Vol. I, Chap. XVII (the advance), XVIII (the capture). The climax of the story, the climbing of the heights, and victory and death of Wolfe are told, pp. 458–76.

Parkman, F. Montcalm and Wolfe (Dent: Everyman's Library), Vol. II, Chaps. XXVII, XXVIII.

Lafayette in America. Trevelyan, Sir G. O. The American Revolution (Longmans, 1912), Vol. IV. His arrival, pp. 218–24; his friendship with Washington, pp. 314–17. The career of **Washington** is well sketched in D. C. Somervell's Studies in Statesmanship (Bell, 1923), Chap. VI.

The Story of Burgoyne at Saratoga. Trevelyan, Sir G. O. The American Revolution (Longmans, 1912), Vol. IV, pp. 159–202.

The Death of Chatham. Green, W. D. William Pitt (Putnam's, 1901), pp. 356–66.

The Fall of Yorktown. Trevelyan, Sir G. O. The American Revolution (Longmans, 1915), Vol. VI, pp. 380–4.

Stories of the Agricultural Revolution. The Story of Otmoor. Hammond, J. L. and B. The Village Labourer (Longmans, 1913), pp. 87–96. Useful in illustrating the bad side of the enclosure movement.

Stories of the Industrial Revolution.

1. The Stories of Telford, Brindley, Stephenson, &c., are given in Smiles' Lives of the Engineers (Murray, 1904). 5 vols.
2. The Story of Francis Place's Boyhood. Wallas, G. The Life of Francis Place (Longmans, 1898), Chap. I. An excellent story for illustrating industrial life and troubles at the end of the eighteenth century.

See also stories on nineteenth-century history.

The Story of Captain Cook. The stories of the second and third voyages (1772–5 and 1776–80) are both contained in

Captain Cook's Voyages. (Dent: Everyman's Library.)

Stories of Mungo Park. The Travels of Mungo Park. (Dent: Everyman's Library, 1907.)

The Story of the Fall of the Bastille. Madelin, L. The French Revolution (Heinemann, 1916), pp. 69–83. This account is not only very exciting, but it is in accordance with the findings of modern research. There has been a considerable revision of the traditional story.

The Story of the Flight to Varennes. Madelin, L. The French Revolution (as above), pp. 188–95. Full story in Lenotre, G. (tr.) The Flight of Marie Antoinette (Heinemann, 1906).

The Fall of the Monarchy, August 10th. Madelin, L. The French Revolution (as above), pp. 265–73. The King's death, pp. 317–24.

The Fall of Danton. Madelin, L. Danton (Heinemann, 1921), pp. 328–63.

The Battle of the Nile. Mahan, A. T. Life of Nelson (Sampson Low, 1899), Chap. X. Also in Fitchett, W. H. How England Saved Europe (Smith Elder, 1899–1900). Vol. I, Period III, Chap. IV. (N.B.—The sea fights of 1797 will be found in the same volume.)

Napoleon's coup d'état, 18th Brumaire. Madelin, L. The French Revolution (as above), pp. 608–23. See also Rose, J. H. Life of Napoleon I (Bell, 1902), Vol. I, pp. 220–8. The whole career of Napoleon is well and briefly sketched in D. C. Somervell's Studies in Statesmanship (Bell, 1923).

The Story of Beethoven. Parry, C. H. H. Studies of Great Composers (Routledge, 1887), Chap. VI. Has enough human interest to fascinate children to whom his music as yet means nothing: acts not only as an introduction to his name, but as an illustration of revolutionary feeling and its relation to the career of Napoleon (pp. 170–1).

The Baltic Expedition and the Battle of Copenhagen. Mahan, A. T. Life of Nelson (Sampson Low. 1889), Chap. XVI. For the actual fighting, see pp. 476–89. Also Fitchett, W. H. How England saved Europe (Smith Elder, 1899–1900), Vol. II, Period IV, Chap. VIII.

Trafalgar and the Death of Nelson. Mahan, A. T. Life of Nelson (Sampson Low, 1899), Chap. XXIII. This is a wonderfully told story from the human and dramatic standpoint. There has been some controversy as to tactics: any teacher who wishes to study it is referred to Appendix XII in Grant Robertson's England under the Hanoverians.

Death of Moore at Corunna. Napier, W. F. P. History of the War in the Peninsula (Routledge), Book IV, Chap. V. A selection of Napier's stories of the Peninsular War has been edited by H. Strang. 1913.

Fitchett, W. H. How England saved Europe (Smith Elder, 1899–1900), Vol. III, Period V, Chaps. VII, VIII.

The Lines of Torres Vedras. Fitchett, W. H. How England saved Europe. (Smith Elder, 1899–1900), Vol. III, Period V, Chap. XVII. The stories of Badajos and Vittoria are told in the same volume.

The Story of Waterloo. Fortescue, J. W. A History of the British Army (Macmillan, 1920), Vol. X, pp. 345–93. Fitchett, W. H. (as above), Vol. IV, Period VI, Chaps. XII–XX.

The Story of Napoleon at St. Helena. Lord Rosebery. Napoleon: the Last Phase, e.g. Chap. VIII; the question of custody. Chap. XIV; the supreme regrets. Chap. XVI; the end.

D. The Nineteenth Century

The Story of Wilberforce. From the Life by R. Coupland (O.U.P. 1924).

The Story of the Boyhood of William Lovett (1800). The Life and Struggles of William Lovett, with an introduction by R. H. Tawney (Bell, 1920), pp. 1–24. Gives a picture of the social life of the time and how a poor boy was educated.

The Story of a Yorkshire Riot. Charlotte Brontë. Shirley. Chaps. XVIII, XIX.

Story of the March of the Blanketeers, 1817. Hammond, J. L. and B. The Skilled Labourer, 1760–1832 (Longmans, 1919), pp. 343–9.

The Story of the Luddites. Hammond, J. L. and B. The Skilled Labourer, 1760–1832 (Longmans, 1919), Chap. IX.

The Story of Peterloo. Hammond, J. L. and B. The Town Labourer, 1760–1832 (Longmans, 1917), pp. 89–92.

Story of the Repeal of the Combination Acts. Wallas, G. The Life of Francis Place (Longmans, 1898), Chap. VIII.

The Story of the Reform Bill of 1832. Trevelyan, G. M., Lord Grey of the Reform Bill (Longmans, 1920). The Bill introduced, debated and defeated, pp. 280–96; the election, p. 297; the Bill thrown out again, pp. 306–10; examples of popular feeling, pp. 321–7; the third Bill introduced, p. 329, &c.; the final victory, pp. 348–9.

The Story of Lord Shaftesbury. Hammond, J. L. and B. Lord Shaftesbury (Constable, 1923). His unhappy childhood, pp. 1–4; the state of the factories and how Ashley took up their cause, Chap. II; the passing of the Ten Hour Bill, Chap. X, &c.

A Story of the Poor Law of 1834. Charles Dickens. Oliver Twist, Chaps. II, III.

The Story of the Dorchester Labourers, 1834. Webb S. and B. The History of Trade Unionism (Longmans 1920), pp. 144–8.

The Story of Disraeli's First Speech. Monypenny, W. F. The Life of Benjamin Disraeli (Murray, 1912), Vol. II, pp. 1–16. Or the story of Disraeli's youth and first speech could be told from the brilliant sketch by A. Maurois (Lane, 1927).

The Story of a Lancashire Strike. Mrs. Gaskell. North and South. The relevant parts of Chaps. XV (the masters' side), XVII (the men's side), XXI, XXII (the riot), and the end of Chap. XXVIII (breakdown of the strike).

A Story of the Chartists. Charles Kingsley. Alton Locke. Chaps. II and X (the conditions that bred Chartism), XXXIII and XXXIV (what became of the charter). This story is included for the sake of completeness: it would require very careful treatment to be suitable for children.

The Repeal of the Corn Laws. Trevelyan, G. M., The Life of John Bright (Constable, 1913), pp. 135–53.

The Story of a Bad School (Boys). Charles Dickens. Nicholas Nickleby. Chaps. VII, VIII, XIII.

The Story of a Bad School (Girls). Charlotte Brontë. Jane Eyre, Chaps. V, VI, VII, VIII.

A Story of Rugby School. Tom Brown's School Days. Chaps. V, VI, IX. These stories show the changes in school life made by the influence of Arnold, and are a good contrast to the story of Squeers.

The Coming of Garibaldi. Trevelyan, G. M., Garibaldi's Defence of the Roman Republic (Longmans, 1907). His youth, Chaps. I and II; the Legion and the formation of a Roman Republic (1849), pp. 87–92.

Story of the Fall of Rome, 1849. *Ibid.*, Chap. XI.

The Escape of Garibaldi, 1849. *Ibid.* The death of Anita, Chap. XV; the escape, Chaps. XVI and XVII.

The Story of Mazzini. Bolton King. Mazzini (Dent, 1903). His youth and exile, Chap. I; the making of Young Italy, Chap. II; life in London, Chap. V; examples of part he played in the freeing of Italy, e.g. his Roman triumvirate 1849, pp. 128–38; final efforts and death, pp. 213–21.

The Coup d'État of 1851 and how Louis Napoleon made himself emperor. Guedalla, P. Louis Napoleon (Longmans, 1923), Chap. V.

Stories of the Crimea. Kinglake, A. W. The Invasion of the Crimea. (Blackwood, 1888.) E.g. Alma, Vol. III; the Light Brigade, Vol. V, p. 166 *et seq.*; Inkerman, Vol. VI. For Florence Nightingale, see her biography by Cook, and the sketch in Eminent Victorians by Lytton Strachey.

A Story of the Indian Mutiny. The Siege of Lucknow. Forrest, G. W. A History of the Indian Mutiny (Blackwood, 1904), Vol. I, Chaps. VIII–XVI.

The Story of the Interview at Plombières, 1858. Thayer, W. R. The Life and Times of Cavour (Constable, 1911), Vol. I, pp. 526–33. It is easy to find stories of Garibaldi, but rather hard to find a story interesting to children that introduces Cavour. The secrecy of this interview, however, is attractive to them and it is useful in showing the connexion between the Italian story and Louis Napoleon.

Story of the Battle of Calatafimi, 1860. Trevelyan, G. M., Garibaldi and the Thousand (Longmans, 1909), Chap. XIV. A dozen splendid stories might be made from this book: the story of Calatafimi has been chosen as the turning point of Garibaldi's Sicilian campaign and because it displays the peculiar quality of his leadership.

The Battle of Volturno, 1860. Trevelyan, G. M., Garibaldi and the Making of Italy (Longmans, 1911), Chap. XIII.

The Result of Garibaldi's Victory, 1860. *Ibid.* Victor Emanuel marches triumphant through Italy and meets Garibaldi, pp. 266–72. Garibaldi retires to Caprera, pp. 284–7.

The Story of the Outbreak of the Franco-German War. Headlam, J. W. Bismarck (Putnam's, 1899), Chap. XIII (includes the story of Bismarck and the famous telegram of Ems). The story of Bismarck's career as a whole is well sketched in D. C. Somervell's Studies in Statesmanship (Bell, 1923), Chap. VIII.

The Story of Sedan. P. Guedalla. The Second Empire (Constable, 1922), pp. 416–29.

The Siege of Paris. Maurice, C. B. The Franco-German War (Sonnenschein, 1900). The besiegers, pp. 272–7; example of the fighting, pp. 285–8; the bombardment and state of the besiegers, pp. 309–17; the fall of Paris, pp. 323–7. This story is written from a German point of view.

The Story of the Foundation of the German Empire. Headlam, J. W. Bismarck (Putnam's, 1899), Chap. XIV.

The Story of Khartoum. See 'Eminent Victorians,' by G. Lytton Strachey. Gordon's own journal of events at Khartoum has been published by A. E. Hake (Kegan Paul, 1885).

The Story of Livingstone. Livingstone described his Travels in Missionary Travels and Researches in South Africa (Murray, 1899) and a Narrative of an Expedition to the Zambesi (Murray, 1865). A brief group of extracts with a biographical note by G. S. Maxwell is published by J. Brodie: The Brodie Books, No. 24.

See also H. M. Stanley: How I Found Livingstone. Sampson Low. 1874.

The Story of the Dockers' Strike. Smith, H. L. and Nash, V. The Story of the Dockers' Strike. (Fisher Unwin.)

Stories of Modern Exploration. See Nansen, F. Farthest North. 2 vols. (Constable, 1897.) A selection entitled Episodes from Farthest North is published by Harrap, 1927. Shackleton, Sir E. H. South (Heinemann, 1922). Scott, R. F. Scott's Last Expedition (Murray, 1923). Norton, E. The Fight for Everest (Arnold, 1925). Amundsen, R. My Life as an Explorer (Heinemann, 1927).

VI

SELECT LIST OF HISTORICAL FICTION FOR CHILDREN

THE makers of this select list offer it to the public with all proper diffidence. No one is more conscious than they of the difficulties of such a selection, involving as it constantly does a choice between what children would like to read and what the history teacher would like them to read. The main aim has been to find in each period books that are actually within the children's powers, and that would at the same time help and not hinder their historical knowledge. The search has not been an easy one, and has occupied the spare time of a special committee during the better part of two years. A very large number of stories, amounting to several hundreds, was first sifted in a preliminary reading by elementary school teachers who considered in their choice the attractiveness and suitability of the books to the children whom they taught. The desire to keep the list really juvenile in character has been responsible for the omission of several famous adult historical novels. The list was then submitted to a number of history specialists, each of whom took a group of books in the period of which he had particular knowledge and re-considered them from the point of view of reasonable accordance with historical truth. This, of course, in a child's story can only be a matter of degree, and those who dislike to allow such reading to their pupils can make out a case: but the general opinion is that the reading of historical stories does interest children in great events and familiarize them with great names. Finally the much shrunken list was given a third sifting by experienced teachers; and the result is set out below.

The main difficulty encountered in the final choice was, of course, the wide variety that exists among the powers and interests of different children. It is impossible to generalize accurately. Books that seem to an adult the very acme of stodginess will often be read and re-read with sparkling eyes by some child; and every teacher knows that an intelligent child of ten from a bookish home will read with interest books that a slower child with few academic advantages cannot read alone at fourteen. For this reason the committee members were soon obliged to abandon their own childish memories as a guide. People who teach when they grow up were generally rather bookish when they were small; and the memory of having enjoyed *Hereward the Wake* at nine and *Romola* at fourteen is not really much help in deciding what can be read in Standard IV and Standard VII. It seemed therefore more useful to consult the children themselves as to modern tastes. A number of schools was asked to co-operate by encouraging their pupils to report in a very simple form on the history stories they knew best. They were asked only to give the name of the book and to answer the question, 'Would you recommend this book to some one of your own age?' It was impressed on them that an *honest* answer was desired; that their teacher really wanted to know what books would be enjoyed by other boys and girls. A certain number of replies, in spite of this, bore traces of a misguided politeness; but there were enough honest answers to give some indication of what modern children think of historical fiction.

It was clear, in the first place, that the recognized classics are not read with ease by the average child. It was impossible to doubt the sincerity of the little girl who, faced with the question, 'Would you recommend *A Tale of Two Cities* to some one of your own age?' returned the simple answer, 'I would not recommend it to any one of any age'. Sydney Carton has died in vain as far as she was concerned. 'I do not recommend this book to some one of my age,' writes a fourteen-year-old of *Ivanhoe,* with really touching humility, 'because it is dry the whole way through; but to an intelligent reader, I do'. Another reader dismisses *The Three Musketeers* even more brusquely. 'I would not recommend it to anybody. It is very dry; old-fashioned and hard to understand. You cannot make head nor tail of the story.' *Westward Ho!* gets some commendations, but they are generally guarded. 'It is a bit stiff.' 'It is more fit for a boy or girl of seventeen or eighteen.' *Kidnapped* 'needed a lot of explaining'. 'A grown-up person might like it.' 'I would not recommend this book to a friend of my age,' says some one else of *Guy Mannering*. 'Perhaps a student or doctor may approve of it. Most of the book is about science, also it has a stiff and dry beginning and perhaps somebody very clever in astrology may like it.' 'I supplied a copy of *Ivanhoe* to the class library,' writes one boys' teacher, 'but it has no dirty finger-marks on it yet—a bad sign from the point of view of popularity.'

Are these comments natural or deplorable? Many of the committee thought them deplorable, and were inclined to blame the softness of modern education as destroying children's appetite for strong meat. 'We had dull textbooks and read Scott for pleasure: they have attractive textbooks and they regard Scott as harder than their lessons,' might stand as a summary of this opinion in its extreme form. On the other hand, it was pointed out that most of the classical authors of historical fiction were not regarded as children's writers in the hey-day of their fame. Scott wrote for adults, and all references in contemporary literature to his admirers show them as at least adolescent in age. Jane Eyre read his poetry in her lonely moorland cottage, but there are no indications that she expected such serious reading of Adèle. Charlotte Yonge's novels describe more than one enthusiast for Scott, but they are all in the later 'teens. The character and style of his writings suited the taste of the nineteenth century, but they are not on the whole popular even among adults of to-day; why should children find them more attractive? The general conclusion among people of this opinion was that children of an older generation read Scott because there was nothing really childlike accessible for them to read instead; that what was required in the present day was not to urge children back to writers of the past but to supply books written with understanding of a child's point of view, and that a tremendous opportunity is waiting for anyone who can supply such a need. It must be left for the individual reader to decide which of these views he feels to be the more sound, and whether he will try to teach his pupils to read the old authors or try to find newer books which they can read with more spontaneous interest.

If he decides to make an effort to keep Scott's and Kingsley's memory green (and the sympathies of the editor lie that way), the children's answers supply him with a few helpful hints. It is clear that the greatest difficulty lies in *beginning* the book, grasping the characters' names and relationships, and following the exposition of the story. One reporter writes of *Ivanhoe*, 'I should recommend this book to some one of my own age, because although the beginning was not interesting the ending makes up for it'. More definite still is the evidence of a girl of thirteen, who would recommend *Woodstock* to a friend 'if I knew she had patience enough to get to the understanding part'. A boy says of *Westward Ho!* 'If they got down to it, they would find it interesting and adventurous; if not, parts are dry'. A girl who 'cannot say that she really likes *A Tale of Two Cities*' would not recommend it to younger children 'because the first two or three chapters are not really interesting and so they would not read any more'. All this goes to suggest that while exceptional children will read the older authors without help, a far larger number would read a part of the book with spontaneous interest if the teacher had read the beginning with them; and it might be of the greatest value in forming a habit of private reading if the teacher could from time to time introduce a new book to promising children and leave them to finish it for themselves when the interest of the story had once gripped them.

The other difficulty, which is much harder to tackle, is the difficulty of vocabulary. Weyman's *House of the Wolf* was not recommended 'because the words are rather hard, and it is also hard to follow'. *Ivanhoe* is 'certainly not recommended, because the words are too long to be understood. Also the characters do not speak much.' 'Some girls', plaintively adds a reporter of eleven, 'do not like hard books with pharagraphs of description.' Is the remedy here to give an abridged copy in which some of the 'pharagraphs of description' are omitted? Opinions differed; finally it was decided to include references both to the full text of the classical stories and to abridgements of them, and leave it to the individual teacher to decide what is best suited to his class. The old guard was eager again to point out that if children are always spoken to and written for in words they understand, their vocabulary will not develop after the age of twelve or thereabouts and they will never in their lives be able to read a really well-written adult book. This is perfectly true; but the development must be a question of degree. There is not the slightest hope that a child will read for entertainment a book which requires constant reference to a dictionary, and there are many Senior School children who could not read Scott without one.

What do modern children like? First and foremost they seem to like Henty. He, almost alone of the old names, has survived the Great War and the coming of cinemas and comic papers. 'I would recommend this book to any boy because he would like the fighting in it.' 'This book gives every detail of the battle of Agincourt which rouses one's blood up when one reads it.' 'A truly exciting book.' So ran the comments. 'G. A. Henty still holds undisputed sway', writes a teacher. 'Personally I think he understood the boy mind as few authors have, before or since.' This popularity is much to be commended, for although Henty's books are not all historically sound, there is no doubt that they tend to arouse an interest in serious history, and are therefore a help to the teacher. But not all the favourites are so accommodating. *The Scarlet Pimpernel* gained more vivid eulogies than any other book; but the delightful antics of Sir Percy and his followers, written purely for entertainment, give a very one-sided view of the Revolution to a child who has no background of knowledge about it, especially as there is practically nothing that can be read by way of counter-balance. After some discussion the committee decided to include these books in the list on the ground that anything that encourages private reading has some justification, and to issue this warning in the preface. Among modern children's writers, Herbert Strang is deservedly far the most popular, as well as being the most helpful to the teacher.

The books fall mainly into three classes. There is the leisurely, old-fashioned story, full of incident and generally containing a good deal of historical reference: there is the rattling adventure story: there is the domestic and sentimental story. Of these classes girls read all three, and boys the first two; in each case, the first class is the least popular. But there is of course tremendous variety in the attractiveness of each class or of any book to particular children. Even among the members of a single committee there was considerable difference of opinion as to the suitability of books, a difference arising out of the variety of teaching experience represented there. The children of a slum school are quite two years behind the children of a better district in reading powers; and the secondary and central schools are generally ahead of the senior school children. In the list given below the books are roughly grouped as suited for Juniors (eleven years and under), Seniors (eleven to fourteen years) and fourteen years upwards. It is hoped that in the light of the explanatory comment added on each book teachers will be able to translate these recommendations into terms suited to their own pupils' needs and powers. A certain number of out-of-print books are included if experience shows that they are often found in the free libraries.

I. STORIES OF PRE-HISTORY AND PRE-ROMAN BRITAIN

Dopp, K. E. Industrial and Social History Series: **I. The Tree Dwellers. II. The Early Cave Men. III. The Later Cave Men. IV. The Early Sea People. V. The Early Herdsmen.**

Attractively told and purely fictitious stories of primitive life. Suited to very young children and juniors. Harrap.

Hall, H. R. Days before History. An admirable and attractive book in which fact and fiction are carefully distinguished. Deals with the Stone Age. Many excellent illustrations. For Juniors and Seniors. Harrap.

MacIntyre, M. A. The Cave Boy. Simply-written fictitious stories of cave life. For Juniors. Harrap.

Waterloo, S. The Story of Ab. A well-written and interesting story of cave life, giving a good idea of the laws of necessity in primitive times. For Seniors. Black.

Hall, H. R. The Threshold of History. Does for the Bronze Age what 'Days before History' did for the Stone Age.

Lamprey, L. Children of Ancient Britain. A story of pre-Roman Britain containing a good deal of information as to the condition and occupations of the people. For Juniors and Seniors. Harrap.

Stevinson, E. Pictures of Social Life. Charming little stories of children in different social settings from the earliest times to the fourteenth century in England. Very useful for Juniors. Harrap.

N.B.—Kipling's **Just So Stories** contain some delightful imaginary reconstructions of the origin of writing, &c.

II. STORIES OF ANCIENT EGYPT

Baikie, J. Wonder Tales of the Ancient World. Tales from Egyptian literature. Valuable, but not easy in style. For fourteen years and upwards. Black.

Henty, G. A. The Cat of Bubastes. A long but interesting story of life in ancient Egypt. For fourteen years and upwards. Blackie.

Lamprey, L. Children of Ancient Egypt. Very attractive and useful. A good deal of information as to Egyptian social history is interwoven with the story of a little girl. Seniors. Harrap.

Stowell, T. In the Days of the Pharaohs. A most useful simple story of the period of Rameses II. For Juniors. O.U.P.

III. STORIES OF GREEK HISTORY

Buckley, E. F. Children of the Dawn. 2 vols. Greek myths simply and yet vividly told. For Seniors. Macmillan.

Kingsley, C. The Heroes. Every child should have a chance of reading these nobly told stories of Perseus, the Argonauts and Theseus. For intelligent Juniors and for Seniors. Macmillan.

Stawell, M. and **Marvin, F. S. The Story of the Iliad.** Far the best, most simple and most classical in spirit of the many retold versions of Homer. For Juniors and Seniors. Dent.

Stawell, M. and **Marvin, F. S. The Adventures of Odysseus.** The companion volume to 'The Story of the Iliad'.

IV. STORIES OF ROMAN HISTORY

Kipling, R. Puck of Pook's Hill. Contains some fascinating stories, although they express the personality of the writer rather than the character of his period. A Roman Centurion describes to two bewitched modern children life on Hadrian's Wall. For intelligent Juniors and Seniors. Macmillan.

Henty, G. A. Beric the Briton. A story of Roman Britain and Boadicea. For Seniors. Blackie.

Lamprey, L. Children of Ancient Rome. A good deal of information in a fictitious setting. Useful, but not exciting. For Juniors and Seniors. Harrap.

Lamprey, L. Children of Ancient Gaul. Contains very useful descriptions of Gaul before and during the Roman occupation. For Seniors. Little, Brown and Co.

Macaulay. Lays of Ancient Rome. Children generally enjoy the spirited rhythm of this verse if it is read aloud to them. Legends of early Rome. For Juniors (if read aloud) and Seniors. Longmans, etc.

Mattingly, M. Marcus the Briton. A very useful story of Roman Britain in the third century. For Seniors. O.U.P.

Wallace, L. Ben Hur. A story of life in the Roman Empire at the time of Christ. Generally speaking, it is too long and old-fashioned for children, but some seem to be reading it as a result of seeing the film. For Seniors and upwards. Harper.

V. STORIES OF THE DECLINE OF ROME

Church, A. J. The Count of the Saxon Shore. Too long and full a story to interest the average child. Contains a good account of the Roman evacuation of Britain. For Seniors and upwards. Seeley.

Kingsley, C. Hypatia. A vivid story of life in the later Roman Empire: shows the development of Christianity and the coming of barbarians into the Mediterranean world. For fourteen years and upwards. Macmillan.

VI. STORIES OF THE EARLY SAXONS TO THE TIME OF EGBERT OF WESSEX

Strang, H. Olwyn's Secret. A very useful story of the struggle between Saxon and Celt, including a description of a ruined Roman villa. Simply told for juniors. O.U.P.

Marshall, H. E. Stories of Beowulf. Simply, but very well told, keeping as much as possible to the words of the poem. Eleven years and upwards. T. C. Jack.

Markham, Sir C. R. The Paladins of Edwin the Great. A story of King Edwin of Northumbria, partly founded on Bede. Fairly good. For Seniors. Black.

Lynn, Escott. Edric the Outlaw. A story of the days of Egbert, introducing Charlemagne and the beginnings of the Danish invasions. Top classes of Senior Schools. Chambers.

Baldwin, J. The Story of Roland. The romance of Roland told in a form suitable for the teacher to re-tell or read to the children. Harrap.

VII. STORIES OF THE PERIOD OF THE DANISH INVASIONS TO THE NORMAN CONQUEST

Clouston, J. Storer. Vandrad the Viking. A well-written story which would hold children's interest and give them a sense of the romantic adventurous character of the Vikings. For Seniors. Nelson.

Snedden, G. Leaf and Thorkel. A thoroughly good story, vividly and simply written, and giving in an interesting way much useful knowledge of Viking raids, institutions and social life. For eleven years upwards. Harrap.

Wilmot-Buxton, E. M. Tales from the Eddas. Excellently told simple stories of Norse gods and legends. For Juniors and Seniors. Harrap.

Fenn, G. Manville. The King's Sons. An attractive simple story of King Alfred's childhood. Most of the details are, of course, purely fictitious, but the tale would appeal to young children. For Juniors. Ernest Nister.

Henty, G. A. The Dragon and the Raven. Long, but adventurous and interesting. Useful to teacher in introducing Danish raids in countries other than England. For Seniors. Blackie.

Whistler, C. W. King Alfred's Viking. Useful as introducing the first English fleet, but not a very attractive story. Fourteen years and upwards. Nelson.

Whistler, C. W. A Sea Queen's Sailing. A well-told, adventurous story, about A.D. 935 in date. Good descriptions of Viking invasions and life among Saxons and Danes. For Seniors and upwards. Nelson.

Whistler, C. W. Dragon Osmund. A good story, with whose historical background the author has taken considerable trouble. Introduces details of the battle of Brunanburh. For Seniors and upwards. Nelson.

Whistler, C. W. A Son of Odin. Rather long but interesting romance of old Norway and the coming of Christianity. Date about A.D. 995. Fourteen years and upwards. Nelson.

Haggard, Rider. Eric Brighteyes. A romance of Norse life in Iceland. Several children describe it as 'thrilling'. Fourteen years and upwards. Longmans. Longmans also publishes a competent abridged edition.

Crake, A. D. Edwy the Fair. A story of the days of King Edwy and Dunstan. Long, but well told. For Seniors and upwards. Longmans.

Leighton, R. Olaf the Glorious. The life of King Olaf told in story form, half historical, half legendary. Introduces the battle of Malden. Fourteen years and upwards. Blackie.

Crake, A. D. Alfgar the Dane. Long and old-fashioned in style, but very interesting. Deals with the massacre of S. Brice's Day, the fighting of Edmund Ironside and the accession of Cnut. Seniors and upwards. Longmans.

Strang, H. Cedric the Saxon. A simple yet delightful and very instructive story of a Saxon boy's heroism in the time of the second Danish Invasion. For Juniors. O.U.P.

Durrant, W. S. Bevis of Hampton. A romantic half legendary story which had its origin in pre-Conquest England but which, being written down at a later date, often illustrates the atmosphere of later medieval days. For Seniors. Harrap.

Gerrould, G. H. Sir Guy of Warwick. See note on 'Bevis of Hampton'.

Surrey, G. S. A Northumbrian in Arms. A rather long but interesting story. Gives some idea of conditions in England immediately before the Conquest, and of the hostility of the Saxons to Edward the Confessor's Norman favourites. Ends with the battle of Hastings. For Seniors. O.U.P.

VIII. STORIES OF THE PERIOD OF THE NORMAN CONQUEST (1042–1100)

Yonge, C. The Little Duke. Is technically outside this group in date, but prepares the way for understanding the Conquest by describing the Normans in France and the difficulties surrounding a young feudal lord. An excellent artistic story. For Seniors. Bell. An abridged edition by O.U.P.

Crake, A. D. The Rival Heirs. Gives a strong idea of the contrast between Norman and Saxon, but is old-fashioned in style and has a strong Saxon bias. For Seniors. Longmans.

Henty, G. A. Wulf the Saxon. An adventurous exciting story. Gives a full account of the life of Harold and of the Hastings campaign. Seniors. Blackie.

Kingsley, C. Hereward the Wake. One of the best adventure stories ever written. Based on the legendary accounts of Hereward's feats ; it is not intended to represent accurate history. For intelligent Seniors and upwards. Macmillan. The O.U.P. publishes an abridged extract entitled **'Hereward's Last Fight'**, which would encourage children to read the real book.

Reed, M. B. The Foundling of Thornesford. A simply-told tale of Norman and Saxon. For Seniors. Arnold.

Strang, H. A Little Norman Maid. A very simply-written pleasant story which would give an incentive to further reading. For Juniors. O.U.P.

Strang, H. and **Aston, J. In the New Forest.** Describes the hatred and unrest caused by the Norman settlement. For Seniors. O.U.P.

Kipling, R. Puck of Pook's Hill. 'Young Men at the Manor' is a vigorous story of the Norman occupation, and **'Old Men at Pevensey'** tells of feudal life under Henry I. Excellently told stories. For Seniors. Macmillan.

Gullick, M. E. The Little Swineherd. A very simple little tale of the time of Rufus. For Juniors. Nisbet.

Hollis, G. In the Days of S. Anselm. This would give children a strong impression of the exactions of William II and the inevitability of Anselm's quarrel with him ; but it is not easy reading. For Seniors and upwards. Sheldon Press.

IX. STORIES OF THE TWELFTH CENTURY (1100–1216)

(*a*) HENRY I.

Pollard, E. F. A Saxon Maid. A pretty and simple story of the marriage of Henry I. For Juniors. Blackie.

(*b*) STEPHEN.

Whistler, C. W. A rather long but interesting story illustrating the misrule under Stephen and the Civil War. Shows the feeling of the age towards the Jews. For Seniors and upwards. Nelson.

(*c*) HENRY II.

Bennett, G. R. Boys of the Border. A story of the Welsh Marches in the time of Henry II. Seniors. Blackie.

Seth-Smith, E. K. Sir Ranulf. Deals with a pilgrimage to Glastonbury. Contains good accounts of Henry II and Hugh of Lincoln. For Seniors. Sheldon Press.

(*d*) RICHARD I AND THE THIRD CRUSADE.

Henty, G. A. Winning his Spurs. An adventurous story of the third crusade and the captivity of Richard I. For Seniors and upwards. Sampson Low.

Scott, Sir Walter. Ivanhoe. A splendid story of England in the time of the third crusade, though the hostility shown between Saxon and Norman is not historically sound at this date. A good abridged edition is by Gilliat, E. (Rivington).

Scott, Sir Walter. The Talisman. Again, one of the most famous of Scott's tales. Deals with Richard in Palestine. Abridged by Gilliat as above.

Strang, H. and **Stead, R. Lion Heart.** An excellent tale of the Welsh Marches and the third crusade ; an interesting story, and would also give a very good idea of the line of march and chief events of the Crusade. For Seniors. O.U.P.

Barham, A. M. The Namesake of the King. A good story, told with skill and full of interest. Deals with the last days of Richard I. For Seniors. Sheldon Press.

(*e*) JOHN.

Edgar, J. G. Runnymede and Lincoln Fair. A good but long and hard story. Fourteen years and upwards. Dent: Everyman's Library.

Hollis, G. Spurs and Bride. An interesting, well-told story, introducing Magna Carta. For Seniors and upwards. Sheldon Press.

Kipling, R. Puck of Pook's Hill. 'The Treasure and the Law.' A highly fictitious, fascinating story of King John, the Jews and the Charter. For Seniors. Macmillan.

(*f*) ROBIN HOOD STORIES.

Finnemore, J. The Story of Robin Hood. Episodes in the spirit of the ballads. For children of eleven and upwards. Black. Boys' Library.

Gilbert, H. Robin Hood and his Merry Men. Episodes based on the ballads. For Seniors. Jack.

Gilliat, E. In Lincoln Green. A continuous story. For fourteen years and upwards. Rather an old book. Seeley.

Gilliat, E. Wolf's Head. See note to 'In Lincoln Green', to which this story is a sequel.

Lynn, Escott. When Lion Heart was King. A continuous story. For fourteen years and upwards. Blackie.

Lynn, Escott. Robin Hood and his Merry Men. See note to 'When Lion Heart was King'. Chambers.

Marshall, H. E. Robin Hood. From 'Told to the Children' series. For Seniors. Jack.

McSpadden, J. W. Stories of Robin Hood and his Merry Outlaws. Stories re-told from the ballads. Harrap.

Tilney, F. C. Robin and his Merry Outlaws. Episodes based on the ballads. For Juniors. Dent.

Wilson, C. and **McSpadden, J. W. Robin Hood.** Episodes told in the spirit of the ballads. For Juniors. Harrap.

Wilson, W. Stories of Robin Hood. The Merry Men of Sherwood. For Juniors. Aldine Press.

X. STORIES OF THE THIRTEENTH CENTURY (1216–1314)

(*a*) HENRY III.

Ker, D. The Earl's White Cross. A very good story of Henry III and Simon de Montford, introducing the battles of Lewes and Evesham. Interesting, and gives a good account of social life, as for instance in the description of Oxford. For Seniors. Chambers.

Harrison, F. De Montfort's Squire. A fairly good story of the Barons' Wars, De Montfort and Evesham. Introduces Roger Bacon. For Seniors. Sheldon Press.

Wilmot-Buxton, E. A Little Book of St. Francis. Charming and simply-told stories and legends. For Seniors. Burns, Oates, &c.

(*b*) EDWARD I AND II.

Gilliat, E. The King's Reeve. An interesting and lively story, based on ballads. Describes the social life of the period, Glastonbury monastery and the Welsh wars. For fourteen years and upwards. Seeley.

Kyle, E. Gilbert the Page. A good and exciting story of William Wallace. Eleven to thirteen years. O.U.P.

Henty, G. A. In Freedom's Cause. The story of Wallace and Bruce; adventurous, but not one of Henty's best. For Seniors. Blackie.

XI. STORIES OF THE FOURTEENTH CENTURY (1327–1399)

(*a*) Edward III.

Andrews, J. C. Lords' Men of Littlebourne. Very useful. Good, lively sketches of social life in a fictitious setting. For Seniors. Harrap.

Bearne, C. The Cross of Pearls. A simply written story of the Jacquerie and of the Hundred Years' War from the French point of view, showing the effect on peasant life. For Seniors. Sheldon Press.

Hollis, G. Hugh the Messenger. A good, lively, interesting story, describing events from the English and French points of view. Introduces Queen Philippa and the burghers. For eleven years and upwards. Sheldon Press.

Elrington, H. In Queen Philippa's Days. An interesting and simply-told story, showing not only the victories of the Black Prince, but the burden they imposed on everyday people. For Juniors. O.U.P.

Henty, G. A. S. George for England. Good adventure story. For Seniors. Blackie.

Fairless, M. The Gathering of Brother Hilarius. The story of a young novice who goes out into the world in order to understand the claims of life. Has an imaginative appeal for the exceptionally thoughtful child. Introduces the Black Death. For fourteen years and upwards. Murray.

Yonge, C. M. The Lances of Lynwood. Very good indeed. A romantic story of knightly chivalry with the Black Prince in Spain. Fourteen years and upwards. Dent: Everyman's Library.

Doyle, Sir A. Conan. Sir Nigel. An exciting, vivid romance, introducing the Black Prince and Poictiers. Historical background very good. For fourteen years and upwards. Smith Elder.

Doyle, Sir A. Conan. The White Company. A sequel to the above, and of the same quality. Deals with the age of Du Guesclin. Smith Elder. Longmans has published an edition adapted to schools.

Strang, H. and **Stead, R. With the Black Prince.** A good, reliable and simply-written story. Covers the course of the French Wars from Sluys to Poictiers and illustrates the social background. For Seniors. O.U.P.

Harding, T. W. The Abbot of Kirkstall. A pretty, romantic story of the Black Prince and the last days of Edward III. For Seniors and above. Heffer.

(*b*) Richard II.

Hardwick, J. C. Master and Man. An interesting story told in simple and vivid language. John Ball a leading character. Describes the social unrest and intrigue leading to the Peasants' Revolt. For Seniors. Sheldon Press.

Bevan, T. Red Dickon the Outlaw. An adventurous story, illustrating the Peasants' Revolt, especially in St. Albans. Introduces John Ball, Wat Tyler, Jack Straw. For fourteen years and upwards. Nelson.

Converse, F. Long Will. A charming literary romance of the Peasants' Revolt, introducing Wat Tyler, John Ball, and Langland. Valuable, but for the exceptional child of over fourteen: language hard. Dent.

Hollis, G. Philip Okeover's Pagehood. A good, lively story of the Revolt. For Seniors. Sheldon Press.

Crake, E. E. Dame Joan of Pevensey. A fairly good story of about 1390, introducing pirates, John of Gaunt, and the defence of Pevensey Castle. For Seniors. Sheldon Press.

Henty, G. A. The Lion of St. Mark's. A tale of Venice in the fourteenth century. Good account of trade and quarrels between rival cities. Seniors and above Blackie.

XII. STORIES OF THE FIFTEENTH CENTURY

(*a*) Henry IV.

Henty, G. A. Both Sides of the Border. Vivid and readable story of Scotch and Welsh wars. Interesting on weapons and on the life of a great fifteenth-century noble household. Seniors and over. Blackie.

Elrington, H. In the Days of Prince Hal. An interesting story of life in the New Forest under the Forest Law. Introduces Prince Henry. Seniors and over. Blackie.

(*b*) Henry V.

Strang, H. and **Aston, J. Claud the Archer.** Very good. A romantic, exciting story, and also gives a good account of Agincourt and social life in England. For Seniors. O.U.P.

Westerman, P. F. Under King Henry's Banner. A spirited story of adventures at Harfleur and Agincourt. For Seniors. Pilgrim Press.

Yonge, C. M. The Caged Lion. A story of Henry V and the captivity of James I of Scotland. Excellent background and characterization. For fourteen years and over. Macmillan.

(*c*) Henry VI and the Wars of the Roses.

Green, E. Everett. A Heroine of France. A good and sympathetic story of Joan of Arc. For Seniors and over. Nelson.

Twain, M. Personal Recollections of Joan of Arc. A most delightful book. The recollections of Sieur Louis, Joan's friend. Based on the evidence at the trial. For fourteen years and over. Chatto & Windus.

Bevan, T. Held by Rebels. A spirited and readable tale of Cade's rebellion. For Seniors and upper Juniors. Collins.

Elrington, H. Page or Prentice. A pleasant, readable story of everyday life in the time of the Wars of the Roses. Deals with the introduction of printing. For Juniors and early Seniors. O.U.P.

Stevenson, R. L. The Black Arrow. A story of high literary quality; describes the character of the wars. For fourteen years and upwards. Macmillan, &c.

Strang, H. and **Lawrence, G. For the White Rose.** Very good. A story of the wars and of merchant life in London. Instructive, yet interesting. For Seniors. O.U.P.

Lynn, Escott. Under the Red Rose. An interesting, adventurous story, though long. Gloucester is the villain, and the murder of the princes is described. For Seniors. Cassell.

Elrington, H. The Luck of Chevril. An attractive story, illustrating town life and the wool industry at the end of the century.

(*d*) European Stories of the Fifteenth Century.

Eliot, G. Romola. Only the exceptional child would read this learned story of Italian life in the Renaissance; but some of the beautifully-written episodes might be read by the teacher. Blackwood, &c.

Hollis, G. The Blessed Bands. A story of the Medici and Savonarola in Renaissance Florence. Well told and interesting. For Seniors. Sheldon Press.

Reade, C. The Cloister and the Hearth. This classical story of fifteenth-century German Life will be found too long by most modern children. There is a good abridged extract published by the O.U.P., entitled 'Gerard's Last Journey', and another in Nelson's 'Books Within Books' Series.

Scott, Sir Walter. This century is represented by **The Fair Maid of Perth, Quentin Durward** (introducing a wonderful study of Louis XI of France) and **Anne of Geierstein** (Charles the Bold). Dent: Everyman's Library.

Yonge, C. M. The Dove in the Eagle's Nest. An excellent romantic story of merchant and feudal life in Germany. For fourteen years and over. Dent.

XIII. STORIES OF THE TUDOR PERIOD

(*a*) Henry VII.

Haggard, Sir Rider. Fair Margaret. A well-told story of life in England and Spain. Introduces Ferdinand and Isabella. For fourteen years and upwards. Hutchinson.

(*b*) Henry VIII.

Ainsworth, Harrison. Windsor Castle. A long story in an old-fashioned style, but containing a good deal of romantic pageantry. The story introduces Anne Boleyn, Sir Thomas Wyatt, Henry VIII, Wolsey, etc. Harrap.

Crake, A. D. The Last Abbot of Glastonbury. A good story of the dissolution of the monasteries, strongly siding against Henry VIII and his agents. For Seniors. Mowbray.

Gough, E. P. The Forest Shrine. Quite a good story of the dissolution and the Lincolnshire Rising. Contains account of life in a monastery. Cromwell presented in a very unfavourable light. Sheldon Press.

Hollis, G. My Lord of Reading. Describes the dissolution of the monastery at Reading. Sheldon Press.

Lee, A. The Call of the Night Rider. A very good story of Tyndale's life, describing the translation of the Scriptures, the flight to Germany, and Tyndale's connexion with Luther. For fourteen years and upwards. Morgan & Scott.

Manning, A. The Household of Sir Thomas More. A charming vivid narrative ; the diary of More's daughter. For fourteen years and upwards. Dent: Everyman's Library.

Nicholson, R. T. The Tudor Necklace. A fanciful story of a modern character who returns in a dream to the time of Henry VIII and is regarded as a wizard. Introduces Dean Colet. For Seniors. Sheldon Press.

Yonge, C. M. The Armourer's Prentice. A good sound story ; through the careers of two boys introduces the figures of Henry VIII, Wolsey, More, and Erasmus. For Seniors. Macmillan.

(*c*) Edward VI.

Plunket, I. L. Joanna of the Little Meadow. A simple, exciting story useful for social background. For Juniors and Seniors. O.U.P.

Twain, M. The Prince and the Pauper. The story of how Edward VI changes places with a little beggar boy. A vivid, humorous, and eminently readable fantasia. For Seniors. Chatto & Windus.

(*d*) LADY JANE GREY AND MARY I.

Ainsworth, Harrison. The Tower of London. A long but interesting and romantic story of Lady Jane Grey and Wyatt's Rebellion, &c. For fourteen years and upwards. Harrap. There is an abridged edition published by Jack.

Green, E. E. Under Two Queens. A rather long but fairly interesting story of Lady Jane Grey told by her companion. For Seniors. Shaw.

(*e*) ELIZABETH.

Bennett, J. Master Skylark. The story of a boy whose gift for singing brings him to London and into the company of actors. Introduces Shakespeare and Ben Jonson. A story that would interest children. For Seniors. Harrap.

Bevan, T. Sea-dogs all! Long, but adventurous. Raleigh at court and sea adventures. For fourteen years and upwards. Nelson.

Collingwood, M. Across the Spanish Main. An adventurous story of two boys, pirates, and the Inquisition. For Seniors. Blackie.

Gullick, M. E. Only Master Shakespeare. The adventures of Shakespeare's godson, who finally comes to London and acts in one of his plays. For Seniors. Nisbet.

Henty, G. A. Under Drake's Flag. A stirring story of Drake, the Spanish Main, and the Armada. For Seniors and upwards. Blackie.

Kingsley, C. Westward Ho! A glorious story of sea adventure and the Armada. Anti-Catholic. Harrap. There are abridged editions published by Nelson, Arnold and Longmans.

Lane, M. S. Freda of Long Dyke Farm. A charming and simple little story for Juniors. Introduces Elizabeth and the Ridolfi Plot. O.U.P.

Leighton, R. Hurrah! for the Spanish Main. A long but exciting story of Drake's third visit to Darien. For fourteen years and upwards. Melrose.

Leighton, R. The Golden Galleon. Difficult language, but exciting story; Sir Richard Grenville and the Revenge. For fourteen years and upwards. Blackie.

Leighton, R. Under the Foeman's Flag. A long but thrilling story of the Armada as seen from the Spanish point of view. For fourteen years and over. Melrose.

Plunket, I. L. Daily Life in Tudor Times. A modern 'John Bull' disabled by an accident pays a visit to his village in Tudor times, and also visits Tudor London. Very useful for social background. For Juniors and Seniors. O.U.P.

Reed, Talbot Baines. Sir Ludar. Good account of England and Ireland under Elizabeth. The story of the Armada told from the point of view of an English apprentice who is prisoner on a Spanish ship. For fourteen years and upwards. Religious Tract Society.

Scott, Sir Walter. Kenilworth. One of Scott's finest novels for romance, drama and pageantry. The story of Elizabeth, Leicester and Amy Robsart. Harrap or Dent. A fairly good abridged edition published by Macmillan and another by Rivington.

Strang, H. A Gentleman-at-Arms. The adventures of a young Elizabethan in Ireland, Spain, France and the Netherlands as related by himself in later life. Attractively told. For Seniors. O.U.P.

Strang, H. and **Stead, R. A Mariner of England.** A simple, instructive and interesting account of the main events of Elizabeth's struggle with Spain, woven into a very fascinating story. For Seniors. O.U.P.

Strang, H. With Drake on the Spanish Main. A thoroughly exciting story of Drake's visit to the Spanish Main, finding of treasure, and sight of the Pacific. For Seniors. O.U.P.

Westerman, P. 'Gainst the Might of Spain. A boy's story of treasure-hunting, the Inquisition and the Armada. For fourteen years and over. Pilgrim Press.

Whitham, G. I. Basil the Page. A simply-told and very attractive story of an Elizabethan boy, introducing Leicester, Mary Queen of Scots and Drake. For Seniors. Wells, Gardner.

(*f*) EUROPEAN STORIES.

i. *Italy.*

Hollis, G. The Blessed Bands. See under Fifteenth Century.

Surrey, G. S. 'Mid Clash of Swords. A story of the Italian Cities. Illustrates the chaos of politics after the French invasion. For Seniors. O.U.P.

ii. *Spain.*

Haggard, Rider. Fair Margaret. See under Henry VII.

Stables, G. Westward with Columbus. Rather long and old-fashioned in style, but gives a good account of the youth and adventures of Columbus, including the voyage of 1492. For Seniors. Blackie.

iii. *Spain and the Revolt of the Netherlands.*

Henty, G. A. By Pike and Dyke. Long, stirring and adventurous. Ends with the death of William the Silent. For fourteen upwards. Blackie.

Henty, G. A. By England's Aid. A continuation of the subject of 'By Pike and Dyke'. For fourteen years and upwards. Blackie.

Orczy, Baroness. Leather Face. Story of the struggle of the Netherlanders against Alva. For fourteen years and upwards. Hodder & Stoughton.

Strang, H. Silver Shot. A very good and simply-told story of war in the Netherlands, 1593. For Seniors and top class of Juniors. O.U.P.

iv. *France.*

Hare, C. Bayard. A charming popular biography retailing the adventures of Bayard. For Seniors. Dent.

Henty, G. A. St. Bartholomew's Eve. A good romantic tale, full of incident. For Seniors. Blackie.

Weyman, S. A Gentleman of France. A story of the age of Henry of Navarre. Court intrigues connected with rival religious factions. For readers of over fourteen years. Harrap.

Weyman, S. The House of the Wolf. A good description of the French nobles and religious factions. Deals with the massacre of St. Bartholomew. For fifteen years and upwards. Nelson.

XIV. STORIES OF THE STUART PERIOD

(*a*) James I.

Ainsworth, W. H. The Lancashire Witches. Interesting, but long and old-fashioned in style. For fourteen years and upwards. Routledge.

Ainsworth, W. H. The Star Chamber. Deals with the court of James I and the monopolists. For fourteen years and upwards. Routledge.

Finnemore, J. The Renegade. A story of the Barbary pirates; exciting, but contains accounts of cruelty. Black.

Fox, A. Wilson. Too Near the Throne. The romantic story of Lady Arabella Stuart; of no great historical importance. For Seniors. Sheldon Press.

Lee, A. The Maid of the Mayflower. An interesting and useful picture of the sufferings of the Puritans in the time of Elizabeth and James I. For Seniors.

Scott, Sir Walter. The Fortunes of Nigel. A wonderful picture of James I and his court. Dent: Everyman's Library.

(*b*) Charles I and the Civil War.

Bowen, M. The Governor of England. Useful and good ; excellent portraits of chief personalities ; but too difficult for the average child. For readers of over fourteen years. Methuen.

Cooper, Mrs. Frank. True to the King. An abridged edition of the old tale of 'Hide and Seek'. Story of attempted capture of Royalists by Ireton, whose character is taken from Clarendon's 'Great Rebellion'. On Royalist side. For Seniors. Sheldon Press.

Gilbert, B. John of the Fens. A story in the vein of Henty about Cromwell and his Ironsides. For fourteen years and upwards. O.U.P.

Groves, J. P. Charmouth Grange. Old-fashioned in style, but includes accounts of several of the most famous battles of the Civil War. For fourteen years and upwards. Sampson Low, &c.

Hayens, H. For Rupert and the King. A well-written story of a boy's adventures in Prince Rupert's army. On Royalist side. Very readable. For Seniors. Sheldon Press.

Henty, G. A. Friends though Divided. A story of boy friends on opposite sides. Includes Charles' imprisonment and Cromwell's campaigns in Scotland and Ireland. For fourteen years and upwards. Frowde and Hodder.

Hinkson, H. A. The King's Liege. A story on the Royalist side of the discontent leading up to the Civil War. Of no great historical value, but readable and simple. For eleven to fourteen years. Blackie.

Hollis, G. In a Royal Nursery. A story of the children of Charles I, told from the Royalist standpoint. Not very important historically, but recommended as interesting by a number of girls. For Seniors. Sheldon Press.

Lane, M. S. The Silver Thread. Readable, but not of great historical importance. Royalist point of view. For Seniors. O.U.P.

Marryat, Captain. The Children of the New Forest. The story of a Royalist family during the time of Charles I's imprisonment. Old-fashioned and full of detail, but a number of modern children seem to like it. Routledge.

Moore, D. A Nest of Malignants. Contains little historical information, but is a readable story of the exploits of some children who help in the escape of Charles II after Worcester. For eleven to fourteen years. Sheldon Press.

Moore, D. A Brave Little Royalist. The history is very superficial; but little girls would be certain to like the book and to feel an interest in the Royalist fortunes. For Juniors. Nisbet.

Quiller-Couch, Sir A. T. The Splendid Spur. A well-written story of everyday life in Stuart times, and of the adventures of a Royalist in the Civil War. For fourteen years and upwards. Nelson.

Scott, Sir Walter. The Legend of Montrose. The Royalist campaigns of Montrose in Scotland. Dent: Everyman's Library.

Strang, H. and **Stead, R. One of Rupert's Horse.** Very useful. The adventures of a young Cavalier from 1642–9, introducing all the chief battles, yet interesting and simply told. For Seniors. O.U.P.

Westerman, P. F. The Young Cavalier. A good story of the wars, introducing Edgehill and Carisbroke Castle. For Seniors and upwards. Pearson.

Whitham, G. His Majesty's Glove. A romantic interesting story, though of no particular historical value. For Seniors. Nelson.

Whitham, G. Dick Chester. A very readable pro-Royalist story, of no great historical value. For Seniors. Blackie.

Anon. Brave Dame Mary. The siege of Corfe Castle, quite well told from the Royalist point of view. For Seniors. Sheldon Press.

(*c*) The Commonwealth.

Caine, O. V. Wanderer and King. A well-told and useful account of Charles II's adventures after Worcester. For Seniors. Nisbet.

Drinkwater, J. Oliver Cromwell. An imaginative piece of work, which has been appreciated by several of the elder children. An excellent corrective to the numerous pro-Royalist stories. Sidgwick and Jackson.

Lane, M. S. The Wild Bird. A good and interesting story of the wanderings of Charles II told from the Royalist point of view. For fourteen years and upwards. O.U.P.

Lynn, E. The Twenty-Five Swordsmen. An adventurous story of Worcester and the Commonwealth; illustrates the divisions of families by party strife. Ends with Restoration. For fourteen years. Chambers.

Scott, Sir Walter. Woodstock. A fine story; but the picture of Puritans is highly unfair. A story of the oppression of the Royalists during the Commonwealth.

Whitham, G. The Last of the Whitecoats. Introduces the siege of Holt Castle, and the fight at Worcester. Quite interesting. For fourteen years and upwards. Seeley.

(*d*) CHARLES II.

Ainsworth, W. H. Old St. Paul's. The long, detailed but vivid story of London life in the Restoration period, introducing the Plague and Fire. For fourteen years and upwards. Harrap.

Blackmore, R. D. Lorna Doone. The famous picture of the countryfolk of Devon at the end of the seventeenth century. Too difficult in style for most children. Dent : Everyman's Library.

Clare, A. The Carved Cartoon. The Story of Grinling Gibbons. An old book, but well written and charming, and recommended by several girls. Sheldon Press.

Leslie, J. Red Roof Farm. A simply-told story of how a Royalist family recovered its fortunes after the Restoration ; has a good social background. For Juniors. O.U.P.

Henty, G. A. When London Burned. Long, but vivid and interesting. London in the Plague and Fire. For Seniors. Blackie.

Hope, A. Simon Dale. A drama of foreign politics at the time of the Restoration. Too adult for the average child. Methuen.

Graeme, J. The Fortunes of Harold Borlase. A straightforward, rattling adventure story ; introduces Blake and the Dutch Wars, the Plague and the Moors at Tunis. For Seniors. Sheldon Press.

Scott, Sir Walter. Old Mortality. The story of the Scottish Covenanters and Grahame of Claverhouse. Dent : Everyman's Library.

Scott, Sir Walter. Peveril of the Peak. A fine story of the Restoration, introducing Charles II, the revelations of Titus Oates and the ' Catholic Plot '. Dent : Everyman's Library.

Strang, H. Martin of Old London. A good and useful story of social life and the Great Fire. O.U.P.

Westerman, P. F. A Lad of Grit. A good story of sea adventure in the Restoration period, mentioning the Dutch Wars. For Seniors. Blackie.

(*e*) JAMES II AND THE REVOLUTION.

Bevan, T. Rebels and Rogues. An interesting and adventurous version of Monmouth's rebellion, introducing Sedgemoor and Judge Jeffreys. For Seniors. Nisbet.

Doyle, Sir A. Conan. Micah Clarke. The story of Monmouth's rebellion. Very good, but too difficult for most children. Murray. Longmans publish an abridged edition, which should prove useful.

Finnemore, J. The Lover Fugitives. A story of escape after Monmouth's rebellion and the return to safety with William III. For Seniors. Pearson.

Gilson, C. The Sword of Freedom. The story of the adventures of a Whig who is concerned in the conspiracy against James II. For Seniors. O.U.P.

Lynn, E. A Cavalier of Fortune. A good, romantic story of Monmouth's rebellion, which paints James II in very black colours. For Seniors. Chambers (abridged ed.).

Masefield, J. Martin Hyde. The story of a boy in Monmouth's rebellion. Full of vivid and well-described incident; an excellent story. For Seniors and upwards. Wells, Gardiner, &c.

Masefield, J. Captain Margaret. A fine, stirring story of adventure at this period on the Spanish Main. Nelson.

Rhoades, W. In Stirring Times. A useful and realistic story of James' reign after Monmouth's rebellion, and of the growing feeling against him. For Seniors. O.U.P.

Pollard, E. F. The Lady Isobel. A story of the Scottish Covenanters, introducing Andrew Morton; ends with the coming of William III as the champion of religious toleration. For Senior girls. Blackie.

Strang, H. Winning his Name. A very good, adventurous story bringing in the popular feeling against the Declaration of Indulgence, and the Trial of the Seven Bishops. For Seniors. O.U.P.

Yonge, C. M. A Reputed Changeling. A story of everyday and court life under James II; includes a picture of James at St. Germains. Macmillan.

(*f*) WILLIAM III.

Hayens, H. The Honour of a Royall. Quite a good story of the Jacobite unrest under William III; useful as showing how loyal the Royalists were to James II, and how little he deserved it. For Seniors. Collins.

Henty, G. A. Orange and Green. A good adventurous story of William in Ireland, and the battle of the Boyne. For fourteen years and upwards. Blackie.

Lindsay, H. The Jacobite. Quite a good tale of Jacobites at St. Germains at the close of the century. Picture of London life. For Seniors. Chatto & Windus.

Strang, H. Humphrey Bold. A good, spirited and useful story of a boy who is thrown on the world, and who fights by sea in the wars of William III against the French. For Seniors and upwards. O.U.P.

See also the note on **M. Bowen's** books under European History below.

(*g*) Anne.

Green, R. E. Tom Tufton's Travels. A story of London life and Marlborough's wars. For Seniors. Nelson.

Henty, G. A. The Cornet of Horse. The Bravest of the Brave. Two adventurous stories of the wars against France. Good and spirited. For Seniors and upwards. Sampson Low and Blackie, respectively.

Lynn, E. For Name and Nation. A vigorous exciting tale; introduces Marlborough's wars and social life. For fourteen years and upwards. Chambers.

Strang, H. The Adventures of Harry Rochester. With Marlborough to Malplaquet. Two excellent stories which introduce a good deal of the history of Marlborough's wars in an interesting way. For Seniors. O.U.P.

Thackeray, W. P. Esmond. A wonderful, intimate and interesting picture of the great events and characters of Anne's day; could not be read by children, but passages could be read to them. Dent: Everyman's Library.

(*h*) Stories of European History of the Seventeenth Century.

Bowen, M. I will Maintain. The Defender of the Faith. For God and the King. A fine trilogy on William III, but too difficult for the average child. Methuen.

Bramston, M. The Thorn Fortress. A very useful and interesting story of the sufferings of a village during the Thirty Years' War, 1618–48. For Seniors. Sheldon Press.

Doyle, Sir A. Conan. The Refugee. A tale of Louis XIV, the Huguenots and the Revocation of the Edict of Nantes. An excellent story, but rather old for the average Senior school child. For fourteen years and upwards. Murray.

Henty, G. A. Won by the Sword. A stirring tale of the Thirty Years' War. For Seniors and upwards. Blackie.

Townshend, D. Whither; the Story of a Flight. A simply-told story of the flight of a Huguenot family to England after the Revocation of the Edict of Nantes. For Seniors. Sheldon Press.

XV. STORIES OF THE EIGHTEENTH CENTURY

(*a*) STORIES OF THE JACOBITE RISINGS.

Buchan, J. A Lost Lady of Old Years. A tale of the '45. For fourteen years and over. Lane.

Lee, P. The Northumbrian Rebel. An interesting though not always well-written story of a boy's adventures in the rebellion of '15. Brings out the causes of its failure. For Seniors. Pilgrim Press.

Orczy, Baroness. Beau Brocade. An exciting story written in bad English. Introduces highwaymen, travelling, the aftermath of the rebellion of '15, and village life in the early eighteenth century. For fourteen years and upwards. Hodder & Stoughton.

Poynter, H. M. A Fair Jacobite. A rather charming story of a spirited girl who goes to visit the Stuarts in exile at St. Germains just before the rebellions of '15 and '45. For fourteen years and upwards. Nelson.

Scott, Sir Walter. Some of Scott's most famous novels centre round the Jacobite movement. **The Black Dwarf** describes the Jacobite party before 1715. **Waverley** is the story of the rebellion of '45, and has always proved one of the most popular of the novels. **Rob Roy** introduces Jacobite intrigue. **Redgauntlet** shows the decline of Jacobitism. **The Heart of Midlothian,** of the same period, deals with the Porteous Riots in Edinburgh. All in Dent: Everyman's Library.

Stevenson, R. L. Kidnapped. Catriona. Finely-told tales of adventure in Scotland and abroad after the failure of the rebellion of '45. Contrasts the Highland and Lowland temperaments. For Seniors and upwards. Cassell, &c.

Strang, H. The Cave in the Hills. An interesting and instructive tale of the rebellion of '45. Very useful. For Seniors. O.U.P.

Strang, H. Honour First. An excellent story of the '45 rebellion, skilfully blending history and romance. The story of a boy who becomes messenger to the Pretender. Brings out causes of failure. For Seniors. O.U.P.

Watson, F. Muckle John. An interesting and good story of the effect of Culloden and the escape of the Prince. For Seniors. Black.

(*b*) SMUGGLING AND PIRATE STORIES.

Most of these contain little or no historical information, but they are good stories.

Bourne, L. R. The Channel Pirate. An exciting sea story of smuggling at the end of the seventeenth century. For Seniors. O.U.P.

Stevenson, R. L. Treasure Island. A gloriously sensational story, of high literary quality. For Seniors and upwards.

Strang, H. Bastable Cove. A short and very simple story of a boy's adventures with smugglers in 1806. For Juniors. O.U.P.

Strang, H. The Adventures of Dick Trevanion. An exciting sea story of the early nineteenth century; incidental reference only to French wars. For Seniors. O.U.P.

Strang, H. Jack Hardy. The daring escapades of a boy in warfare against smugglers in the early nineteenth century. For Seniors. O.U.P.

(*c*) THE WESLEYAN MOVEMENT.

Charles, E. Diary of Mrs. Kitty Trevelyan. This is probably too old-fashioned and quiet in tone for the modern child. But it is a charming picture of everyday life in the eighteenth century and of the Wesleyan Revival. For fourteen years and upwards. Nelson.

(*d*) ANGLO-FRENCH WARS IN INDIA AND AMERICA.

Fox, A. W. A Regular Madam. A readable story of a girl who goes to seek adventures in North America. Introduces the capture of Quebec. For Senior Girls. Macmillan.

Henty, G. A. With Wolfe in Canada. A good interesting story of the fighting in America and the taking of Quebec. For fourteen years and upwards. Blackie.

Parker, Sir Gilbert. The Trail of the Sword. The Seats of the Mighty. Two excellent novels of French Canada but beyond the scope of children's reading.

Quiller-Couch, Sir A. T. Fort Amity. A fine romantic story of French-Canadian life and the wars of Montcalm and Wolfe. For fourteen years and upwards. Dent.

Strang, H. One of Clive's Heroes. A very good, simply-told and useful story of life on the high sea and in India. For Seniors. O.U.P.

Strang, H. Rob the Ranger. A very good story of life in the backwoods and the Canadian wars. For Seniors. O.U.P.

Strang, H. and **Laurence, G. Roger the Scout.** Deals with the results of the '45 rebellion in Scotland, and the Canadian wars before the taking of Quebec. For Seniors and upwards.

Thackeray, W. P. The Virginians. A well-described picture of eighteenth-century life in America and England, introducing George Washington. Too difficult for children, but some episodes might be read to them. Dent.

(*e*) The Gordon Riots.

Dickens, C. Barnaby Rudge. A great classic. Quite a good abridged edition is published by the O.U.P.

Moore, D. Pamela's Hero. A well-told lively story of London life and the riots. For Seniors. Blackie.

(*f*) The French Revolution.

Practically all these books are strongly anti-Jacobin.

Bearne, Mrs. C. In Perilous Days. A story of the escape of one member after another of a noble French family from the Jacobins. Not very exciting. Sheldon Press.

Brereton, F. S. Foes of the Red Cockade. An exciting adventurous story of the rebellion in La Vendée, and the Reign of Terror. For Seniors. Blackie.

Coleridge, M. The King with Two Faces. A dramatic romance, mainly of Swedish history, but introducing the French Revolution and the flight to Varennes. Full of interest for intelligent children of fourteen years and upwards. Arnold.

Dickens, C. A Tale of Two Cities. A great classic.

Henty, G. A. In the Reign of Terror. An exciting story, including most of the well-known episodes of the Revolution. For fourteen years and upwards. Blackie.

Martineau, Harriet. Peasant and Prince. A fair account of the Revolution period for children, including much interesting detail, but not much story. For Seniors. Ginn.

Moore, D. Adventurers Two. The escapes of an English boy and girl during the Vendean rising. For Seniors. Sheldon Press.

Orczy, Baroness. The Scarlet Pimpernel series includes **The Scarlet Pimpernel, The Elusive Pimpernel, I will Repay, Lord Tony's Wife, The League of the Scarlet Pimpernel, The Triumph of the Scarlet Pimpernel,** and **Sir Percy Hits Back.** See note in preface.

(*g*) The Napoleonic Wars.

Doyle, Sir A. Conan. Uncle Bernac. A story which introduces Napoleon's attempts to invade England. For fourteen years and upwards. Smith, Elder.

Doyle, Sir A. Conan. The Adventures of Gerard. The Exploits of Brigadier Gerard. Spirited, humorous stories that stick at nothing. For Seniors and upwards. Nelson.

Doyle, Sir A. Conan. Rodney Stone. A story of prize-fighting in the Napoleonic era. Introduces Nelson. Smith, Elder.

Finnemore, J. The Story of a Scout. A story of guerilla warfare in the Peninsula, in the period leading up to Burgos and Vittoria. Historical background too vague to be of much use. For fourteen years and upwards. Pearson.

Fraser, E. Jack Chaloner. A good romantic narrative, but highly coloured; deals with the naval war under Nelson, and its effects at home. For readers over fourteen years. Hutchinson.

Gilson, C. The Lost Empire. An adventurous story of Napoleon and Nelson and the Egyptian campaign. For Seniors and upwards. O.U.P.

Gilson, C. The Spy. A sensational story of the Peninsular War, heartily recommended by several boys. For Seniors. O.U.P.

Henty, G. A. At Aboukir and Acre. Adventurous detailed story of Napoleon in Egypt. For fourteen years and upwards. **By Conduct and Courage.** A story of Nelson, introducing in the second part the battles of '94 and '97 in considerable detail. For fourteen years and upwards. **The Young Buglers.** A very good account of the Peninsular War, detailed, romantic, but accurate. For readers over fourteen years. **Through Russian Snows.** A good story of Napoleon's retreat from Moscow. For fourteen years and upwards. **With Moore at Corunna.** Deals with the years 1808 and 1809. A substantial story, less accurate and good than 'The Young Buglers'. For fourteen years and upwards. All published by Blackie, except 'The Young Buglers' (Hodder and Stoughton).

Marryat, Captain. It is doubtful whether the stories of this writer are still read by boys; here is a list of his sea stories of the eighteenth and nineteenth centuries: **Frank Mildmay. Jacob Faithful. Newton Forster. Mr. Midshipman Easy. Peter Simple. The King's Own** (a tale of the mutiny at the Nore). Routledge.

Moore, D. The Luck of Ledge Point. A charming little story of 1805, but not very useful historically, although it contains slight pictures of the Emperor, Berthier, &c. For Seniors. Blackie.

Newbolt, Sir Henry. Taken from the Enemy. A story of Napoleon at St. Helena. For Seniors and upwards. Chatto & Windus.

Stevenson, R. L. St. Ives. The romantic story of a French prisoner of war. For fourteen years and upwards. Heinemann.

Strang, H. Boys of the Light Brigade. A vivid attractive story of the Peninsular War 1808–9, containing excellent detail as to the taking of Saragossa, etc. For readers of over fourteen. **In Trafalgar's Bay.** Chiefly a picture of home life in the period. For Juniors. **Our Great Adventure.** As above; for Juniors. O.U.P.

XVI. STORIES OF THE NINETEENTH CENTURY

(*a*) Stories of Social Life.

Brontë, Charlotte. Shirley. Contains vivid picture of the coming of the Industrial Revolution, and the effect of the Napoleonic wars on trade. Dent: Everyman's Library.

Craik, Mrs. John Halifax. Rather long and adult for modern children, but very useful in describing the coming of the machines and the corruption of Parliamentary elections before the Reform Bill. There is a simplified extract entitled **'John Halifax's Boyhood'** published by Nelson.

Eliot, George. Silas Marner. An excellent picture of how industry was carried on before the factory system became universal. For beauty of language and characterization this story is unsurpassed, and much of it is simple enough for children. Dent: Everyman's Library.

Henty, G. A. Through the Fray. A good, interesting and true account of the Luddite riots in a Yorkshire village. For Seniors and upwards. Blackie.

Weyman, S. Chippinge. An excellent story of the Reform Bill, introducing the Bristol riots; but difficult for children. Smith Elder.

(*b*) The Crimean War.

Henty, G. A. Jack Archer. A long, but interesting and good story, introducing Alma, Inkerman and Balaclava. For Seniors and upwards. Sampson Low.

Lynn, Escott. Blair of Balaclava. A good and vivid story. For fourteen years and over. Chambers.

(*c*) The Indian Mutiny and Indian Wars.

Jackson, A. F. Heroes of the Chitral Siege. A straightforward well-told story of the Afghan Wars. For Seniors. Sheldon Press.

Henty, G. A. In Herat and Cabul. Through the Sikh Wars. For Name and Fame. All published by Blackie.

Lynn, E. A Hero of the Indian Mutiny. Long, but fairly interesting. For fourteen years and over. Chambers.

Strang, H. Barclay of the Guards. A good and exciting story, bringing in Lawrence. Gives a good idea of the attitude of the natives. For Seniors. O.U.P.

(*d*) THE WAR OF ITALIAN INDEPENDENCE.

Henty, G. A. Out with Garibaldi. For fourteen years and upwards. Blackie.

(*e*) AMERICA IN THE NINETEENTH CENTURY.

Stowe, H. B. Uncle Tom's Cabin. The well-known story of slave atrocities, parts of which are still read with interest by children.

Stables, G. For Life and Liberty. A fairly good and interesting story of the American Civil War. Style not very good. For fourteen years and upwards. Blackie.

(*f*) THE FRANCO-GERMAN WAR.

Henty, G. A. The Young Franc-Tireurs. A very good story, informative, spirited and interesting. For fourteen years and over. An abridged edition has been published under the title of '**The Boy Heroes of France**'. Whitcombe and Tombs.

(*g*) AFRICA IN THE NINETEENTH AND TWENTIETH CENTURIES.

Henty, G. A. The Young Colonists. A story of the Zulu and Boer Wars. Blackie.

Henty, G. A. The Dash for Khartoum. With Kitchener in the Soudan. Blackie.

Gilson, C. In the Land of Shame. A vivid story showing the conditions in East Africa round about the Zambesi River about 1890, and describing the slave trade. For fourteen years and over. Boy's Own Paper.

(*h*) CHINA.

Gilson, C. The Lost Column. A most exciting story of the Boxer Rising. For Seniors. O.U.P.

Henty, G. A. With the Allies to Pekin. A story of the Boxer Rising. Blackie.

VII

THE TEACHING OF PRESENT-DAY AFFAIRS

NOT much more than twenty years ago, the history course in many schools and colleges ran from A.D. 1066 to 1837. Little effort was made to trace the origins of the society and political situation revealed to William the Conqueror when he invaded England; and as little effort was made to explain social and political conditions in the present day to the young adventurers who were to explore an England of the future. Teachers were rarely successful in giving the impression, if indeed they attempted to give it, that they and their pupils were actually living in the midst of a historical period, that its great movements and institutions were continuous with those of an earlier age, and that one reason for learning about the past is to understand the present. Between the facts of a history text-book and the facts of everyday life as children could observe and understand them, there stretched a wide gulf; it was little wonder if the actors and events on the far side of that gulf seemed as remote and unreal as the figments of a dream.

Such at any rate were the memories of those who attended the Civics Committee of the Handbook: and their purpose was to look for means of *bridging the gulf between the history lesson and the children's own social experiences.* Their aim, in this connexion, was not to prepare the few for the enjoyment of history as an academic subject but to prepare the many for the practical demands of civic life. They desired to link together the past, the present and the future by helping children to understand something of their present social environment, to discover its connexion with the past history they had learned, and to look forward in a natural way to holding certain rights and responsibilities in regard to it when they should grow up. Having defined an aim, the Committee then set to work to discuss, first, by what methods the children could best approach the work; secondly, what the course should include; and thirdly, what books and equipment would be most useful.

I. METHODS OF APPROACH

The Committee members began by setting aside the possibility of approaching the subject through some one class-book. They did so partly because they had found no book quite to their mind but chiefly because they wished to follow the bent of the class of thirteen-year-old girls who were to take the experimental course. If the educational system is working as it should, the majority of children who like books and reading have left the school before reaching the top classes, and those who remain prefer practical and active work. The aim was to rouse their interest in examining or questioning the familiar details of their own neighbourhood, and to bring in books in a secondary way, as useful for reference and explanation.

Several suggestions were made. One head-master explained his method of teaching civics through arithmetic lessons, using E. & J. Riley's Arithmetic of Citizenship (Sidgwick & Jackson, 1922. Teacher's book, 2*s.* 6*d.*, class book, 2*s.*), which he found excellent and practical. Another proposed that the work might be grouped round a survey of the various buildings of the district, and that the children should set to work to discover what past history and present problems were connected with the residential quarter, the schools, the town hall, the factory, the churches and railway stations. Another experimented successfully with a scheme in which a family of people named Smith came to settle in the neighbourhood. They had first to find a house, and their requirements and chance of satisfaction were investigated. Then they settled down, among the protests of Mrs. Smith that her kitchen was inconveniently planned and that she had no 'separate front door'. The children went to school, won scholarships or entered industry, and had varied careers. Mr. Smith took part in the outstanding occupation of the district, joined a trade union, and in the ripeness of time stood as a candidate for the Town Council. Mrs. Smith shopped, washed clothes, patronized Co-operative Stores. conducted her offspring to the clinic, and took advantage generally of the facilities of her district. The family as a whole had a taste for politics and public events. The Smiths were very successful in interesting the children; but their career had the disadvantage of falling too readily into a story form which left the majority of the class as listeners. The great aim was to find a scheme based on individual observation and inquiry.

The method finally decided upon was to set a question paper covering each part of the course and let the children find out as many answers as possible from their own observation and from a class library. Such a course involved a considerable amount of work, which would probably be most easily achieved in other districts, as in this one, by a committee of teachers and social scientists working together. Shared out among the group, the work was not formidable: one teacher, for instance, prepared the section on co-operation, another drew up an admirable summary of the work of local and central government in the district, and all joined in the search for suitable books. The brunt of the work was borne by the teacher of the first class taking the course, without whose powers of organization the experiment could never have been carried through. Each paper was thoroughly discussed by the Committee before it was given to the children: and after they had finished, it was discussed again and handed on in a revised form to the second school undertaking the experiment. In their discussion of the general principles of the course the Committee had the very great advantage of visits from Mr. Tawney and from Mr. Farquharson of Leplay House; and they found the local and public bodies to whom they applied for information most helpful and friendly.

The papers were generally given out to the girls with an introductory talk, but their work was almost entirely individual. Everything that they could discover for themselves was written in green ink, information from books was entered in red. They got a certain amount of help from home; some of the fathers became really interested, particularly in Paper V. It was possible for the children to handle four sets of encyclopædias, and a few special books on each paper. These were put in a separate book rest, and during the lesson they were distributed among the class. Each girl answered those questions with which her book dealt, and as the work proceeded the books were passed from group to group until the whole paper was answered. Any child unable to proceed was required to work at a special topic, such as 'The Repair of the Roads' (in Paper II), or to revise from her history notebook any matter specially relating to a paper. The main practical difficulty during the first experimental working of the course was the scanty supply of books, a scantiness which was inevitable while the Committee members were still exploring the children's literature of the subject. It is hoped that the bibliographies subjoined will help to remove the difficulty of choice of books; but teachers desirous of trying the course should be warned of the importance of securing plenty of duplicates in the class library. It need not be said that the scope and nature of the questionnaires must be determined to some extent by the books that are available. There are several topics, as for instance Trade Unionism, where very little of the reading is directly suited to children. But it was generally found that children could use for reference a far more difficult book than they could read continuously, as long as the question was simple and the page reference clear.

When the class had finished a paper one oral lesson on the corrected work was usually given. This often took the form of a general reconstruction of the paper, each girl being called on to read her answer to one question: and while obviously the papers of the best girls were most useful in regard to the hard questions, there were plenty of simple answers which gave the weaker girls a chance to make their contribution. At the end of the whole course the children revised their material, and were given a test. This was done for the sake of thoroughness. But the Committee did not feel that the value of the course was gauged by the amount of knowledge shown under test conditions; the value lay rather in the girls' increased interest in their surroundings and their readiness to regard public events as something important to them, not as something alien and beyond their ken.

II. THE NATURE OF THE COURSE

It is undeniable that 'civics' teaching has not always a good name in educational circles. The teacher of civics is sometimes considered a crank; the pupils are sometimes pitied for learning anything so dull. The reason for this is not far to seek. The Committee began its work by analysing and discussing the subject-matter of all the children's books written on the subject, and soon found itself in a position to make a general criticism. With very few exceptions these books began by describing the King, the Cabinet and Parliament and went on to describe the judicial system, the army and navy, the machinery of local government and finance. It is obvious that these topics are as remote from the children as any topics of past history can be. They describe an elaborate central organization, complicated by a thousand traditions, which never touches the life of children directly and which is of pressing practical importance to the adult worker only in times of emergency. These books, in their naïve assumption that the most important factor in everyday life is the activity of the State, were turning their backs on social realities. The children had far more direct contact with voluntary activities such as Sunday schools, co-operative societies and hospitals than they had with the activities of the State. In short, the Committee soon reached the point of condemning the general plan of almost all children's civics books and endorsing heartily the Board's suggestion that 'any attempt to deal elaborately with the parts of the British Constitution, the local government of the country or the administration of justice, is wearisome and must be largely unintelligible to children'. Teaching about institutions should be the climax, and not the starting point, of a civics course.

The Committee thus arrived at certain definite principles. Civics teaching should not be taken as a separate subject but should form an integral part of the history course. It should, when possible, be placed at the end of the syllabus and taken in the last term of a school career, so that it acts at once as a climax to history-teaching and a preparation for life; but besides this the spirit of civics teaching should penetrate the whole course, so that in innumerable small ways the children are prepared for the work before they attack it directly. The material for teaching should be limited by the children's own social experiences, and should be local, concrete and practical rather than abstract and general. It should start with the home, the street and the school, and proceed outwards from these as the children's horizon widens. It should deal with the district before dealing with the nation. Above all, it should deal with voluntary social and economic activities before dealing with the impersonalized activities of the State. From all this it follows that a civics course must be adapted to the school and the neighbourhood, and that no general course could be drawn up for universal application ; but it was decided to work out a course suited to a Deptford girls' school and ask volunteers in other districts to see whether the course could be adapted to their needs. This second inquiry was undertaken by another S.E. London school of rather more well-to-do girls, and by a boys' junior technical school at Rochester, whose work developed on most interesting lines.

The Deptford scheme was divided into six parts, each intended for a fortnight's work, to be carried out by the top class :—

1. Housing.
2. Local Communications.
3. Local Occupations.
4. Voluntary Social Activities in the District.
5. Local Government.
6. Central Government, and its Activities in the District.

The Rochester school adapted this scheme to an experimental course of regional survey work. All the pupils taking part in the work came from good artisan homes scattered over a large provincial town and the surrounding country, an area favourable to geographical study. The regional survey course was in fact substituted for geography as a school subject, and the various aspects of civics in relation to local study found a place in the course as a necessary part of the observational work. The course was taken by a special first-year Form, the ages of the pupils ranging from twelve to fourteen, and was planned to cover three school terms with two hours' class work each week.

The relation of the Deptford and Rochester experiments was one of a friendly interchange of ideas. It is not possible, even were it desirable, for one school to adopt the questionnaire of another. Differences of sex, age and local environment will dictate wide differences of method and syllabus. The record of these experiments is not put forward as one to be copied literally by other teachers but as containing suggestions which they might be able to adapt to their own needs.

PART I. HOUSING

About three miles from the crowded streets of Deptford lies the new L.C.C. estate of Downham, whose houses, small though they are, allow of a personal cleanliness and privacy in sleeping arrangements unknown to the two-roomed Dept ford homes. One house in ten of this estate is reserved for Deptford people, and the population is slowly beginning to empty itself into wider spaces. This is a social change which the girls can observe for themselves and which interests them. One or two families moved out to Downham while the course was actually in progress: one of the girls' fathers had helped to build the houses there. It was an ideal moment, not only for discussing the housing problem, but for giving prospective emigrants some ideas about how to use the little modern houses when they got them; for although comparatively few of the girls' parents make the move, the girls themselves stand a good chance of living on a Council estate when they marry. Most of the children were thoroughly familiar with crowded household conditions in their own homes, had never seen anything different, and would naturally have tended to reproduce the arrangements they knew even in conditions where better ones were possible. The first attempt to get the girls to contrast a two-roomed tenement home with a modern dwelling drew out the naïve remark, 'I would rather have a house with three bedrooms than with one (for an imaginary family of six people) because then I could take in lodgers'.

The Committee members could therefore set to work with definite aims in view. They wanted to show the girls how the housing problem had arisen from nineteenth-century social conditions as they had recently been studied by the class: to discuss the defects of present-day housing conditions; to help the girls to break away from these conditions with which they were so familiar and conceive of a better organization of housework and family life. A question paper was drawn up on these lines, and the class set to work to discover the answers. A summary of the question paper is given below; the parts quoted in full are given in italics.

INTRODUCTION

1. *You know that since the beginning of the Industrial Revolution towns in England became much larger and more*

crowded, and there were not enough good houses for the people. Since the Great War there have been fewer houses than ever because the cost of building is so high. (Refer to your notes on North of England industrial towns or to Unstead, 'The British Isles to-day', pp. 81, 82, 85, 93, 95.)

2. *You know too that houses are generally built and planned by people who do not know much about housework.*

From these two facts have arisen the HOUSING PROBLEM, which every girl ought to think about.

I. FIRST LET US SEE WHAT IS WRONG WITH MANY MODERN HOUSES. *Read pages* 23 *and* 24 *of 'A Working Woman's House' and page* 3 *of the Medical Officer's Report for Deptford* (1925).

Using these and one or two other books [1] the children were asked to comment on faults of housing under various headings ; some, such as overcrowding, bad water supply and sanitation and lack of repair, were particularly connected with a poor district : others, such as inconvenient housework arrangements, might affect any type of house. It may be noted in passing that the girls' natural reserve in regard to their own homes was fully respected : they were referred to books to find instances of overcrowding in other districts, although their teachers knew that they could have found instances in their own streets. On such subjects they were absolutely silent, with a fierce protection of their homes' privacy, although they would talk freely on questions of floods, water supply and lighting in regard to which they felt no responsibility. In the boys' school, which was of a more prosperous type, this difficulty did not exist, and the work could be based more directly on observation and survey. The following exercise, for instance, enabled the boys to find out for themselves that towns develop definitely marked zones of social well-being and that these zones are connected with geography.

On your copy of the town (or parish) map draw a red pencil line along the rows of houses which are seriously defective or in which, if you had your choice, you would not care to live.

II. NOW LET US IMAGINE WHAT WE SHOULD LIKE HOUSES TO BE. This was the crucial part of the paper and considerable space was given to it. The girls were taught to understand a plan and were then allowed to use a small class library

[1] **For full Book List, see Section 3 below.**

with numerous plans and pictures. They were asked to answer questions so framed as to extend their ideas or to give them a chance of expressing an opinion. Here are some specimen questions : the first two are planned to show how to use a modern house, the second two deal with questions of general hygiene, the third two are matters of opinion.

Imagine a family of father and mother, two boys, two big girls and a baby. In the books in your class library you will find several plans of houses. (Reiss, p. 50. Working Woman's House, pp. 16, 17. Everyday Architecture, pp. 43, 78, 80, 81, 84.) Choose one, and trace or copy it. Show how you fit the family into the bedrooms.

What is the importance of having a bathroom in a house? Do you want hot water laid on? Do you want a bath even if hot water is not laid on? Which is the most convenient place for a bath, upstairs or down?

Would you rather have a sunny house or one that gets little sun?

Where do you think the larder should be in a house?

Would you rather have a parlour and a small living-room or one big room?

Do you think it best to have cooking done in the scullery with the help of gas or electricity, or would you rather do it in the living room with coal? The answer to this last question was pretty general ; they would rather do it in the scullery so that it shouldn't make the room smell, but it must nevertheless be done in the living-room because you can't have two fires going.

The boys covered the same ground, but as they had more time and were dealing with a more compact unit than a part of London they were able to add exercises on town planning. These exercises were based on the following introductory suggestion :

You will realize that our town has grown up slowly and that factories and houses have been built where they could be fitted in. If you were asked to re-plan the town and make it a better place in which to live and work, say what steps you would take. If there are streets of houses or factories which you think should be pulled down, what would you build on their sites? Where would you like to build new houses in place of those you have demolished? You would probably like more open spaces with grass and trees. Where in the new town would you like these?

The work on this section ended constructively :—

III. Now let us find out what is being planned and done to get Better Houses. This section consisted of six short questions.

What different people or groups of people undertake to build houses?

What is done to prevent the private builder from building very small, bad houses?

How is the borough council helped to build houses?

Can you find out any houses built by the Deptford Council since the war? (Use the Borough Guide, pp. 54–5.)

Can you find out what the Downham estate is, and how many houses there are given to Deptford people?

What do you think you yourself can do to end the housing problem?

Most of the girls, who had heard of Mr. Baldwin's Franchise Act, said that they would vote for people who would give them better houses. No one at first suggested that a good housekeeper can make a better home in a bad house than a sloven can; but this point was arrived at in the course of oral work.

This paper as a whole roused great interest and enthusiasm among the girls and led some of the least bookish among them to look at books with affection, provided that they contained plans.

The work undertaken by the boys was rather differently oriented. Survey work on housing conditions has a stronger appeal to boys than the domestic side of the housing problem. Questions about the pupils' own homes revealed the prevalence in the town of a type of residence which could be readily distinguished as the 'artisan' house. Its merits and defects were considered and compared on the one hand with those of 'residential' houses and on the other with 'slums'. This rough threefold classification was found to work satisfactorily in the Medway towns, and was used in a survey of the borough of Rochester. Field work was carried out with the aid of six-inch scale maps cut into sections, and the collected results of the survey were displayed in colours on a fair copy of the map. Many striking facts about the distribution of housing types were discussed, and have been frequently raised in connexion with such later aspects of the regional survey as communications and physical features. The outline maps used in the housing survey were engineers' prints from a tracing of the six-inch Ordnance Survey map. Other copies have been set aside to show in colour the distribution of open spaces, parks, recreation grounds, allotments and the sites of houses known to have been built before 1850.

PART II. LOCAL COMMUNICATIONS

This paper was, comparatively speaking, a failure as regards the girls' interest. The aim of the Committee had been to help the children to get a clear general idea of the lie of the district and its connexions with the outside world and to connect their present work with the regional work they had done in geography. But girls are so much kept at home by housework and the care of younger children that they had very little knowledge or curiosity even about their own immediate neighbourhood. They did the work steadily and well, but without much interest except in certain places where a connexion was made with local history.

The paper was divided into two sections:—

1. *Communications within Deptford.* They were asked to trace or draw a map, to put in the names of the river and the big road system, to see if they could find in their local history books any reasons for these names, to put in their own school and home and shops and finally to collect the numbers and routes of buses and trams running through the district. They were also asked to compare their map with the map of Deptford made by John Evelyn in the seventeenth century.

2. *Communications between Deptford and other places.* These were taken in order of time, beginning with the river as the most ancient of all highways and going on to roads, railways, underground railways and aeroplanes. Connexions with social and local history were made whenever possible. The girls also found out what cheap fares were offered by railways or buses, and what interesting places could be reached by means of them. Several girls wrote essays describing how roads are made and mended.

This section, which was on the whole unsuccessful with the girls, was very attractive to the boys, who have more opportunities for roving and who found the study of roads, railways and their traffic much more easy to deal with in a provincial town than in the London area. The highways and waterway of Rochester have exercised a profound influence on its history, and considerations affecting them entered into every branch of the work from physical geography to the study of present-day civic organization. In London the great roads tend to become lost in the vast sea of houses and factories; their significance is commonly unsuspected by the inhabitants of the great blocks of slums through which they pass. But in the smaller provincial towns the highways are closely bound up with local affairs and some part at least of their regional significance is familiar to every one. The following questions formed the basis of some useful work on the communications of the Rochester district:—

1. *Draw a map of the streets for a radius of ¼ mile round your home. Carry on the roads upon which there is most traffic. Number them, and at the end of each make a list of the places to which they lead.*

2. *Make a list of roads in Rochester which you believe to be very old. Give your reasons for each statement.*

3. *Make another list of roads whose names appear to have a historical association (e.g. 'New' Road).*

4. *Name all the roads which have public bus services, giving a list of the services in each case.*

5. *How many buses pass along the High Street, (a) in half an hour in the middle of the day, (b) in half an hour between* 4.0 *and* 6.30 *p.m.?*

6. *You will be given a map on a scale of ½ inch to one mile. Carefully line in with red ink all the main roads communicating with Rochester. Number these roads and make a list on paper.*

Example:—3. *The Hoo Road, passing through Strood, Frindsbury, Wainscott, Chattenden, Hoo, Stoke and Grain.*

7. *If you had to drive a car to the following places, state in each case which number you would take:—Westminster, Brighton, Margate, Dartford, Sevenoaks, Guildford, Cambridge, Canterbury, High Halstow, Meopham, East Malling, Ashford.*

The subject of main roads was also taken as the starting point for the study of physical features of the region and a number of instructive road profiles have been made by the boys from information obtained from contour maps. The relations between main roads and housing areas have also been dealt with. The subject of roads in relation to civil administration is important.

PART III. LOCAL OCCUPATIONS

The material for this section in the Deptford experiment was largely based on an inquiry made by one Committee member (a local head mistress) into the occupations of her girls' fathers, mothers, big brothers and big sisters. The occupations were grouped under retail trading, factory work and transport, with a special section on women's work. The aim of the course was to help the girls to realize that they lived in the midst of a complicated division of labour, in the strongest possible contrast with the self-contained home production of earlier times. It was also thought a good part of their training that they should understand something of the nature of men's work, just as the boys were asked to consider methods and devices in housework.

1. *Shops.* The section opened with a historical connexion. *Long ago in the eleventh century when Deptford was a little village called a manor there were no shops in it. Can you find out why this was? (Piers Plowman Histories: junior books IV, V and VI, but especially Book V, pp.* 37–45 *and IV, chap.* 6.)

The girls went on to contrast this with modern Deptford and to make a plan of a stretch of shops in the neighbouring street, discussing which shops were the most numerous, and why. They then found out what laws regulated the hours of closing and how the buyer is protected against short weight or adulterated goods. Every opportunity was taken of referring to such concrete instances of the work of Parliament or the Town Council so that when at last the course arrived at a description of these institutions they should not appear remote from everyday life. The girls discussed whether they would like the shops to be open for longer or shorter hours: the argument was either, 'I would like the shops open longer because of mothers whose fathers come home late with their money', or 'I would not like them to be open longer hours, because the shopkeepers would not get much rest'.

2. *Factories. When Deptford was growing into a little town (about the fourteenth century) goods were made behind the shops by craftsmen. Do the names of any girls in the school show you that they are descended from medieval craftsmen? Do any street names in Deptford show that craftsmen once lived there?* This introduction was greeted with great enthusiasm. The smiths and the tailors were delighted with themselves, and girls who could not find their names in Weekley protested hotly. It was a new idea to realize that one must actually have had an ancestor living in the fourteenth century or in the age of Elizabeth.

If Deptford had been a village with a stable population this interest would have been carried on by the use of the parish register and enquiries from old inhabitants: but London children have lost their background. So the course had to return to a reference to the coming of factories in the Industrial Revolution, and the compiling of a list of factories and works in modern Deptford. This might be extended to the study of a single workshop, with plans and pictures, and a discussion of the things made in it. The section ended with the question: *You remember that workers used to be treated very badly in factories when the Industrial Revolution began. What laws have been or are being passed to make things better?*

3. *Transport.* The girls first found out all that they could about transport as an important local occupation: several of them had fathers who worked on the railway. They went on to the question:

How many things have you used to-day (e.g. tea) that must have been brought to Deptford from far away? The aim here was to lead them to realize the economic interdependence of the world. The same idea is worked out by E. V. Lucas in his story told to Prue, which is included in 'London Lavender'.

4. *Women's work.* The section ended with a discussion on the occupations open to girls in Deptford. This was not a very cheerful topic to the social reformer, and one could not but sympathize with the girl who wrote, 'I do not like any of the jobs I have written above. But I shall have to take one of them if I cannot get the job that is in my mind.'

The Rochester boys carried work on this section a good deal further. The historical and scientific side of local occupations is of special interest in Rochester, and the syllabus was drawn up to include a full survey of modern occupations and an inquiry into their histories and their more primitive prototypes in the pre-Industrial Age. A map was prepared showing the distribution of shops, factories and warehouses in Rochester.

PART IV. VOLUNTARY SOCIAL ACTIVITIES

The Committee regarded this section as the most important part of their work, since these activities give more scope to the ordinary citizen than the management of State affairs can do. In the days of Pericles every individual who was not a slave could exert himself in the affairs of the city. In our days of enormous population and political equality such an ideal becomes impracticable, and democracy must express itself in other ways: by managing the local branch of a trade union, for instance, or taking out shares in the Co-operative, or acting as a local preacher at the Wesleyan Chapel. Any voluntary social activity, from a cricket club to a great hospital, which was prominent in the life of the district was regarded as proper material for this section. In Deptford the list comprised co-operative and friendly societies, trade unions, churches and chapels, hospitals, clubs and societies such as Boy Scouts and Girl Guides, Play Centres, the Country Holiday Fund and the Y.M.C.A.

1. *Co-operation.* This section opened by an inquiry into the historical origins of co-operation. *You have heard in your geography lessons of co-operative societies among the farmers of Czechoslovakia, Denmark and Canada. Many of you buy your groceries at a co-operative society in the New Cross Road. Can you find out why these societies were formed, and by whom? (See 'Co-operation', by Clayton, pp. 5–8, 10, 11, 32. 'Our Story', by Nicholson, p. 4. 'Social Reformers', by Guest, p. 145.)*

The girls went on to discover the essential principle and meaning of co-operation.

If you look at 'Wealth and Work', by G. W. Gough, p. 255, you will see that a man who organizes a business must put some money (called CAPITAL*) into it, and that he must devote his time and talents to running the business. For these services he is entitled to a wage—generally called* PROFIT. *Try to find out who puts* CAPITAL *into the Royal Arsenal Co-operative Society and who receives the* PROFITS. *(Consult Clayton, p. 50, and the R.A.C.S. pamphlet, pp. 6 and 7.)*

What is a member's pass book? Examine one, and see how it is used.

The organization of the local co-operative society was then dealt with, very simply, but bringing out the analogy between its government and representative parliamentary government as the girls had watched it grow in history.

You remember that from the Middle Ages the British people have had the idea that representative government is the best way of managing affairs in our land and in the colonies. In the same way, the co-operative society decided to elect a committee for every big piece of work on hand. Try to find out the main committees and their work.

The section concluded by making a list of the various schemes of the local co-operative society, excluding politics. The girls considered the work of the various insurance and benefit schemes, the coal clubs and convalescent funds, the building department (with local details), the libraries and holiday clubs.

2. *Trade Unions.* This was a very difficult section, both to the Committee and the girls. The girls nevertheless performed their work excellently. The section began—

Trade Unions are most important to people who are going to earn their livings. You will find when you are grown up that there are many problems connected with the future of trade unions. You must get ready to understand these by finding out a little about trade unions to-day. I want you to begin by finding out what a trade union is. You will have a lesson to help you, you can ask father and you can read Jones. Then see if you are able to understand this definition and write in your own words what a trade union is—

'A Trade Union is a continuous association of wage-earners for the purpose of maintaining or improving the conditions of their working lives.' (Webb.)

One girl wrote, 'I think a Trade Union is a society of workers that meet to discuss better conditions of work, better wages'; and another, 'I think a Trade Union is a society of wage earners who get together to help themselves and others who belong to the Trade Union, and who try to improve wages, and conditions of work and living'.

The girls went on to make a short summary from their class-books of the history of Trade Unionism in England; they read pp. 129–33 of 'Everyone's Affairs,' by Dr. Robert Jones (which was found to be the most useful juvenile account of Trade Unionism), and discussed why people joined trade unions; they found out how many people in England belonged to Trade Unions ('Organized Labour,' by Cole, p. 14), and what were the names of the biggest trade unions and their secretaries (Cole, pp. 17–21); they discovered the existence of the Trade Union Congress and noted that representative government was to be found in the Trade Union world as well as in the world of co-operative societies and politics. Finally they considered why there were fewer trade unions among women than among men, and held a debate on the question of trade unions for shop assistants and domestic workers.

It was felt by the Committee on a general revision of this section that although the girls had gained some useful knowledge, the approach had on the whole been too abstract, and that it would have been better to link the work on Trade Unions with the Occupations section, starting from the consideration of the worker's need for security and unity.

3. *Churches and Chapels, &c.* This section was considerably easier to work out ; its main aim was to show the girls how toleration has proved the solution of the religious strife they learned about in history and to emphasize the voluntary social help given by church members to one another. They made a map of the churches and chapels in their neighbourhood and contrasted the varied group with the single building of S. Nicholas marked in Evelyn's seventeenth-century map. They found out from their history note-books the circumstances in which the Roman Catholic Church and the Church of England separated, the Congregationalist, Baptist and Quaker Churches were founded, and the Wesleyan Methodists appeared. They contributed information about the social work of the churches they knew and described the aims and working of the various clubs to which they belonged. It was felt that the general effect of all this was to increase the girls' interest in the public life of their district and to help in breaking down the narrow boundaries in which their hard life of housework confined them.

PART V. LOCAL GOVERNMENT

So much work has been done on the teaching of State institutions to children that the Committee found this and the next section easy work, and the main anxiety was to see how much could be left out. The questions were to be of the simplest and to include nothing that was outside the range of interest of the ordinary citizen. They began by establishing a connexion between the work of the State and the children's everyday lives.

How many things have you used to-day outside your home that you know must have cost money and that you did not pay for at the time? (for instance, the pavement from your house to school).

One girl wrote, 'All the things I use at school, sanitation, water, kerbs, the lighting of the streets, policemen'.

Who does pay for these things? (Try Blakiston, p. 37; Madeley, p. 23; Whiskard, p. 91; or Swann, p. 66.)

How often does your father or his landlord have to pay rates? Where are they paid? How much are the rates in Deptford?

Let us find out who takes care of the money you pay and how it is spent.

You live in the METROPOLITAN BOROUGH OF DEPTFORD. *Now, the Deptford ratepayers chose men as* COUNCILLORS *to sit in the* BOROUGH COUNCIL *and take care of their money and arrange how it shall be used. These men are not paid, but do the work in their spare time. Find out the names of the councillors in your 'ward', that is, in the part of Deptford where you live (Use the Directory, p. A 17). Find out the names of other councillors if you can.*

These councillors were chosen by the ratepayers in an ELECTION. *When was the last election? When will the next be held? When will you vote? (Madeley, p. 21.)*

The councillors choose a MAYOR *every year to be at their head. Who is mayor now?*

The Council has some officers who give all their time to their work and who are paid. Find out the names of the town clerk, the medical officer of health, the assistant officer who is in charge of children's welfare, and the librarian.

The Borough Council divides itself into several committees, one to see after each piece of work. What different committees are there?

The paper concluded with a brief inquiry on the same lines into the work of the London County Council and an explanation of the special position of the City of London and the Lord Mayor, with whose title they were all familiar.

A much fuller local government questionnaire will be found noted in the book list given below (Miss Madeley: Citizen's Handbook). Another useful suggestion made by a Committee member was that the children might build up an exhibit consisting of pictures and notes about all buildings in the district owned by the Local Authority or used for Local Government purposes. The same method could be used by London children in their study of Central Government.

In Rochester there proved to be more opportunities than in London and the larger provincial towns for the study of civic organization and government as evolved by history.

Many grandparents can describe the activities of the beadle, the watch, the poundkeeper, the parish clerk of ancient days and other officials who have been replaced by modern public services. Where living memory provided such information, the greatest possible use was made of it. The changes in civil rights and liberties and the rise of institutions to meet the needs of a changing social life are the more impressive when brought home to the children through their own inquiries and the accounts given by folk speaking from actual experience. From this historical background the boys proceeded to investigate modern administration and civic institutions, including Parishes: the Corporation and its work: Elections: Municipal Officers and their Work: Public Services: Civic Functions and their bearing on History, &c.

PART VI. CENTRAL GOVERNMENT AND ITS WORK

Here again the main point was to leave out all non-essentials and to connect what was included with the children's own experience.

You have seen in the earlier papers how important Parliament is in our everyday life: you have seen, for instance, how laws passed in Parliament help new houses to be built, give shop-keepers their half-holiday, and protect workers in factories. Let us find out how all this is done.

I. *How is Parliament made?* Under this heading the girls found out the names of the two Houses and how each was composed, the name of their own member, and the present qualifications needed by a voter: this was connected with the series of Reform Acts described in their history note-books.

II. *How does Parliament make up the laws?* Here the girls described briefly how a Bill is brought into Parliament, using Blakeston, pp. 19–20. They were told that '*the most important Bills are brought in by the* GOVERNMENT, *that is, by the party that gained most seats in the last election*', and found out the name of the present Government and its chief men. In the same way they dealt with the opposition parties as those '*whose work it is to criticize and discuss the Bills brought in by the Government*'. But no attempt was made to teach more than the names of the great political parties, and this gap was made clear to the girls. '*One of the things that every voter must do is to find out the different policies of these parties and decide which he or she thinks best to vote for in an election.*

Think of this as something that you mean to find out after you leave school.'

III. *How does Parliament govern the country?* Under this section the girls found out the names of the chief government offices and the ministers attached to them, using such books as Swann, Whiskard and Whitaker's Almanack. They went on to a simple explanation of the work of the Cabinet, and found out from their history note-books when and how the Cabinet began to be important. Every opportunity was taken of drawing their attention to topical events such as the introduction of the Budget. But on such niceties as the existence of the Privy Council or the way in which an appeal reaches the House of Lords or who the Chancellor of the Duchy of Lancaster may be, they remain in contented ignorance.

Finally, in order to make the vital connexion between the world as they knew it and the official world which they had been describing, the girls investigated the activities of the State in their own district. The subject as usual was introduced in a very practical way.

1. EDUCATION. *Think of girls who have left this school, make a list of the different kinds of schools to which they have gone and try to say what is the special aim of each kind.* (*See M. Cole* (*Local Government for beginners*), *p.* 73, *and the Borough Guide, pp.* 51, 52, 73, 78.)

The girls worked this out thoroughly, making a list of neighbouring centres of education, discussing the work of each, and discovering what was meant by 'the educational ladder'. They then dealt in a very simple way with twentieth-century legislation for children's welfare.

2. PUBLIC HEALTH. The girls first dealt with the question of individual health, imagining themselves to be mothers of a family and discussing the value of school medical inspection, clinics, and the notifying of diseases. They went on to consider general sanitary conditions and the system for removing house refuse. By frequent repetition throughout the whole of the section it was constantly brought to the girls' notice that public services are not capriciously bestowed by some official. They are paid for by the people and can only be worked successfully by co-operation between the individual and the State. House refuse was a case in point; the girls found that the dustbin must be provided by the householder, but that it is emptied weekly by order of the borough council.

3. Poor Relief was very briefly described, connecting the modern system with the Act of 1834 already known to the girls through earlier history lessons.

4. Recreation. This was fully worked out, since so much of the pleasure of a London child depends upon schemes for public recreation. The girls found out all that they could about the facilities offered by the public baths, made a map of London's open spaces and a list of local museums, and ended by a description of the excellent free library of Deptford and the steps they would take to find the particular reading they wanted, such as the Encyclopædia or 'My Magazine'.

The Deptford course concluded here. But of course it is obvious that with more time at their disposal, the horizon of the girls could have been still further widened. The laws of co-operation and mutual help which, in spite of all our discords, are still obeyed by the vast majority of people during the greater part of their lives, could have been shown to obtain, not only in Deptford and England, but in the family of the British Commonwealth, the family of European nations, and at last in all the varied fellowships of the great globe itself. The course leads naturally outwards from the railway trucks and steamer funnels seen from the windows of a New Cross School to the great routes of world transport and to the relationships and problems of the lands through which they pass. The League of Nations is implicit in the foreign bread and butter and tinned sardines on a London tea-table.

The whole virtue of a course such as is described above is that it should be incomplete, a beginning rather than an end. It should aim less at amassing information than at arousing curiosity, detachment, a power to criticize and a desire to explore. Society, for all the reforms of the last half century, has been to many of these children a cruel enough guardian. There could be no greater danger than to let them grow up regarding her as something static and incapable of change, against whom they may rebel but whom they can never influence. The aim of the course was to show them Society as something which man is slowly shaping to his needs; so that with their sense of righteous discontent there should mingle some sense of power and responsibility, and that side by side with their feeling of injustice in the present they should feel, as they look towards the future, some hope.

III. BOOK LIST

BOOKS ON METHOD FOR THE TEACHER

Gollancz, V. and **Somervell, D. Political Education at a Public School.** 130 pp. Collins. 1918.
Challenging, readable and suggestive.

Penstone, M. M. Town Study. 454 pp. National Society's Depository. 1910. 5*s.*
A suggestive book, specially useful in giving a historical background to modern social problems.

Peverett, G. and **Pike, A. T. Social Survey : a guide to good citizenship.** 51 pp. National Adult School Union. 1924. 6*d.*
Contains suggestions for the social survey of a neighbourhood : would be useful to teacher planning a course.

Showan, P. B. Citizenship and the School. 180 pp. C.U.P. 1923. 7*s.* 6*d.*
Makes suggestions for a four-year syllabus showing how citizenship may be taught in the course of the history and geography lessons.

White, E. M. The Teaching of Modern Civics. 126 pp. Harrap. 1923. 3*s.* 6*d.*
The most useful introduction for the teacher. Contains full suggestions for syllabus and a good bibliography.

GENERAL BOOKS FOR THE CHILDREN

There are many books on this subject, but few suitable : the majority are either dull or horribly didactic or both. The following are among the most useful:—

Jones, R. Everyone's Affairs. 200 pp. Sidgwick & Jackson. 1924. 2*s.* 6*d.*
An outspoken and stimulating discussion on the problems of the modern citizen and how they arose. Should be in every school library as one of the few books that do not approach the subject from the institutional side. Will require teacher's help except for a class of real intelligence. Some interesting diagrammatic illustrations.

Lay, J. S. Citizenship. 280 pp. Macmillan. 1921. 2*s.* 6*d.*
A series of brief common-sense discussions of social topics—health, education, work, government, &c.

Row, E. F. Work, Wealth and Wages. 95 pp. Harrap. 1920. 1*s.*
A very simple, clear and useful introduction to economics for children.

Whiskard, G. How we are governed. 96 pp. Harrap. 1926. 1*s.* 3*d.*

Purely constitutional: an easy impartial account of the machinery of government: could be read by the children alone.

But the general opinion of the Committee was that this work would be better carried on by the use of a varied class library than by a single book. Suggestions for such libraries on each topic will be found below. The books are intended for the teacher's reading and the children's reference. Books which the children found particularly interesting and from which they wanted to read more than the passages marked for them are shown by a star.

PART I. HOUSING

Bournville Housing. 56 pp. Publications department Bournville. 1926. 6*d.*

Useful for illustration: contains good plans.

***Furniss, A. W. S.** and **Phillips, M. The Working Woman's House.** 84 pp. Swarthmore Press. 1920. 1*s.* 6*d.*

Specially interesting to girls. Contains illustrations and plans.

Housing. 190 pp. P. S. King & Son, Ltd. 1928. 2*s.* 6*d.*

The official account of the L.C.C. schemes since 1913. Contains good plans and descriptions of houses.

Housing Manual. 42 pp. H.M.S.O. 1927. 9*d.*

Contains official statement of present needs and aims, with pictures and plans.

Reiss, R. The New Housing Handbook. viii + 195 pp. P. S. King & Son, Ltd. 1924. 2*s.* 6*d.*

A good practical and clear general account.

Reiss, R. The Town Planning Handbook. 130 pp. P. S. King & Son, Ltd. 1926. 4*s.* 6*d.*

A very useful general account.

***Robertson, Sir John. The House of Health.** 186 pp. Faber & Faber. 1925. 3*s.* 6*d.*

Very clear, useful description of 'what the modern dwelling needs to be'. Illustrated.

Robertson, Manning. Everyday Architecture. 176 pp. Fisher Unwin. 1924. 3*s.* 6*d.*

Lively reading, and contains good plans and photos.

The London County Council and what it does for London: Housing. 36 pp. Hodder & Stoughton. 1924. 6*d.*

Very useful to London teachers. Good maps and illustrations.

Town Planning in England and Wales. 23 pp. Ministry of Health. H.M.S.O. 1926. 4*d.*

A brief explanation of recent legislation.

HOUSEWORK. This section applies specially to girls. The main aim is to show them what the industrial revolution is doing in the home and to interest them in the development of labour-saving devices.

Labour-Saving in Small Houses. Garden Cities and Town Planning Association. 28 pp. P. S. King & Son, Ltd. 1922. 9*d.*

Report of a sub-committee of women on the most desirable arrangement of a house, together with criticisms on some modern houses.

Philips, R. P. The Servantless House. 160 pp. Offices of Country Life, Ltd. 1923. 6*s.*

Although this implies a higher standard of living than is usual among elementary school children, it gives useful information and pictures of labour-saving devices.

General Books of Reference :

Borough guide and directory.
Ordnance Survey maps of district.
Medical Officer of Health's reports.
Encyclopædias.

PART II. COMMUNICATIONS

***Griffiths, J. P. Transport.** vi + 245 pp. Philip & Son. 1923. 3*s.*

A very useful children's book, dealing in simple language with roads, canals and railways ; contains a list of more advanced books. Illustrated.

***Penstone, M. M. Town Study** (as above).

Pratt, E. A. A History of Inland Transport and Communications in England. x + 532 pp. Kegan Paul. 1911. 8*s.* 6*d.*

A good historical book of reference for the teacher, informative and concise. Deals most fully with the development of railways in the nineteenth century.

General books of reference as above. Tram map of London for each child. Books on the history of the district.

PART III. LOCAL OCCUPATIONS

Jones, Everyone's Affairs; Lay, Citizenship ; and **Row, Wealth, Work and Wages** (as above).

Cox, E. E. Girls' Work in Trade and Industry. 172 pp. Pitman. 2*s.* 6*d.*

A clear account of various employments.

***Fiennes, G. Getting our Living.** 149 pp. Bell & Sons. 1924. 1*s.* 6*d.*

An excellent and simply-written little introduction to economics. For Seniors. Illustrated.

*(Ed.) **Pollock, M. A. Working Days.** 276 pp. Cape. 1926. 6*s*. The personal records of sixteen working men and women of different occupations, written by themselves. Simple enough for the use of Seniors, who would find it full of interest, but saddening.

Rowntree, S. The Human Factor in Business. 188 pp. Longmans. 1925 (2nd edition). 2*s*. 6*d*.

A more comforting account of conditions in a particular factory.

***Williams, S. A. The Romance of English Trading.** 211 pp. Univ. of London Press. 1928. 2*s*. 9*d*.

A fresh and interesting account for children of the development of trade from simple beginnings to the co-operative store and big shops of the present day. Illustrated.

General books of reference as above.

Part IV. Voluntary Social Activities

Co-operation

***Clayton, J. Co-operation.** 93 pp. T. C. and E. C. Jack. 1912.

A short popular account.

Fay, C. R. Co-operation at home and abroad. 481 pp. P. S. King & Son. 1925. 15*s*.

The standard authority for the teacher.

***Nicholson, I. Our Story.** 84 pp. 1906.

A very simple and interesting survey, written for children. Material was lent by the local Co-operative Society.

Trade Unionism

Appleton, W. A. Trade Unionism. 159 pp. Hodder & Stoughton. 1924. 2*s*. 6*d*.

Appleton, W. A. Trade Unions: their past, present and future. 183 pp. Philip Allan & Co. 1925. 3*s*. 6*d*.

Both straightforward, moderate and fairly popular accounts of the movement.

Cole, G. D. H. Organized Labour: an introduction to Trade Unionism. 182 pp. Allen & Unwin and the Labour Publishing Co. 1924. 6*s*.

A succinct scholarly review of the subject.

Drake, B. Women in Trade Unions. 237 pp. Allen & Unwin. 1921. 8*s*. 6*d*.

Useful to teachers in girls' schools.

Guest, G. English Social Reformers. Book 2. Chapter on Francis Place. Horace Marshall. 1923. 2*s.*

***Jones, R. Everyone's Affairs,** and **Lay, Citizenship,** contain chapters on Trade Unionism.

Lloyd, C. M. Trade Unionism. vii + 194 pp. A. & C. Black. 1928 (3rd edition). 5*s.*

A valuable concise history and description of Trade Unionism for the teacher.

Swann, F. English Citizenship (see below). Contains chapter on Trade Unions and the Labour Movement.

Wallas, Graham. The Life of Francis Place (see in biographical section, p. 152).

*The Children's Encyclopædia is useful on this topic.

General books of reference as above.

PART V. LOCAL GOVERNMENT

An account of the machinery of Local Government can be found in any of the following.

Blakiston, C. H. Elementary Civics. 120 pp. Arnold. 1920. 2*s.* 6*d.*

Clarke, J. J. Outlines of Local Government in the United Kingdom. x + 230 pp. Pitman. 1928. 2*s.* 6*d.*

Cole, M. I. Local Government for Beginners. v + 90 pp. Longmans. 1927. 1*s.* and 2*s.*

Fisher, Mrs. H. A. L. The Citizen. 270 pp. Chambers. 1927. 2*s.* 6*d.*

Madeley, H. M. Key to the Citizen's Handbook. Blackwell. 1926. 2*s.* 6*d.*

Marriott, J. A. R. How we are Governed. 112 pp. O.U.P. World's Manuals. 1928. 2*s.* 6*d.*

Swann, F. English Citizenship. vi + 272 pp. Longmans. 1923. 2*s.*

Swann, F. A Primer of London Citizenship. ix + 118 pp. P. S. King. 1915. 2*s.*

***Whiskard. How we are governed** (as above).

A full questionnaire for children on Local Government is given in

***Madeley, H. M. The Citizen's Handbook.** 32 pp. Blackwell. 6*d.*

Books of reference :

Whitaker's Almanack.
Pamphlet on Public Services issued by the Borough Council.
Others as above.

PART VI. CENTRAL GOVERNMENT

A general outline will be found in **Blakiston, Fisher, Marriott, Swann** or **Whiskard** (as above). A simple historical background is given in **Court, H. M., Story of British Government.** 118 pp. Sampson Low. 1927. 2*s.* 6*d.*

More detail is given in:

Clarke, J. J. Outlines of Central Government. x + 198 pp. Pitman. 1925. 1*s.* 6*d.*

Ilbert, Courtenay. Parliament. 254 pp. Home University Library. 1911. 2*s.* 6*d.*

An admirable summary, especially for its descriptions of the procedure and organization of the House of Commons.

Books of reference.

The Statesman's Year Book.

Others as above.

N.B.—G. P. Putnam's Sons are publishing in The Whitehall Series monographs on the work and history of particular departments. Books on the Home Office, the Ministry of Health, the Post Office, the Board of Education, among others, are already published.